Raymond,

This is your book to keep and read forever.

I hope it helps

Please read it - Just a little at a time, so you can think about it.

D1417367

Table of Contents

FOREWORD...................................6

WITH THANKS..............................7

INTRODUCTION..........................8

SMALL THINGS, BIG PICTURE.........10

A PAINFUL WALK.........................13

HOW CAN I?...............................16

VISIBLE EXPRESSION..................19

MENDING THE BROKEN................22

CHOICE.....................................25

HANDS......................................29

A POWERFUL CORE....................32

ONE IN BILLIONS.......................35

BRUISING...................................38

EARS TO HEAR...........................41

ADJUSTING TO CHANGE..............44

THE STRENGTH OF THE BODY.........48

HEALING WRITING......................51

KEEPING ACTIVE.......................55

DARE TO SING...........................58

PHYSICAL AND FINANCIAL...........61

HAVING HEART...........................65

THE BASICS...............................68

RELAX.......................................72

DREAMS....................................76

A FIRM FOUNDATION...................79

WEEPING...................................82

HOPE..85

SCARS.......................................88

DISRUPTION...............................91

OPPOSING ACTION.....................94

UNIMPAIRED PRAYER..................97

PITY PARTY PITFALL..................101

HIDDEN INSIDE.........................104

SHAKEN...................................107

A SENSUAL PRISON...................110

WAITING FOR DAWN..................113

FACING IT................................116

BREATH OF LIFE.......................119

STATURE..................................122

BONE DRY................................125

EXAM TIME...............................129

INS AND OUTS..........................132

LIVING WATER..........................135

BEHOLD...................................138

WHAT'S THE UPSIDE?................141

REMEMBER..............................144

TENSION RELIEF.......................147

WARFARE.................................150

GETTING A GRIP.......................154

WHAT ARE YOU WAITING FOR?.......157

FIGHT OR FLIGHT?....................160

EXPECTATIONS.........................163

BATTLEGROUND OF THE MIND.......166

RESTING..................................169

SURPRISE................................172

WRAPPED UP............................176

WHEN GOD SAYS NO..................179

SILVER TONGUED?....................183

VISIBLE AND INVISIBLE.............186

TOOTH TRUTH..........................189

LIFE LINE.................................192

NAME IT!..................................195

FIGHTING THE INVASION............198

TO BELIEVE AND TO KNOW............202

WILDERNESS HEAT 205

FINGERS..................................208

HEART FAILURE 211

RUNNING THE RACE....................214

AN OUTSTRETCHED ARM................217

TASTY! 220

JOY..223

WHAT HOLDS YOU UP?.................226

COMMUNICATING 229

THROUGH THE FIRE....................233

TOTAL REMAKE..........................236

LAUGHTER................................239

THE RIGHT STUFF 242

LOVE 245

STRENGTH IN WEAKNESS..............248

TIME IS TICKING 251

LEG WORK................................255

CHRIST IN YOU 258

MOTHERHOOD............................261

THE PERFECT FATHER.................264

HAIR-RAISING LIVES.................267

PARTNERING IN SUPPORT.............270

FILLED WITH WHAT? 274

MIND OVER MATTERS 278

LEFT AND RIGHT......................281

SUCCESSFUL PULLING.................285

SHOULDERING MUCH....................288

SPINNING OUT OF CONTROL..........292

MAN'S ODDS OR GOD'S?.............296

THAT THE BLIND MAY SEE..........299

THE NEEDED KNEE 302

POWER OF TOUCH.......................305

PLENTY OF PURPOSE...................308

PERSISTING PAIN 312

THE CHEMISTRY OF DEPRESSION....315

AGEING...................................318

BODY-CENTRAL..........................321

VOICING IT..............................325

PERSEVERANCE..........................328

LIFE AND DEATH.......................331

THE ANKLE SOLUTION..................335

HOLDING TOGETHER.....................338

RESET....................................342

A NEW THING............................346

CONCLUSION.............................350

SOURCES.................................351

ACKNOWLEDGMENTS 351

HYMNS....................................352

Foreword

I have known Marjorie since high school. The years have been unfairly kind to her, an injustice that becomes glaring with each passing reunion.

Of course, we all hate her for this.

But after she smiles and says hello, somehow recognizing us through the ruins of time, the warmth and goodness of who she is comes out, and we all forgive her.

At least, until the next reunion.

She played tennis back then, if memory serves me, which it does less and less, and has always stayed in good shape. Me, I have to take a nap after tying my tennis shoes. After *each* shoe.

The spiritual life isn't any easier. Life has a gravitation pull it exerts not just on our bodies but on our souls. And the spiritual life that once seemed so effortless now seems so strenuous.

Living east of Eden in a world that resists us, we labor by the sweat of our brow. We labor in birth. We labor in growth. We labor in maturity. We labor in old age.

The New Testament tells us how to live in such a world by using a variety of athletic metaphors. We tend to forget how rigorous some of those metaphors are. And, how important they are if we are to run the race that has been set before us.

Paul makes repeated comparisons between our physical life and our spiritual life. With our Western mindset we tend to separate the two, when, in fact, they are intricately interconnected.

I have not read a book that respects this interconnection as much as Marjorie's book does. She helps us with the spiritual disciplines. Physical therapist, Gayle Griffen, helps with the physical disciplines.

There is something invigorating after a good workout – after the strain, the sweat, and the shower. You'll feel that sense of invigoration with each passing day you spend with these two, gifted, personal trainers. Day by day, you are going to see the results. And you are going to love the results.

I learned a lot when I first read the manuscript– interesting things, things I didn't know. The Scriptures focused me. The stories touched me. And the prayers moved me into a deeper connection with God. Now that the manuscript is in print, I actually plan on doing the physical exercises.

If only I can remember where I put my tennis shoes!

– Ken Gire

With Thanks

Not only do I owe many thanks to the people who shared their stories on these pages, but also to the authors, teachers, evangelists and mentors who have led me into a deeper understanding of scripture and whose insights I have drawn heavily upon: Charles Swindoll, David Jeremiah, Charles Stanley, Phillip Yancey, Ron Hutchcraft, John Eldredge and others too numerous to name.

My heartfelt gratitude goes to author and friend Ken Gire for terrific writing advice and editing as well as for his foreword; to Dr. John Muir for his theological input; to Dr. Joe Dean for checking the medical facts; to Pat Templer for her valuable suggestions; and especially to Mom, whose super editing, counsel and encouragement not only kept me going, but also transformed this book. And I also deeply appreciate my dear husband Joe, who has supported me in every way through health problems as well this two-year writing project. To all the therapists at North Texas Rehab Center, especially my therapist and helper on this book, Gayle, thank you for not only vastly improving my physical life, but for generously sharing your hearts and expertise.

Most of all, I am grateful to my Lord, Who allowed a difficult time in my life to be used for His purposes: to transform me, to ignite a passion within me for the Bible, to reveal new and glorious things about Himself and to give me a means to tell others about His love. He has led me into the abundant life, which has nothing to do with earthly things and everything to do with Him.

Unless otherwise indicated,
Scriptures are taken from the
New International Version of the Bible.

Introduction

*W*hen *suffering and trials shake us* to the core of our being, we need more than human strength. We need God. But what do we do when we can't feel Him near, when we cry with the Psalmist, "My God, my God, why have you forsaken me?" (Psalm 22) How can we instead move to the understanding of another suffering Psalmist: "My health may fail, my spirit grow weak, but God remains the strength of my heart." (Psalm 73:26)

Trust is the key. But how can we develop it? By getting to know God better. And He gives us glimpses of Himself in the astonishing and mysterious workings of our physical body. He also teaches us about Himself through His word. Scripture often ties together the spiritual and the physical, and the devotionals here weave body and soul together, combining interesting physical body facts with biblical truths and spiritual promises.

Trust is a form of spiritual muscle. Developing it requires effort from us, just as building physical muscle does. We must "work out." Our confidence in God is built by getting into His word and studying it to strengthen our understanding of Him, His character, His love, and His passionate desire for a relationship with us. He invites us to come to Him in prayer, too, and He promises wisdom, peace, guidance and strength when we do.

Even though God remains mysterious and often perplexing to our finite understanding, He makes some things perfectly clear: He is not only always *with* us, He is *for* us! He *loves* us. The One who brought light into darkness, order from chaos, and peace out of turmoil, can also bring faith and trust to replace fear and unbelief, if we ask Him.

Each personal story in this book is a testimony to how God strengthened that person's faith, enabling him or her to live victoriously, despite severe trials and unanswered questions. While life threatened to tear these people apart, they were held together instead by spiritual core strength.

Along with spiritual strength, physical core strength also helps us to endure life's demands. Exercise enables us to better cope with stress, pain and limitations. Performing even mild exercise can help build up our body's core muscles (abdominal, back, and pelvic or hip muscles), giving our spine better support and, in turn, improving the strength and function of the head, neck, arms and legs. As the Bible says, the whole body is connected...every part affects the other. So along with spiritual workouts, this book contains gentle exercises (and stretches) for those who are able to perform them.

Through my own health crisis, I learned one of God's primary truths: for those who love Him, He *does* work eventual good even in the most trying of circumstances. The God of all hope never wastes anything in our lives. Just as muscle is built by a tear-and-repair process, it's when we are shaken to the core that we progress from knowing *about* God to better *knowing* Him, and that infuses us with a new strength.

*(Although physical therapist Gayle Griffin helped with the physical exercises, be sure to consult your doctor before beginning. Take care to warm up, and then exercise slowly and carefully. Stop if it produces pain.)

"Strengthen the feeble hands, steady the knees that give way; say to those with fearful hearts, 'Be strong, do not fear; your God will come'...."
(ISAIAH 35:3, 4)

Small Things, Big Picture

BODY BASIC
The pea-sized pituitary gland weighs only a fraction of an ounce, but it plays a key role in the body's chemical processes. It is a very complex, vital organ hanging on a tiny stem from the underside of the brain. But for centuries it was misunderstood and thought simply to be the source of nasal mucus!

SPIRITUAL SPECIFIC
"The kingdom of God is like a mustard seed...though it is the smallest of all your seeds, yet when it grows, it is the largest of garden plants and becomes a tree..." (MATTHEW 13:31)

In the smallest parts of the human body, God reveals something about Himself: He creatively uses little things to make a big difference. In scripture, too, we're shown this pattern. Our all-powerful God came to us as a small, helpless, newborn human being who grew up to free us from sin and death's eternal grip. Our Father, the "Bread of Life," provided tiny, thin flakes like frost called manna to feed thousands of wandering Jews for forty years in the desert.

Our Lord anointed Israel's first human king, Saul, from the smallest tribe of Israel, Benjamin, and the least of all the clans. God also demonstrated His might through David, a faith-filled shepherd boy with an ordinary slingshot and one smooth stone, who felled an armor-clad giant. God spoke to Elijah, not in the wind, earthquake or fire, but in a still, small voice. Our Creator chose a childless man, Abraham, to father the nation Israel at age *100!* God said, "When I called him he was but one, and I blessed him and made him many." (Isaiah 51:2)

Our finite minds can't imagine the divine big picture God sees. But He gives us a good vantage point through scripture to see how He used the trials of His faithful people to serve a meaningful purpose. Those stories can comfort us when we, too, are deeply troubled.

Job, who experienced an enormous amount of life's unfairness, heartbreak and pain, thought that God was alienated from him. But he discovered He was not. In the midst of suffering, Job came to truly *know* the God he had only heard about before. Although God never revealed why He allowed Job to lose almost every earthly thing, He did reveal Himself. And that was enough for Job. After their encounter, God restored Job's health and gave him double the earthly blessings he had lost. This one man's saga, which God made sure to include in His word, has demonstrated for thousands of years a central truth: whether trials are an attack of Satan (as in this story) or the result of sin in a fallen world, no matter how forcefully God's loved ones are buffeted, God's plan and His eventual good purposes cannot be thwarted.

The fact that you are reading these pages shows that God used my own small trials to give birth to this book. It was through pain, limitation, fatigue and fear that I experienced God and His mercies in a new way. Dealing with painful degenerative spine and joint problems as well as a drawn-out "mystery illness," I gained a tiny taste of how people feel who are suffering. And through my broken health, God placed the desire in my heart to reiterate His important message to His people: *He is in it with you.* He loves you, and He never allows you to suffer for no reason.

Our Rock, says, "Listen to Me, you who pursue righteousness and who seek the Lord: Look to the rock from which you were cut and to the quarry from which you were hewn. I, even I, am He who comforts you." (Isaiah 51:1, 12).

We may be only a tiny chip off the Mighty Rock, but we are part of

Him, and He invites us to tap into His solid strength and comfort. We are limited by much, but He is limited by nothing. In God's hands, problems are never pointless, only purposeful. And some day, when we see His big picture, we will understand how all the little pieces fit together.

SOUL THERAPY

All-seeing, all-knowing God,
With my limited view, I easily cave in to frustration.
So when my steps seem too tiny for the long, steep road ahead,
And I'm disappointed by my slow progress and half-hearted hope,
Remind me that no matter how it looks from down here,
You can do great things with small beginnings.
I am thankful that my weaknesses can never restrict
Your bigger purposes for me.

WORK OUT

In exercising, starting small and working your way up to more repetitions and longer sessions is the best way to begin. Today, take a ten minute walk if you can.

JOURNAL

If you don't keep a journal already, begin one. Each day, even if it's just a line or two, write out your feelings, prayers or what you are learning about God through your trials. After a month, read back from the beginning of the journal, and see if there hasn't been progress in faith, health or enlightenment. If there is, thank God for it. If it hasn't happened yet, pray for it to occur.

A Painful Walk

BODY BASIC
As the body ages, it becomes more susceptible to disease, because certain immune system cells begin diminishing in number. Even at a young age, however, the immune system can suddenly go awry and begin attacking its own tissues as if they were foreign, and that causes such autoimmune diseases as rheumatoid arthritis.

SPIRITUAL SPECIFIC
"Honor and enjoy your Creator while you're still young, before the years take their toll and your vigor wanes...In old age, your body no longer serves you so well. Muscles slacken, grip weakens, joints stiffen."
(ECCLESIASTES 12 MSG)

*L*ael, the wife of a college friend of mine, had been athletic most of her life. But before age thirty, she told me, her body felt ancient and pain-wracked as her joints became inflamed and stiffened with rheumatoid arthritis. "My toes and fingers are bent in directions God never designed them to go; my grip and muscles have weakened," she said. After four joint replacements and crying "bottles of tears," she wrote in the margin of her Bible, "Dear Lord, what grief to live old for so long! I long for healing, vigor...no limitations...I long to put on incorruptible flesh."

During the onset of the arthritis she read Philippians 3:8-10 in which Paul says that nothing human compares to the surpassing greatness of knowing Christ. "I want to know Christ," Paul wrote, "And the power of his resurrection and the fellowship of sharing in His sufferings, becoming like Him…" But Lael couldn't identify with that.

"I did not feel more Christ-like because of what I was suffering. I didn't feel like I was becoming more like Him," she said. "I looked in the mirror and saw a stooped, weary creature, puffed by Prednisone, elbows contracted, fingers knotted and swollen." She found it hard "to feel intimate with One who seemed to be lugging a sledgehammer! I could see my life shrinking, not expanding."

Depressed, she questioned and cried out to God. "I tried to cling to a God who seemed distant, because, like Peter, I knew there was nowhere else to go. I claimed His promise that He is close to the brokenhearted (Psalm 34:18). And I began taking prayer more seriously. I asked God to give me more life, more purpose, and to show me where I was choosing my dreams over His."

As a former teacher, Lael knew how to encourage others. So she began taking stock of what she could do to encourage herself and make life more bearable. "I could sit," she says. "So, I decided to sit and read and study Scripture. Sit and write lectures. I could still lecture a class. I could write creatively. I could be grateful there are no joints in my head to get inflamed—the synapses in my brain fire without the least pain," she laughed.

With God's help over the years, step by step, she has found "a rising tide of joy. I know following Jesus doesn't always lead to sunlit fields of laughter and dancing, but our dance with Christ can produce endurance, character and hope. Suffering can open the eyes of our heart to see more of God than we ever imagined. I decided to do what Solomon advised and enjoy my Creator despite the pain. And, in my submission, God has shown me more of His heart and His kingdom. He has opened new doors for me."

Lael wrote and taught a Bible study, wrote a book and has a ministry. She presses on. "The things God prepared me to do—write and teach—don't require much mobility or strong hands," she says, "And that's a mercy."

SOUL THERAPY

Lord, pain is so hard to live with.
It throbs into my very soul sometimes!
Please grant me times of relief.
Show me how to focus my full attention on You instead of the pain.
Remind me of what I *can* do
And help me to pursue it,
So that the enemy misery doesn't win.

WORK OUT

Exercise, stretches and range-of-motion activities several times a day help rheumatoid arthritis and joint problems, and may be easiest to do after a warm bath. For a hand exercise, open your hands and spread your fingers, then close them all as if making a fist without the force. Repeat ten times. For knees, sit on a chair, and from that position straighten out one knee until it is hip level, then bend it again putting the foot on the floor. Repeat ten times (or more), then change legs.

JOURNAL

Write out a prayer asking for God's help in a painful area of your life. Date it, so you can record any later answers to that prayer.

How Can I?

BODY BASIC

Psychological research has shown that gratitude plays a role in both physical and emotional well-being. In one study, two colleagues at the University of Miami (Mike McCullough and Robert A. Emmons, PhD) discovered that the people in the study's "gratitude group" were not only happier than the control and gripe groups, but they also reported fewer health complaints and even exercised more.

SPIRITUAL SPECIFIC

"Give thanks to the Lord, for He is good; His love endures forever. The Lord is my strength and my song; He has become my salvation."

(PSALM 118:1,14)

*S*ometimes it's almost impossible to be grateful*—especially when you or someone you love is suffering. Yet Paul, probably in prison at the time, instructed the Ephesians to always give "thanks to God the Father for everything." (Ephesians 5:19-20) That takes a lot of strength. And, until we can muster that strength, we can more easily obey another scripture, one that says "give thanks *in* all things." Jesus did that before sacrificing Himself on the cross.

When He was struggling with the agony of His upcoming crucifixion, Jesus fervently prayed in the Garden of Gethsemane. We're not told that He thanked God for the privilege of suffering. Instead, He fearfully anguished over "the cup," and said, "Father, if you are willing, take this cup from Me; yet not My will, but Yours be done." (Luke 22:42) Scripture uses "a cup filled with the wine of God's wrath" as a symbol of divine judgment against wickedness, and that cup awaited Jesus, the Perfect One, as He took our sins upon Himself. Jesus knew that cup held not only physical torture, but horrible spiritual agony as He, the Lamb of God, became our substitute. Innocent of any sin of His own, He would endure God's wrath against *our* sin as He died.

Earlier, however, Jesus had demonstrated how to give thanks in all things. That same night, He had given thanks at the Passover Feast for the bread and wine which He said now represented His body and blood, "poured out for many for the forgiveness of sins." He also had expressed appreciation for Mary's earlier anointing of Him with expensive perfume, because "she did it to prepare me for burial." And before He left the upper room and headed toward the Garden, where He faced betrayal and the arrest leading to His death, Jesus led a hymn of thanksgiving—Passover fellowship was concluded with the singing of Psalms 115-118, which glorify and thank God for His love, faithfulness, goodness, mercy and blessing. Jesus gave thanks even as He agonized over what was to come.

He willingly pressed on toward the cross when God didn't remove the necessity for it. He could do it, because He intimately knew and trusted His loving Father. He understood and consented to God's plan, and had no doubt it was right and good, despite how things seemed. He agreed that His people were worth the tremendous price He had to pay, even though the prospect of paying it tormented Him. And because of His own pain and grief, Jesus can sympathize with ours.

A young soldier, who lost a leg in Iraq, described his own method of being thankful during an interview: "The way I stay positive is to appreciate what I still have. I can just look around me and find people who are in worse shape than I am."

Who is it that can't look around and find anyone enduring more than he? Only Jesus—the One Who endured the unimaginable for *us*. He could have chosen to save Himself. But, if He had, He couldn't have rescued us.

Now the resurrected Jesus assures us that He is always with each of us, His followers, whether we feel Him there or not. He is in control of all things, and He will create something positive through the pain. Those promises can kindle our gratitude.

SOUL THERAPY

My Savior, it's so hard to be like You,
Or even like Paul,
And to give thanks in suffering and grief.
But I know I have much for which to be grateful.
And at the top of that list is You and Your sacrifice for my salvation.
Thank You that no matter what else I might lose,
I always have You and Your love.

WORK OUT
Express your thanks to God verbally while moving physically. Start with your feet together. Step sideways to the right all the way across the room. Each time you step, lift your arms straight out to your sides (like a T) and lower them again when you bring your feet back together. With each step, give thanks for a blessing, past or present. Then repeat the process while side-stepping left.

JOURNAL
Record the list of things for which you are thankful and read back over it whenever you need a gratitude boost.

Visible Expression

BODY BASIC
The face has twenty-two muscles on either side of it. Because those muscles are attached to the skin or other muscles instead of bone, even the slightest twitch is visible. We can produce many facial expressions, and they often speak for us.

SPIRITUAL SPECIFIC
"When Moses came down from Mount Sinai with the two tablets of the Testimony in his hands, he was not aware that his face was radiant because he had spoken with the Lord."

(EXODUS 34:29)

*M*oses' *facial expression isn't described* as he delivered the stone tablets of God's law, but we're told that his face glowed so brightly from being with God that "the people of Israel could no more look at him than stare into the sun." (2 Corinthians: 3, MSG) His face reflected God's glory.

Countenance is a look on a person's face that shows his nature or feelings, and the Bible mentions many a face whose countenance told a story. In Genesis, when God accepted Abel's offering and not Cain's, Cain's anger showed on his countenance, and God said, "Why is your face downcast?" God warned Cain if he didn't do what was right, sin would master him.

Cain didn't listen. Sin won, and the jealous Cain went on to commit the world's first murder—killing his own brother, Abel.

Daniel, one of the young Jewish captives in Babylon who was in training to serve the Babylonian King, obeyed God by refusing to eat the defiling royal food of the Babylonians. And it was not only his face that reflected the benefits of his submission to God. His entire body did. While the others ate the royal food, Daniel and his three friends, Shadrach, Meshach, and Abednego, were given permission for a certain length of time to eat a special diet acceptable to God. And, at the end of the test period "their features appeared better and fatter in flesh than all the young men who ate the portion of the king's delicacies." (Daniel 1:15 KJV) So the four were chosen by the King for special service. The exile Daniel became a renowned and influential prophet who was very instrumental for God under both Babylonian and Persian kings.

The stout-hearted, faithful servant Isaiah, the suffering prophet, expressed his determination to continue God's work by saying, "I set my face like flint, and I know I will not be put to shame." And, the martyr Stephen's face reflected God in another way. Falsely accused of blasphemy and brought to trial before the Sanhedrin, Stephen sat through the testimony of lying witnesses. And all those sitting in the Sanhedrin looked intently at Stephen, "and they saw that his face was like the face of an angel." (Acts 6:15)

Writers in the Bible poetically described a sense of God's presence, blessing and deliverance as God's "face" shining upon a person. Psalmists pled with God not to hide His face from them. And God lets His people know that He delights in shining His face upon us. He gave Moses a priestly blessing for Aaron and his sons to pronounce to the Israelites: "The Lord bless you and keep you; the Lord make His face shine upon you and be gracious to you; the Lord turn His face toward you and give you peace." (Numbers 6:24-26) Especially when we are facing difficulties, we need God's countenance to shine upon us!

A precious face that inspires me belongs to a little boy, Josh, whom I see at the therapy pool. About three or four years old, Josh's tiny body is stiff and uncoordinated; his legs don't move, but his adorable face is radiant. He is always smiling. He tries hard to do what his therapist asks of him. Rolling over on the floating mat is a huge challenge, but after great effort, when he finally accomplishes it, he beams. When I look at Josh, I see more than a beautiful handicapped child. I see joy. His determination and attitude make me try harder. He reminds me to be happy with any physical progress, and if there is none, then just to be joyful in trying. Josh doesn't know that I'm watching him. He doesn't know the effect of his countenance upon me. And it makes me wonder: who might be watching me?

SOUL THERAPY

Father, I need Your help in a big way today,
Because when I'm hurting physically,
Even simple challenges seem overwhelming.
Please let Your face shine upon me,
And give me peace.
And as I tackle my tasks,
Help my countenance to reflect
A joyful determination which comes from You.

WORK OUT
It's fun to observe and appreciate some of your face's many muscles. Sit in front of a mirror and do a series of five repetitions of each exercise: raise your eyebrows, wink one eye, wink the other eye, flare your nostrils, pucker your lips, smile your biggest smile, which uses twelve muscles, and hold for ten seconds.

JOURNAL
Write something that will make you smile—a sweet or funny memory you can thank God for, an answered prayer, an unexpected blessing.

Mending
The Broken

BODY BASIC
*Lightweight human bone,
which makes up only
one-fifth of our body weight, has a
compressive strength greater than
reinforced concrete. After a broken bone
heals, it is strongest in the mended area.*

SPIRITUAL
SPECIFIC
*"I have become like
broken pottery...there is terror
on every side...But I trust in
You, O Lord; I say, "You are
my God. My times are in Your
hands..."* (PSALM 31:12-15)

*N*ot only can our bones be literally broken, but trouble and trials can make us feel broken—broken-hearted, broken-spirited. And
the physical, mental or spiritual pain of brokenness may lead to our being
disappointed with God, feeling more inclined to pull away from Him than
to press closer. In Psalm 73, the writer admits he almost fell away from
faith, because he, a godly man, suffered so much misfortune, while evil
men, who "clothe themselves with violence," prospered. "When I tried to
understand all this, it was oppressive to me until I entered the sanctuary
of God; then I understood their [evil-doers] final destiny," he says.

Seeking God's presence in the Temple, the Psalmist is transformed.

He sees the future God has appointed for the unrepentant wicked. And now he knows that his grieved heart and embittered spirit were "senseless and ignorant." He is healed by a renewed appreciation of what he has: a relationship with God, his Refuge. He says to God, "I am always with You; You hold me by my right hand. You guide me with Your counsel, and afterward You will take me into glory. Whom have I in heaven but You? And earth has nothing I desire besides You. My flesh and my heart may fail; but God is the strength of my heart, and my portion forever."

Evil and suffering raise many questions we can't answer. Yet despite wickedness and the resulting grief in the world, God hasn't lost control. He is sovereign and can bring good out of any evil, even including the agonizing death of His own Son.

That truth became real to Edith, a Jewish Hungarian teenager and gymnast bound for the Olympics, when she was imprisoned in Auschwitz during WWII. She told me her story over the phone, saying that both her parents died at that concentration camp. Later, Edith herself, assumed dead, was thrown into a pile of dead bodies. American soldiers, who fought their way through enemy lines and freed prisoners from the death camp, rescued Edith from the pile when they saw her move slightly. She was barely alive.

Edith said that in spite of the evildoers, "I found God at Auschwitz. I discovered the part of me that I never knew was there—the part that the Nazis could not murder. God showed me how to turn hate into pity; the guards were the prisoners, not me. He taught me to look within, when there was nothing good without. My God is that part of me that I cherish today. I am grateful He put me into the world to contribute something to it."

Edith became a psychologist and inspirational speaker. Through her lectures, she teaches others that "It's not what happens to us, it's what we do with it (with God's help)." In a book she's written, Dr. Edith Eger shares her story of victory in the midst of evil, brokenness and terror.

When "there is nothing good without," we need hope. Jesus, the One whose body was broken for our sins, gave birth to hope by defeating death. And no matter what the evils of this world may wreak, the resurrected Christ promises to be the strength of our heart forever.

SOUL THERAPY

Father, sometimes I feel so broken,
And wickedness wields such power!
But Your strength is far greater.
Please rescue me from evil.
Mend my splintered spirit with Your love and comfort,
And turn my fractured places into areas of great strength and faith,
So that I can reach out to others who are shattered
And help them draw closer to You.

WORK OUT

Resistance, impact and weight-bearing activity build bones' strength and density. Warm up for exercise by marching in place two minutes. Then, using a firm chair, sit down and stand up five to ten times (you can do this with a canned good in each hand, too). Or, get a thick book and place it on the floor. Put the balls of your feet on it, with your heels hanging off. Rise on your toes slowly, then lower your heels as far as you can. Repeat ten to twenty times.

JOURNAL

Record any brokenness you feel and bring it to God in prayer. Jesus' prayer that He taught the disciples—the Lord's prayer—begins and ends with the focus on God, with requests sandwiched in between. He was giving us an outline for any prayer. Date your prayer and leave a space under it to record any of God's answers that you see or lessons you learn as time goes by.

Choice

BODY BASIC
Choices, plans and judgments are made in a certain area of the brain, the pre-frontal cortex, which doesn't mature until a person is in his or her mid-twenties.

SPIRITUAL SPECIFIC
...I have set before you life and death...Now choose life, so that you and your children may live and that you may love the Lord your God, listen to His voice, and hold fast to Him. For the Lord is your life..."
(DEUTERONOMY 30:19)

*F*rom the beginning, God gave mankind the gift of choice. Every day we choose from a variety of options—good or evil—which can affect not only our own life, but others'. One person's bad decision (such as driving drunk) may devastate others with its effects. If someone chooses evil, thousands may perish. We have no control over anyone's choices but our own. And sometimes our own poor decisions grieve us. But God offers humankind the right option: life in Him. And He tells us to choose it.

In the Bible we learn that God makes choices, too. He chose Abraham to father the nation Israel, and appointed Moses to lead His people out of bondage. "He chose our inheritance for us," says the Psalmist. But God's choices are often confusing to us. He allowed James to be martyred, but then miraculously saved the imprisoned Peter from the same fate (Acts 12). He softened some hearts and hardened others, like the unbelieving Pharaoh's. And why did Jesus choose Judas to be one of His inner circle when He knew Judas would betray Him? Why does God allow terrible things to happen?

My friend Leslie and I began discussing why God permits tragedies after she experienced one in her own family, one which tore her world apart. She told me that her sister had been in the process of divorcing a verbally abusive husband, and Leslie had been praying for her as well as helping her find a job. Then, Leslie received the unthinkable news that her sister's estranged husband had murdered her, then killed himself. And their two small children were at home at the time.

Leslie was numb and completely devastated. She admitted, "The truth that God is in control all the time over everything, that He is omnipresent and omniscient, and that He cares for His children, were of little comfort to me. If God was truly with my sister, then why didn't He stop the violence? I had been praying at the church altar for my sister for weeks. Why did God answer like that? Since my sister was closer to God through her Bible study than she'd ever been, why didn't He save her?"

Heavy-hearted, Leslie made it through the funeral, supported by an outpouring of love from family, friends, church and her sister's Bible study group. She felt comforted that at least her side of the family took in her murdered sister's children. But then the paternal side of the family took Leslie's family to court, suing for custody. Through twenty long months of anger, grief and battle, Leslie prayed. Under the strain, her health gave way to Grave's disease, a thyroid disorder. "When I so desperately needed strength and endurance, why did God allow me to become physically and mentally incapacitated?" she asked.

Even as she questioned, Leslie nevertheless chose to trust God. "Even when I can't understand His ways, I do believe God's promises and trust His love," she said. "But I'll probably always be seeking answers. Does anyone down here understand these things?"

With her health improved and the court battle over (her nieces are with her side of the family), Leslie says she finds strength by holding fast to what she *does* understand about God. "I have experienced His sustaining power," she said. "He held me up even though I was weak and wanted to cave in to despair. And in the turmoil, even as I asked my questions, God gave me His peace which surpasses understanding. With my prayer life strengthened, I found that sometimes it was my job simply to persevere day to day, loving my Lord and trusting Him to bring good out of the bad."

She clings to scripture as well. One of her favorites is, "We live on, sorrowful...yet always rejoicing." (2 Corinthians: 6) "I've learned that it's up to me to 'count it all joy,' even when I don't *feel* joyful. I had to *choose* to find joy and to give thanks for every blessing I could count—a loving family, and things that symbolize my sister. I rejoice that He's with my nieces, and has given them a loving Christian home. And I rejoice that even though I'll never understand why God allowed the murder, I know that He was with my sister, holding her in His arms as she fell.

"My bright and beautiful sister was like sunshine in our family," she continued. "And I believe she would use the words from a familiar hymn to say to me, "Cheer up, my sister, live in the sunshine. You'll understand it all by and by.'"

Christ comes into our battered lives knowing how we feel. And even though He doesn't always provide answers in this life, He affirmed "I love you" with His own suffering and sacrificial death. He came to destroy sin and death, "the last enemy," by His death and resurrection. And He promises us His comfort until He comes in final triumph over evil.

SOUL THERAPY

Giver of Grace,
I know You grieve
When Your good gift of choice
Is twisted by sin and used destructively.
Please guide my decisions so that they please You.
And although I can't control another's choices,
I can turn to You for refuge
When I am deeply wronged or harmed by them.
Please strengthen me to trust Your love
Even as I ask questions.

WORK OUT
Choose Paul's prayer for believers in Ephesians 3:16-19 as part of your reading today and pray it for yourself.

JOURNAL
Reflect on Paul's words, or write your own prayer asking for whatever strength, focus, wisdom or refuge you need.

Hands

BODY BASIC
When a baby is born, his hands can grip strongly enough to support his body weight. (But don't test it.) An adult can exert a grip of about ninety pounds.

SPIRITUAL SPECIFIC
"For I am the Lord, your God, who takes hold of your right hand and says to you, Do not fear; I will help you."
(ISAIAH 41:13)

God is Spirit, and doesn't have hands as we know them, but He speaks of His figurative hand in scripture. He said (Jeremiah18:6), "As the clay is in the potter's hand, so are you in My hand, O house of Israel!" God's mighty hand, which He uses in the Bible for both discipline and deliverance, is continually molding His people to be more like Him. His "fingerprints" are all over our life, especially in hard times.

God in the human form of Jesus used His hands for earthly as well as divine jobs. As a toddler, Jesus clutched His parents' fingers, and as a carpenter, He built with His hands. As Messiah, He served and touched to heal. He multiplied and broke bread, and He clasped His hands in prayer. His hands cooled fevered brows and restored people to life.

As Christians, we are in God's hands, and we represent Him. When

Peter met a paralytic who begged for money, he said, "Silver or gold I do not have, but what I have I give to you. In the name of Jesus Christ of Nazareth, walk." Taking him by the right hand, Peter helped him up, and the man walked. (Acts 3: 6-7). Although the power was God's, the hand that reached down to the man was Peter's.

When I met Beth at an organizational dinner, I shook her right hand, but didn't notice that her left hand was a prosthesis. As we got to know each other, she told me the story of a terrible accident that had changed her life. An art major in college in the seventies, Beth had just completed a sculpture and was mixing clay in a large machine in the shop. Through a mistake in handling the unfamiliar machine, her left hand was caught by blades and torn off. Doctors were unable to save the hand.

"I was in the hospital, then in rehab going through all the stages of grief, anger and denial," Beth told me. "I was down. I was a cute little sorority girl with a *hook*! I didn't know how I'd dress myself or what kind of life I'd be able to live. And I needed an advocate to say, 'Here's how you do things.' But there was no one! So, naturally, I was overwhelmed. But finally, the nature that God gave me re-surfaced. I didn't like wallowing in the negative—that's such a waste. So I looked for the positive: what can I learn? How can I make this constructive? My God-given faith told me that losing a hand was something that God had allowed to happen, whether I was ready or not. So I made a conscious decision to use my life to glorify Him by being an example of 'You *can*!'"

And she did. Beth got a prosthesis to replace the hook, finished her degree, married, and had children, "and did all those little things like braiding hair and tying shoes." She became a hospital advocate for amputees, encouraging them. She survived a divorce, then widowhood in the midst of a later happy marriage. She ran the family ranch and opened a Bed and Breakfast to help make ends meet. Later, she wed again and now ranches with her new husband. She sails boats and arranges flowers in her free time!

"I've had my ups and downs," she said, "But I realize that as I've gone through life, each lump and hump has turned out for good in some way. And it's built my faith. I know if I didn't go through Point A, I'd never get to Point B in life. And what God has for me at Point B is so much better. So I focus daily on God and try to give Him control."

She also takes comfort in God's promise, "...Do not fear, for I am with you...I will strengthen you and help you; I will uphold you with My righteous right hand."

SOUL THERAPY

Almighty God, who measured the earth's waters
In the hollow of Your hand,
You mark off the entire cosmos
With the breadth of Your hand,
Yet You offer that hand to me.
"You have searched me and You know me...
You hem me in – behind and before;
You have laid Your hand upon me."
And wherever I am—including on the far side of a turbulent sea,
"Even there Your hand will guide me,
Your right hand will hold me fast."
Thank You.

(TAKEN FROM ISAIAH 40 AND PSALM 139)

WORK OUT
*Squeeze balled-up Play-Doh® or
a small foam ball, and hold the
squeeze for about five seconds.
Repeat ten times. Then use the
other hand. Alternate right and left
hands two to three times.*

JOURNAL
*How have you seen God's hand in
your life?*

A Powerful Core

BODY BASIC
Your "powerhouse" or core stomach muscles are important in helping support the spine and keep the body stable. Tightening those muscles first when exercising benefits your whole body.

SPIRITUAL SPECIFIC
"Proclaim the power of God...the God of Israel gives power and strength to His people." (PSALM 68: 34-35)

*A*lthough I had been walking two miles a day, the pain from bulging discs in my neck and back forced me to quit. As she worked me out in water therapy, my therapist, Gayle, told me that weak stomach muscles had contributed to my lower back problems, and my weak lower back, in turn, had added to upper spine and neck trouble. "Your stomach and back muscles form a girdle that supports the spine by tightening at the same time," she explained. "When the abdominals get weak, it's as if someone untied the girdle!" The disc deterioration in my arthritic spine was partly due to poor core strength.

To maintain proper muscle balance, I had to start "from the inside out," developing and maintaining my core muscles with Gayle's specially-designed water workouts. As I did each exercise, I tightened my "abs" and buttocks, so that my core muscles were exerted along with whatever part of my body I was exercising. I grew stronger all over, but especially my core, and my back steadily improved.

Spiritual "muscle" is the same—it must be strengthened from the inside out. I have found that when I deliberately engage God, my true Core Strength, in everyday circumstances, He influences my actions—like when I decide to pray for the people in the very slow line I'm in, it helps keep me from fuming. When I "tighten my faith" through quiet times of Bible reading and prayer, I am better braced for what trials lie ahead. Memorizing comforting scriptures and sharing them builds my spirit, too.

The Bible has been given to each of us as our basic piece of work-out equipment. It comes with a Trainer, the Holy Spirit, who knows exactly what we are capable of and helps us achieve it—even if it means suffering some pain.

We rarely enjoy the process, but we *do* gain in pain if we allow it to draw us into knowing God better and depending on Him more. We experience His power best when we have none of our own.

My cousin, Edward ("Ned") Sheldon, exemplified that. He was a renowned and successful playwright in the 1920s, the toast of society, when he was stricken with paralyzing rheumatoid arthritis at the height of his career. Bedridden and eventually blind, he could have turned away from God. Instead, he turned *to* Him. And Ned was an inspiration to all who came to his bedside. Ann Morrow Lindbergh called him her most unforgettable character. As he lay immobile in his bed, he said, "If I had to choose, I would choose this physical condition with the spiritual growth it has brought me to the pleasure of returning to my old life." Although Ned's motion was severely limited, nothing hindered his movement toward God, his Core Strength.

SOUL THERAPY

Almighty God, my power is in You.
When life's trials slam me to the ground,
Please out-muscle any defeat and despair
That attempt to pin down my spirit.
Fortify my faith and endurance.
Lift me with Your Holy Spirit,
And make me strong to the core.

WORK OUT

Lie on your back, knees bent with your feet on the floor (or bed). Tightening your stomach, pull your belly button toward the floor until your low back is flat against the mat or bed. Hold it tight for twenty seconds. Repeat ten times. Then, move your arms in a variety of directions while keeping your abdominals tight. For instance, keep your arms straight as you raise them one at a time over your head and lower them back down to your side. Then clasp your hands together, and keeping arms straight move them back and forth over your head and back down. Repeat ten times.

JOURNAL

How is God your spiritual Core Strength? Write down some ways you can engage God today in every chore.

One In Billions

BODY BASIC
Among the billions of people on earth, each person, except identical twins, has his own distinctive DNA, the chemical molecule of heredity. And even identical twins have something to set them apart – their fingerprints.

SPIRITUAL SPECIFIC
"So God created man in his own image...male and female, He created them."
(GENESIS 1:27)

Each person on the planet is unique with one-of-a-kind fingerprints and genetic markers. God's creativity is as limitless as He is, yet we, as His diverse creation, still have one thing in common: we were originally made in His image. Sin has since taken us far from our original perfection. But God sent His Son to save us from that sin, and Christ is "the radiance of God's glory and the exact representation of His being." (Hebrews 1:3)

Jesus came to save all shapes, sizes, and colors of humanity. As our Creator, He understands each personality, our pluses, minuses and handicaps. He meets us where we are, allowing us to approach Him in faith with whatever doubts, anger, limitations or problems we bring with us. And

He mysteriously can use everything that sets people apart—even if it's a physical or mental handicap—for His glory and His purposes.

A minister named David, who told me his story by phone, said that he and his wife were taken by surprise by their son's handicap, because their baby had appeared normal at birth. They had taken their beautiful son home and prayed over him every night. But when he was three, the boy was diagnosed with autism. "My wife and I struggled with grief, confusion and anger, wondering if God had ignored our prayers," David said. But they nevertheless pressed ahead to find out all they could about their child's condition to help him. And, as he learned about autism, David learned some things about himself and God.

"I began seeing parallels between autism and my own faith life," he said. "I wanted to help and train my son to have normal face-to-face interactions. I wanted to get through his peculiar patterns and barriers, and connect with him. His struggle to make progress with me relationally helped me see my own spiritual autism as I struggled to relate to my invisible Father," he said.

"Just as we are training our son, I believe God is training me, drawing me out of patterns that paralyze my capacity to know Him. As I've focused more deeply on God and listened to Him more, I have connected with Him on a new level. I am being freed from worrying that God cannot be trusted just because He does not act according to my script. He often responds in ways I don't expect."

After much work, David's son began making eye contact. "And just as my wife's and my heart soared with delight when our son began making eye contact with us, I know God delights in His children looking at *Him* and knowing His love."

Although David and his wife continue to grapple with their son's challenges, they also want to take the pain and turn it around. "This experience has given us compassion for parents with children who have special needs," he says. "Before this, I would feel sorry for those parents, but I wouldn't truly understand. Now I do. We've started a ministry at our church for the parents of special needs kids—giving the parents a night out once a month. We have as many as 150 kids there, with nearly as many church volunteers each time. It's a little thing, but it means a lot to those parents. Starting that program probably wouldn't have occurred to us if we hadn't experienced our own special needs."

As David learned first-hand, our Designer is always creating something—giving us a deeper knowledge of Him, greater grace, or perhaps even a special outreach—as we press on through physical, mental or emotional challenges. And, when we seek Him, He faithfully works with us to bring eternal gain from our pain.

SOUL THERAPY

My Creator, when I feel discouraged, afraid or trapped
By the unique demands of caretaking,
Or by my own limitations,
Show me how to turn the pain around.
Help me to reach out with kindness,
Patience and perseverance.
Please enable me to see beyond temporary human disabilities
To Your image in each person—
A beautiful, eternal image which will be revealed fully one day,
When the chains of life fall away.

WORK OUT
Pray for someone you know with a challenged child or a handicap of their own, and look for ways that you can encourage them.

JOURNAL
Make a list of things that make you—or the loved one you are caring for—unique. What things are good and not so good? If you can't think of positive gifts, ask God to open your eyes to them. Write out a prayer asking God to take both the positive and negative things you've listed, and use them or change them for His glory. (And don't forget to record any answers or revelations you get as time goes on.)

Bruising

BODY BASIC
Bruising is caused when tiny blood vessels are damaged or broken and blood leaks into tissues under the skin causing a black and blue color. Women bruise more easily than men, and most bruises take two to four weeks to heal.

SPIRITUAL SPECIFIC
"The Spirit of the Lord is upon me, because He hath anointed me to...set at liberty them that are bruised."
(LUKE 4:18 KJV)

Sin has bruised mankind since the beginning of the Bible, when Satan entered God's perfect Garden to tempt Adam and Eve to do things his way instead of God's way. God already had His plan in place for mankind's redemption, however, and His curse on Satan included the first promise of the Savior. God told Satan that the woman's seed, her future offspring, Christ, would crush his head, "and thou [Satan] shalt bruise His heel." (Genesis 3:15 KJV) God's prophecy portrayed the damage done by the nails that were driven through Jesus' ankles and heels on the cross (where His hands were nailed, too), as He suffered and died for our sins. But Jesus' later resurrection struck the destroying blow to Satan's head.

For now, Satan is active in this fallen world, but his time is short, because his bruising is fatal.

Christ's superiority to Satan is revealed all through the Bible—from His encounter with Satan in the wilderness to His casting out of demon spirits from self-destructive people, to His defeat of death. In the synagogue in Nazareth, Jesus read one of Isaiah's prophecies which said, "…He has anointed me to…set at liberty them that are bruised." And then He said, "Today this scripture is fulfilled in your hearing." (Luke 4:18-21 KJV) Jesus fulfilled many other ancient prophecies. One that seems to encapsulate His mission says, "He was "bruised for our iniquities…and with His stripes we are healed." (Isaiah 53:5 KJV)

My church friend Kathie needed healing from the bruising of abuse she suffered for much of her life. It began with sexual abuse when she was only four. Growing up in an alcoholic home, Kathie "escaped" at age fourteen into the arms of a man who turned out to be an abuser himself. She lived in fear, trapped in a situation she didn't know how to escape. "One night I read my Bible and prayed that God would keep him away from me, but he came home and began beating me while I was asleep. I was so angry at God! I cried out to Him, 'Am I such a bad person that you listen to everyone but me?' I really thought it happened to me because I was bad.

"I didn't know how much I mattered to God," she continued. "I pictured Him like my earthly father—someone who sat in a recliner and kind of watched me. Yet, deep in my heart I knew God was with me and was helping me. Looking back, I see how He helped me grow stronger instead of getting beaten down or going insane. He kept me alive several times, putting a stop to the abuse suddenly. Finally, I grew feisty enough to take some personal responsibility and get away from the man."

After that, Kathie struggled through a "rescue marriage" that ended in divorce. She then met the man who has been her husband for more than twenty-five years, and he has seen her through therapy and an emotional recovery. She said, "At age thirty-six, I fully gave my life to Christ in baptism, and it was the first time I felt truly clean after all I'd been through. He gave me a whole new life. God has saved me every way a person can be saved. And after that baptism, I realized what God could do through the pain and evil that had been in my life—He and I could use it to help other people."

Kathie began several successful recovery ministries at the church where she and I are members, and the groups continue to grow under her leadership. "A huge part of my healing," she told me, "has been in realizing how intimately God knows me and how deeply He loves me. One of my favorite Psalms is 139, especially verses 13-18, and I share it with everyone I can."

SOUL THERAPY

Please, God of all comfort,
Don't allow the horror, sadness and wickedness of this fallen world
To warp my idea of who You really are
And how much You love me.
Deliver me from evil!
Give me the strength to walk out of every darkness
And into Your light.
Mend my bruised spirit with Your mercy.
And help me to pass it on.

WORK OUT
Read Psalm 139. Some of Kathie's favorite lines are in verses 13-26: "I praise You because I am fearfully and wonderfully made; Your works are wonderful, I know that full well. My frame was not hidden from You when I was made in the secret place. When I was woven together in the depths of the earth, Your eyes saw my unformed body. All the days ordained for me were written in Your book before one of them came to be."

JOURNAL
Write what that Psalm means to you.

Ears To Hear

BODY BASIC
In a tiny space, the ear's many delicate parts cause an amazing chain of events, taking sound-bearing airwaves and creating, with the brain's help, meaningful noises. Hearing, however, can be impaired by many causes, including illness, injury, age or genetic conditions.

SPIRITUAL SPECIFIC
"He who has ears to hear, let him hear." (MARK 4:9)

W*hen He spoke, Jesus said many times in the gospels,* "He who has ears to hear, let him hear." He said it to let people know that what He told them was important, and they should listen. But He knew that plenty of people would choose not to hear. And there were some, like many religious leaders, who were so infuriated by what they *did* hear that they plotted His death. Others—such as the believing disciples—heard, but often didn't understand, and Jesus always explained it to them later.

Although He healed the physically deaf, Jesus did not unstop the ears of hearing people who refused to listen to Him. Throughout history, Israel had often turned a deaf ear to God. "You have seen many things, but have paid no attention; your ears are open, but you hear nothing."(Isaiah 42:20) Scripture relates story after story of people who failed to listen to God and regretted it.

Because of the stubborn, unhearing disbelief of the chosen Jews, Gentiles were given the chance to hear God's Good News of salvation. And all who believed were saved.

Believers' ears receive God's message, and God says He will listen to us, too: "Does He who implanted the ear not hear?" (Psalm 94:9) He promises to answer the prayers of the righteous person. And even though Paul reminds us in Romans 3 that "there is no one righteous [in right standing with God], not even one," God makes us in right standing through faith in Christ. "The eyes of the Lord are on the righteous and His ears are attentive to their cry." (Psalm 34:15) Reminding ourselves of those promises and claiming them can help when we feel alone and wonder if God is listening

The late Helen Keller, an acquaintance of my great-grandmother, and perhaps the most well-known deaf (and blind) person in America, must have felt totally isolated in her dark, soundless world as a child. Her amazing tutor and friend, Anne Sullivan, helped her out of that dark silence by teaching Helen words spelled out by Anne's fingers into Helen's palm. The world suddenly opened to Helen when she caught on. Anne remained her companion throughout her life, even helping Helen get a college degree by translating books and lectures into her hand. Later Helen, an author, speaker and activist for helping others, said, "Although the world is full of suffering, it is also full of the overcoming of it."

God has always helped His people to overcome. An unseen but loving Companion and Teacher, He spells out His hope and love for us in the Bible, opening up a new world. He doesn't require good physical ears to hear Him. He speaks to minds and hearts. And He makes a promise that we can look forward to: "No eye has seen, no ear has heard, no mind has conceived what God has prepared for those who love Him."

SOUL THERAPY

Lord, if it becomes difficult to hear the voices dear to me,
And I feel isolated,
Please encourage me with Your promise
That You are always attentive to my cries.
Show me ways to connect with those I love,
No matter what shape my hearing is in.
And when it seems to me that You are being silent,
And Your answers are far away,
Remind me that You are not distant,
But are always at work for me.
Give me ears perfectly attuned to Your message of love.

WORK OUT

Tune in to your favorite music CD and, as you do, give ear to the rhythm. Exercise by marching in place to the beat. Involve your arms, too—waving them in rhythm the way a music conductor would. (Your core will benefit from this exercise, too, if you tighten your abdominal muscles as you do it.)

JOURNAL

Others can "hear" your faith story by reading your writing. Record how you came to faith, or your struggles in coming to faith. Then, if one day you choose to share your testimony, you'll have it ready.

Adjusting
To Change

BODY BASIC
The body is designed to adapt to changes, continually adjusting to circumstances and surrounding conditions in order to keep the body's internal environment stable. Most of the time a person is not conscious of how his/her body is adapting. However, paraplegia, a complete or partial lack of motor function in the lower half of the body, affects the body's sensory and systemic functions, so the paraplegic must make conscious modifications as circumstances change.

SPIRITUAL
SPECIFIC
He changes times and seasons..." (DANIEL 2:21-22)

*O*ur changeless God fashioned an ever-changing creation, and He gave the human body the automatic ability to adjust to many of those changes. However, when our life shifts in a new direction because of injury, illness or tragedy, it often requires that we make mental, physical and spiritual adaptations that aren't automatic.

A fellow alumnus of my college, Brian, found that plenty of adjustments were required of him when he was thrown from a horse and broke his back. He'd been married only three months when the accident occurred. And when he awoke from a week-long coma, "I didn't know who I was or who my wife was," he told me. When Brian's memory finally started returning, his doctor spoke words to him that he wished he could forget: "You will never walk again." Brian admits that he was so depressed, he was suicidal.

A police officer, Brian knew his future was dramatically changed. He was angry at God and searching for life-answers. "I turned a corner several months after the accident when I went to a men's church retreat. The speaker said, "You can't do anything about the past, but you can do something about the future—your faith and attitude are the key.' When I took stock of the positive, I realized I could still love and laugh—I still had everything that truly lasts. My wife is wonderful. And God is for me. I took to heart the Bible verse, 'If God is for me, who can be against me?' God was sending me people and opportunities. My job was to take hold of His gifts and press on."

Brian told me that once he had won the battle in his mind, the battle with his body became less difficult. "I began finding ways to get through life. If I can't do something, I use my mind and find ways to get around it or fix it. The accident has made me more compassionate, too, and I understand what I am here to do now. I talk to people to raise awareness about disabilities. I tell them that we wheelchair-bound people are the same as everyone else, we just sit down more! I encourage handicapped people not to give up, and I've helped counsel some young people through their anger. I want to give others hope that a full life can be led from a wheelchair."

Brian's full life has required many adjustments in home, work and travel. But with his wife's help, he has made them. The first three years after the accident, Bryan was in rehabilitation and worked part-time as an investigator while his wife worked full-time. Then he worked at another job until a big event called for further adjustments—his wife gave birth to quadruplets!

"God would not have given us four kids if He knew we couldn't handle them," Brian says. "As my wife recovered, I was able to get into a nighttime routine where I could feed and change all four babies within an hour. My wife went back to work after six weeks, and I stayed home to raise the kids with help from church friends and both grandmothers. The kids have been my best friends and a great help to me since they were as small as two. I think God knew I needed a small army! They're now in school. I work as a substitute teacher, make furniture, and ranch a little."

Because he has some sensation in his legs, Brian believes he will walk again. He pushes hard to make that hope a reality. He continues to challenge himself. And in a daring test to celebrate his fortieth birthday, he tried sky diving. "It was great!" he says with a smile.

SOUL THERAPY

Jesus, You know all about adjusting and persevering—
You gave up Your glory as God and adapted Yourself
To life as a man—a man of sorrows.
Thank You.
When I'm grieved by the loss of abilities or strength,
Enable me to rebound from the disappointment
And make the changes required in my life.
Remind me that no matter what I lose,
You, Lord of Hope, are with me and for me.
You are my one unchanging constant.
Please lift my spirits as I lean on You.

WORK OUT

Make your exercise today a little more difficult by making adjustments such as adding a little weight, more repetitions, or changing the angle of exercise, such as walking uphill.

JOURNAL

Record some adjustments you've had to make and think of ways God has helped you through. If you have frightening changes ahead of you, ask the Holy Spirit to empower you to accomplish them. Reading back over ways God has strengthened you in the past helps to build trust as each new trial arises.

The Strength Of The Body

BODY BASIC

No part of the human body can work independently. All eleven of our organ systems must coordinate to keep us alive. And our 600 or so individual muscles must work together, too, to support and move the body. Even the blink of an eye uses two or more skeletal muscles! The body's many parts enable the whole to function.

SPIRITUAL SPECIFIC

"The body is a unit though it's made up of many parts. God has arranged the parts of the body just as He wants them to be."

(1 CORINTHIANS 12: 12,18)

*W*hen my massage therapist Teresa works on her clients, they usually comment on her very strong hands. Yet she told me that when her clinic has its annual fun day, which includes games and hand strength contests, she can't even get on the chart for hand strength. "My hands are actually very weak. It's using body mechanics, the leverage of my whole body during a massage that makes it seem as if my hands are strong," she says.

Leaning in and using leg muscles puts power behind her hands. And, by using her whole body along with her forearms and elbows in a massage, she keeps from exhausting her hands. That way, she has the energy to keep massaging all day.

When used properly as an entire unit, our body strength multiplies the power of our individual parts. God uses that analogy in the Bible, telling us that each of us is a member of the body of Christ, and we are strongest when we utilize the whole "body" by allowing other Christians to add their strengths to ours. Christ, our Head, shares His power with us as well.

When I was physically restricted by fatigue and pain, Teresa's helpful massages and encouragement helped. So did the prayers of many. But I was frustrated and embarrassed that my own contributions were so limited. How was I benefiting the body?

That question made me read 1 Corinthians 12:12-27 with new interest. Contrary to how I felt, the words assured me that "those parts of the body that seem to be weaker are indispensable." Doing whatever I *could* do—even when it was "only" to lend a listening ear to someone or to pray with and for another—was important.

And my friends demonstrated for me that "There should be no division in the body, but...its parts should have equal concern for each other. If one part suffers, every part suffers with it; if one part is honored, every part rejoices with it." Through those who exemplified that verse, I learned the great importance of obeying it.

The Message, a Bible paraphrase, reiterates the correct lifestyle: "In this way, we are like the various parts of the human body. Each part gets its meaning from the body as a whole, not the other way around. The body we are talking about is Christ's body of chosen people. Each of us finds our meaning and function as part of His body." (Romans 12: 4-5)

Despite my limitations, I had meaning and function just being a part of the body of Christ. I decided to do my small part, whatever it was, and quit fretting. Instead I'd pray that my kind, helpful friends would find it "more blessed to give than to receive."

SOUL THERAPY

Father, sometimes I feel like a burden to others,
When I can't do much for myself.
And occasionally I even wonder if I weary You
With my many requests for help.
But You've encouraged me to come to You
With every need.
And You've provided me with a body of believers
Whom You've promised to bless when they give.
Help me to do my part for others, too,
So that we are all built up in strength and purpose.

WORK OUT

Lie down and stretch your whole body—point your toes and reach your hands over your head and hold it a few seconds, breathing deeply. Then relax. Next, move your feet up and down, bending at the ankle, ten to twenty times. After that, open your fingers wide, then close your fists ten to twenty times. Finish with head motions: Gently bring your head up from the bed and toward your chest, slowly lower it again five to ten times. If you can't perform the movements, think of someone who needs an encouraging phone call and give them a brief call.

JOURNAL

How can you contribute to the body of Christ?

Healing Writing

BODY BASIC

Writing emotionally and thoughtfully about a traumatic experience benefits not only a person's mental health, but also physical health. Studies by clinical psychologists and immunologists at Southern Methodist University and Ohio State University College of Medicine proved that people who vented their feelings through writing achieved improved immunity: they produced more of the immune system's "killer cell," or T-cell, which attacks viruses and other invaders.

SPIRITUAL SPECIFIC

"Jeremiah composed laments for [dead King] Josiah..." (2 CHRONICLES 35:25)

*D*avid *wrote out his feelings in Psalms,* and the writer of Lamentations devoted his whole poetic book to a series of laments over Jerusalem's destruction and the people's slaughter, starvation and exile in 586 B.C. In both books, while pouring out their troubled souls, the writers also re-focused on God's goodness, hope, love, faithfulness and salvation.

When troubles strike, a journal is a good starting place for recording anger, pain, fear, grief, frustration and every hurtful feeling. My friend Katie found "huge relief" in allowing herself to cry out on paper and in prayer through a long series of problems that left her feeling depressed, hopeless, lonely and exhausted.

"All my life, I've been a rescuer and nurturer," she admitted to me as we rocked and talked on her front porch. "And alcoholism in my family has been a major issue. In the late eighties, I found myself trying to rescue my brother, who later died as a result of alcoholism. I felt under terrible pressures at home, too—my husband was a banker in a collapsing banking system, and I was distraught over our family finances. Then my father, who had also been an alcoholic, died. I thought my faith was strong, but I was tired and wrung out, depressed and feeling hopeless. I did lots of crying out to God as I struggled to handle life. Because I needed to express my feelings, one day I picked up a yellow legal pad and began journaling. I didn't believe anyone in my family valued how I felt or realized how their actions were affecting me. My life seemed as though it were being controlled by their destructive choices; I felt bitter and angry. Then I would feel guilty for feeling bitter! Sometimes I would write so hard, the page would rip. Everything just billowed out. It was extremely therapeutic.

"Then in the nineties, there were more family deaths and our teenage son began to rebel," Katie continued. "Once again, I was thrown into depression. But I kept journaling and found I liked writing. I began recording positive events. Every day I would write about something I was thankful for, and I began to feel better. I wasn't so caught up in others' missteps or my own when I began concentrating on what I was thankful for. And I started noticing God at work. I was led to a community Bible study, where I met some amazing Christian women who helped me on my faith walk. We eventually moved to the country, and I found being close to nature refreshing.

"Just as things began improving, we were blindsided again. Our son became addicted to drugs, and we were under tremendous financial stress trying to get him into a treatment center. For an entire year my husband and I lived on a powder keg, praying constantly for our son, trying to be peaceful as he continued to have life-threatening emergencies.

"Then, when we were away on vacation, our son called crying, 'I don't want to die!' He was obviously extremely distraught and wandering along a busy highway. With God's help, I was able to calmly talk him to a hospital, while my husband contacted friends to meet him there. When that painful emotional ordeal was over, I hung the phone up, curled into a fetal position on the floor, and began crying uncontrollably. I couldn't take anymore! Suddenly, I felt God holding me, protecting me. And a dear friend who was with us on vacation came to our room to pray with me, allowing me to purge a lot of my pain. That was a turning point.

"Even though I still wanted to protect my son, my husband and I chose to stay on our vacation. It was then I finally realized I am not in control of anyone's choices. But I can make my own. I don't have to be sad and in pain forever. I can feel the feelings and express them, but I don't have to be consumed by them. I can take good care of myself—and I've chosen to do that with journaling, Bible study, prayer and yoga.

"And it seemed after that," Katie went on, "From that terrifying phone call onward, my son has drawn closer to me and to God. He is on his journey; I am on mine. I don't have it all figured out. I'm just confident in God, because He has been faithful. What I know for sure is that when I am in communion with Him, I have peace."

SOUL THERAPY

Father, family problems are the most painful kind!
But I guess You know all about that with Your wayward family.
Even though You are my beloved, Perfect Parent,
I disappoint You over and over again.
Thank You for reassuring me of Your love and forgiveness

In Your written message to me,
And for using those words
To lead me on Your path to peace.

WORK OUT

One of Katie's favorite yoga poses is the Warrior Pose, because as a prayer warrior, she enjoys opening herself up to God. To do the pose: start in a star position: arms straight out to the side with your feet facing forward and spread wide. Then turn and point your left foot to the left (so that your foot is in line with your outstretched left arm and your head is turned to look in the direction your left arm is pointing). Slowly bend the left knee, so that the knee is in line with the ankle, sinking into a lunge position. (Don't sink too far—don't let your knee get ahead of your foot and ankle.) Hold for thirty seconds. Then slowly straighten the left knee, turn the left foot back to the front and stand in the star position again. Then make the same moves with the right foot. Repeat five times to each side.

JOURNAL

Record whatever is weighing on your heart, and pray over the situation. Add some things you are grateful for, too.

Keeping Active

BODY BASIC
Our Designer created the body to be active. Not only do muscles need activity to prevent atrophy, but the body's 143 joints need movement to keep them lubricated and prevent stiffness.

SPIRITUAL SPECIFIC
"For the word of God is living and active....it penetrates even to dividing soul and spirit, joints and marrow..."
(HEBREWS 4:12)

By staying physically and mentally active, we help to keep our body working correctly. By daily reading God's word, which is living and active, we help keep our faith moving and growing, too. God's message, which was written over the course of 1,500 years, was not just written for ancient times. It is for us today. Knowing the Bible's timeless truths is essential for our spiritual well-being.

Kris Meyers, author of *Discover Bible Basics*, points out that the Bible was written by all sorts of God-inspired people: nomads, shepherds, kings, soldiers, prophets, fishermen, historians, tax collectors, prisoners and a doctor. More than forty authors on three continents—Africa, Asia and Europe—in three languages—Hebrew, Aramaic and Greek—wrote God's message, never realizing their writings would be part of a greater book. And yet there is one consistent central idea that unifies all the writings over the centuries: God's salvation by grace. And that was accomplished through the work of the "Word made flesh," Jesus Christ.

Despite the fact that the Bible reflects the religious, political and social conditions of another time, its truths are still dependable. God's Word still can guide every sort of person in every time and place, no matter what the circumstances.

In the New Testament, Peter reminds readers, "We did not follow cleverly invented stories when we told you about the power and coming of our Lord Jesus Christ, but we were eyewitnesses of His majesty." Jesus, who ushered in the New Testament, quoted the Old Testament in His teachings, giving His stamp of affirmation to those time-worn stories. More than that, He used scripture to rebuke Satan's temptations in the wilderness. In His prayer for His disciples He said, "Sanctify them in the truth; Your word is truth." (John 17:17) Not only is the Word of God living and active, but "the word of our God stands forever." (Isaiah 40:7-8)

The Dead Sea Scrolls, discovered in 1947 in sealed clay jars hidden in caves near the shores of the Dead Sea, were dated from the third century BC to AD 70. They included copies of every Old Testament book except Esther. Comparing those scrolls to the standard Hebrew Masoretic text revealed that the Hebrew Old Testament we read today is the same one that Jesus read. No matter what else changes, God's word does not.

The importance of God's word was highlighted in a story I read of a Buddhist woman in Thailand named San, who became a Christian after her mother told her about Jesus. She enjoyed church and listening to Bible discussions, but never felt the need to explore the Bible for herself. Learning from others was better, she thought, and she was skeptical about the value of a Bible. Finally, at the urging of her Christian friends, she prayed about whether to get a Bible, and felt God directing her to do it.

That year, San became ill. Feeling alone and afraid, she turned to her Bible. It became her cherished source of comfort and hope. Her love for God's word grew, and the few doubts she had about the Christian faith dissolved. It was a turning point in her life. When San's health improved, she began sharing God's word with those who were sick and in need of hope. She continues to do so.

The Bible, the best-selling book in history, has survived banishment, burnings and controversy. It lives on and is essential to a healthy faith life. God's word keeps us moving toward Him and His best.

SOUL THERAPY

Wonderful Word of Life,
Thank You for Your living truth,
Your limitless love, and Your awesome power.
When my physical activity is restricted,
When my mind and spirit feel stiff with discouragement,
Please stir my faith and lift me up.

WORK OUT
You can be active even from a sitting position. Try "chair jogging:" lift each foot slightly off the ground one at a time as if you are jogging and continue it for one to two minutes.

JOURNAL
Write a favorite scripture to begin memorizing as you repeat the exercise.

Dare To Sing

BODY BASIC
Singing uses a different part of the brain from speaking. People who have difficulty with speech, such as stroke victims or persons who stutter, can usually sing without a problem.

SPIRITUAL SPECIFIC
"But I will sing of Your strength, in the morning I will sing of Your love...O my Strength, I sing praise to You."
(PSALM 59:16-17)

*M*any great hymns were composed through suffering. Fanny Crosby, who wrote "Blessed Assurance" and thousands of other hymns, was blind. Horatio Spafford, who had repeated tragedy in his life, including four daughters who died in a shipwreck, wrote "It Is Well with My Soul." Natalie Sleeth, while afflicted with MS and hearing that her husband had been diagnosed with cancer, penned the words to her Hymn of Promise: "In the bulb, there is a flower, in the seed, an apple tree"... expressing her hope of things "God alone can see."

A favorite hymn of mine with a haunting melody and wonderful words by Katharina von Schiegel and Jean Sibelius is entitled "Be Still, My Soul." It says, in part: "Be still my soul; the Lord is on your side. Bear patiently the cross of grief or pain; leave to your God to order and provide; in every change God faithful will remain. Be still, my soul: your God will undertake to guide the future, as in ages past. Your hope, your confidence let nothing shake; all now mysterious shall be bright at last. Be still, my soul: the hour is hastening on when we shall be forever with the Lord, when disappointment, grief and fear are gone, sorrow forgot, love's purest joys restored."

Despite their circumstances, these hymn writers and others learned the art of keeping their focus on God. Jesus, too, sang a hymn before going out to the Mount of Olives just before His arrest. When Paul and Silas were locked into stocks in prison, their bodies raw from a brutal whipping, they still vocalized hymns to God while the other prisoners listened. Singing during a dark time takes courage.

I've discovered that sometimes when I'm struggling with anger, pain or a bad attitude, and I'm not in the right mood to pray, I can sing first—even something as simple as "Jesus Loves Me." It changes my focus and softens my heart so I can talk with God. Paul told the Corinthians, "I will sing with my spirit, but I will also sing with my mind." Using my mind to concentrate on God's awesome attributes as I sing a favorite old hymn lifts my spirits and my hopes. Then I'm able to ask Him to adjust my attitude about a trying situation or person, about problems or poor health.

A broken heart may make us feel like we'll never sing again, but we can still read or listen to the words of hymns or Psalms to soothe our spirit. The lyrics remind us that our Helper is not only beside us but offers us courage and comfort. As the hymn "Amazing Grace" says, "'twas grace that brought me safe thus far, and grace will lead me home."

SOUL THERAPY

My great and awesome Savior,
Only You can help my soul sing to You
Despite what my body or mind is enduring.
When I feel worn down by worries,
Tune my thoughts to You, my Hope and Strength.
You are my Blessed Assurance that no matter what life demands,
I can depend on You.

WORK OUT
If you feel like it, belt out your favorite hymn. If you don't, read over the words of "Be Still My Soul" (in the second paragraph of this reading) and turn it into a personal prayer.

JOURNAL
Pen meaningful lines from hymns you know.

Physical And Financial

BODY BASIC
Food is essential to life, because without it, the body will begin breaking itself down to make the fuel to function – first using its stores of glycogen, then body fat, then protein in muscles and cells – until, finally, death occurs. Acquiring the basic necessities of life such as food generally requires money.

SPIRITUAL SPECIFIC
"When the money of the people of Egypt and Canaan was gone, all Egypt came to Joseph and said, "Give us food. Why should we die before your eyes? Our money is used up."

(GENESIS 47:15)

*W*hether we barter with goods, service or money, it costs us to live as well as to keep our body healthy. Part of sin's curse was that man would have to struggle for survival. When Christ came, His forgiveness didn't change the need for money in this transitory life, but He taught His followers not to be lovers of money. He said, "Do not store up for yourselves treasures on earth, where moth and rust destroy, and where thieves break in and steal, but store up for yourselves treasures in heaven... For where your treasure is, there your heart will be also." (Matthew 6:19)

Jesus' brother James wrote that God especially blesses "those who are poor in the eyes of the world" by making them "rich in faith."

Jesus instructed His people to help provide for one another, too. He sent His twelve disciples out to teach in His name, and said, "Take nothing for the journey except a staff—no bread, no bag, no money in your belts." God Himself promises to be our Provider, and He often delivers through His believing people.

Some college friends of mine, Tricia and Joe, began their life journey together after graduation and went on to become successful, high-profile community leaders. They worked hard in their clothing store to provide for their family. But when the oil industry collapsed in the early 1980s, their oil-rich West Texas town was especially hard hit. Customers could not pay their built-up charges, and Tricia and Joe lost their store. Forced to declare personal bankruptcy, they emptied their savings account, cashed in insurance policies, and did all they could to pay their business's bills.

"Bankruptcy is embarrassing," Tricia said. "I felt like we'd been a failure. It's a horrible feeling to owe people. Even though we were basically victims of a collapsed economy, I couldn't get past wondering what we could have done differently. I kept torturing myself and Joe with 'should haves' and 'what ifs.' I couldn't let go of trying to fix it, to be in control again."

Tricia took five jobs, riding her bike to work when their second car broke down, and Joe commuted to attend college twelve hours a day to get his teaching certification. "We had three children, no money, our marriage was in trouble, and I was angry with Joe for seeming at peace when I wasn't. Finally, Joe said to me, 'You won't give up trying to control things. You are standing in God's way of blessing.' I was shocked and fought back. But after an all-night discussion, we knelt together and prayed. It was a turning point for me—a time of *real* personal bankruptcy. The kind where I had to give everything to God and let go. I discovered what Joe said was true. As long as my worries were at the center of my attention, I couldn't know or see God's blessing. God had a plan in it, and I had to take myself out of the picture. I had to submit to Him.

"After that night," she continued, "I began seeing His blessings like I never had before. I'd always gone to church and believed in God, but I'd never felt a need to know much scripture or to pray for specifics. However, one of the jobs God provided for me was in our church's youth ministry, so I was forced to get into the Bible. I began growing spiritually, and my faith and trust deepened. As I grew, I began appreciating Joe's integrity and spiritual example, and that re-ignited my love for him.

"That Christmas, we decided as a family not to give each other gifts, but to adopt a family worse off than we were. Someone in our church got wind of it and anonymously brought *us* groceries and a $500 check in an envelope so that we could give our own kids Christmas gifts. Nearly twenty years later, we still hang that crumpled envelope on our Christmas tree to remind us of God's provision and His blessings through His people."

Tricia and Joe are now financially on their feet, and she says, "When you finally get past your hard times, you can look back and see so much good that God accomplished through it. Our hard times opened many doors to a much richer life for us spiritually, to new careers that are deeply satisfying, and to stronger family bonds." Tricia understands more fully what Paul meant when he wrote: "Command those who are rich...not to put their hope in wealth, which is so uncertain, but to put their hope in God who richly provides us with everything for our enjoyment." (1 Timothy 6:17-19)

SOUL THERAPY

Generous Giver of every good gift,
You provided Your disciples with net-breaking catches of fish,
Tax coins from a fish's mouth,
Bread for thousands from a boy's small lunch,
Choice wine from water—
Yet I become anxious so easily when money is tight.
You taught us to pray "give us this day our *daily* bread,"
But I often project my financial fretting into the future.
Please help me to "be anxious for nothing,"
But to daily deposit all my trust in You.

WORK OUT

How can you help someone today?
Let that be your exercise.

JOURNAL

If you are job hunting or
financially anxious, write a specific
prayer for God not only to provide
for you, but also to open your eyes to
see His blessings even in hardships.
Don't forget to record answers as
they occur!

Having Heart

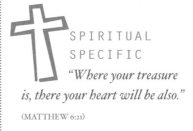

BODY BASIC
As long as it is surrounded by the proper nutrients, a heart muscle can beat completely on its own, even after it's removed from the body.

SPIRITUAL SPECIFIC
"Where your treasure is, there your heart will be also."
(MATTHEW 6:21)

The heart is symbolically the center of everything—thoughts, emotions, character, imagination and desires—and the Bible says it can be evil or pure, soft or hard, lifted up or grieved, wise or foolish. It can be courageous or trembling, lowly or haughty, thankful or ungrateful, filled with love or hate, etc. But we're told the most important thing we can do with the heart is to love and believe. "Love the Lord your God with all your heart," God says. (Deuteronomy 6:5)

When my friend Carla continued serving in Bible study while growing thinner and weaker fighting terminal cancer for four years (doctors said she'd only live for two), some of us asked, "How does she have the heart to go on?" We asked the question even though we knew the answer. Her determination and heart came from faith and love. She didn't fear death—

she was ready for eternity whenever God wanted her. But she also wanted to live, to take care of her husband and love her family as long as she could. I never heard her complain. She just kept going, encouraging others with God's words and her strong faith. When the doctors finally said one day, "There's nothing more we can do," Carla, with the same sweet smile she carried all through her illness, finally went to bed for good. She died two days later at age fifty-five.

The witness of Carla's faith and strength was powerful. She exemplified the verse, "Let us draw near to God with a sincere heart in full assurance of faith…Let us hold unswervingly to the hope we profess, for He who promises is faithful." (Hebrews 10:22-23).

I admit, however, that I wondered why God allowed Carla's suffering. It's still a mystery to me. But, the words of the friendly, powerful lion figure Aslan in C.S. Lewis's *The Horse and His Boy* remind me that God provides just what each individual needs in his or her darkest hour. In Lewis's book, the boy Shasta has just learned from Aslan that the lion himself had been behind circumstances that Shasta found terrifying. Upon Aslan's explanation, Shasta discovers that Aslan had used those frightening experiences to save Shasta's life. However, when Shasta learns that Aslan also was the lion who wounded his friend, Shasta asks, "What for?" At that, Aslan replies, "Child, I am telling you *your* story, not hers."

That's where trust comes in. I have to trust God's heart for Carla just as Carla trusted God with her whole heart. In this life, I'll never know her full story, but God and Carla have it all worked out.

SOUL THERAPY

It's so heart-wrenching to watch a loved one suffer, Lord.
Sometimes it seems worse than being afflicted myself.
But You would understand that—
No one suffered more than Your beloved Son did for us.
Thank You for His gift of salvation.
I come to You now in Jesus' dear name,

Asking for Your relief for _____.
Help _____ and me, too,
To hold unswervingly to Your hope.

WORK OUT

Get your heart rate up with jumping jacks. If you can't jump, try this modified version: Stand with your feet together, arms at your side. Step with your right foot out to the side while raising your arms above your head to clap. Return your foot back in place and bring your arms back to your side. Then do the same movements with your left foot and arms. Alternate sides and repeat thirty times.

JOURNAL

Express your heart—write out your questions to God and ask Him to lead you to verses in scripture that will build your trust in Him, even when you lack answers.

The Basics

BODY BASIC

The cell is the basic element of life, and each of us begins as one tiny egg cell fertilized by a sperm. Cells divide and multiply until, when we are fully developed, we have trillions of them in all sizes, shapes and types. Although each cell contains all the genetic instructions for the whole body, only certain instructions are active in each cell. For instance, even though your arm muscle cells contain information about the color of your eyes, only the muscle directives are active. Each cell is specialized to perform its fixed function, while working cooperatively with the other cells.

SPIRITUAL SPECIFIC

"Before I formed you in the womb, I knew you..."

(JEREMIAH 1:5 NIV)

God, who is the "basic element" of our spiritual life and created every microscopic detail in our body, has always known every intimate secret about each of us. And even before you or I were a cell, He had established our individual purpose. Along with giving human beings responsibilities, our awesome Maker endows people with amazing capabilities for discovery and knowledge. Nevertheless, because the basics about God Himself are never-ending, our human comprehension of Him will always be limited.

For now, wrote the Apostle Paul, we see "but a poor reflection" of God. But in eternity, "we shall see [Him] face-to-face. Now I know in part; then I shall know fully, even as I am fully known."(1 Corinthians 13:12) Even though it's impossible to completely know Him while on earth, we can learn more about God every day through His words in the inspired writings of the Bible. Getting to know Him better helps us to trust Him more, especially during trials that test our faith.

In the Bible, God reveals Himself as the Intricate Designer of all things, who remains personally involved with His creation. He even watches "when the doe bears her fawn." Our eternal God says, "I am He; I am the first and I am the last. My own hand laid the foundations of the earth, and My right hand spread out the heavens..." (Isaiah 48:12-13)

Yet "long before He laid down the earth's foundations, He had *us* in mind, had settled on us as the focus of His love, to be made whole and holy by His love." (Ephesians 1: 4 MSG) Nothing gets in the way of God's love, not even mankind's sinfulness or any life-shattering circumstances, not even our doubts and confusion.

In fact, it's through circumstances that strip us of our own resources that God seems to teach us the most about Himself and His love. In those times of dependence on Him, we gain *personal* knowledge about the Comforter dwelling within us, the Strength who sustains us, the Lord who seeks us. We come to better know the Lover of our souls whose intention for us is wholeness and holiness, even if we can't see it now.

A friend of mine told me that her father, Jerry, discovered the tenacity of God's love at a low point in his life. Trapped on a path of self-destruction, Jerry was desperate when he finally returned to the God who was pursuing him. When I talked to Jerry, he related that although he had been reared in a churchgoing family, "I knew only enough about God to run to Him in a crisis." When he felt God calling him into ministry, he was so overwhelmed that "instead of obeying, I ran *from* Him. And afterward, I had difficulty in every area of my life—with relationships, with coping, with living. When, in spite of myself, I did achieve something like a top management position, I would drink myself out of it. I was obviously trying to destroy myself, and I didn't know why."

Finally, after one especially regrettable weekend of heavy drinking and resulting trouble with his angry wife, "I felt desperate for help," he said. "I just fell to my knees and said, 'God, take this away from me!' I surrendered to Him then and there, gave Him my life. I was totally serious. Repentant. And miraculously, I was instantly healed of the desire to drink. As part of my promise to my wife, I also called Alcoholics Anonymous the next morning."

He continued, "God is the key to everything. No matter where else we turn for help, the bottom line is that God is the key. Getting to know Him isn't an overnight learning experience, but we can find Him in His word and through prayer. The devil doesn't want any of us to win. But Jesus is greater than Satan. And the better we know Jesus and His love, the better life becomes."

That's been Jerry's basic message as a minister for the last twenty years.

SOUL THERAPY

Father, You designed each of my cells with a precise function,
And created me with a distinct purpose, too.
Thank You.
Help me not to fear Your plans,
But to trust You and cooperate,
Making Your wishes mine
And fulfilling them in Your power.

WORK OUT

Sit tall on the edge of your seat and take in ten slow breaths, which will send oxygen to every cell. Then, abs tight and arms straight, lift your hands slowly over your head as you inhale, then lower them as you exhale. (You can do this with your hands in front of you or at your sides.) Be sure to keep your abs tight the whole time. Repeat ten times. As you lift your hands, envision them holding each of the gifts and talents God has given you. Then symbolically hand them back to Him to use for His glory.

JOURNAL

What gifts did you hand to God, and how do you plan to use them for Him?

Relax

BODY BASIC
According to the Mayo Clinic, the process of relaxation, which decreases wear and tear on the mind and body from life's challenges, is essential for stress management, and it benefits overall health. Our skeletal muscles, which must relax as well as contract as they move the body, offer a demonstration of the importance of relaxation. If they are contracted for too long, such as when a soldier stands immobile and at attention for a prolonged period of time, the muscles will fatigue and stop contracting. Then, the soldier will collapse!

SPIRITUAL SPECIFIC
"What I'm trying to do here is get you to relax, not be so pre-occupied with getting so you can respond to God's giving. Steep yourself in God-reality, God-initiative, God-provisions. You'll find all your everyday human concerns will be met."
(LUKE 12, MSG)

"*You are stiff as a brick!*" my therapist Gayle commented. I was floating on my back in the warm water pool, buoyed by flotation devices, while she held my head, trying to gently move it from side to side to coax some flexibility back into my neck. "Can't you just relax?"

"I'm terrified," I admitted. "My neck has been hurting so bad that I'm afraid for you to pull on it."

She comforted me. "This is what I've been trained to do. I won't hurt you. You have to trust me. You have to relax in my hands, or I can't help you."

I never knew it could require such heavy concentration and prayer to relax! It took several sessions for me to become comfortable with Gayle. My trust grew the more I spent time with her and recognized her knowledge, skill, gentleness and commitment to my recovery. Sure enough, after several weeks, my neck muscles began responding to the treatment. When driving, I could actually turn my head to check for traffic instead of twisting my whole body.

Gayle's words return to my mind often. "Trust me. Relax in my hands or I can't help you." Do you ever feel frustrated and frantic when a problem arises and you can't do all the things you need to do, especially within your limitations? Then do you overdo and, as a result, experience pain, fatigue and more tension?

When I feel overburdened, I have to force myself to stop, relax and truly concentrate on God's characteristics in order to place myself, my life, responsibilities and problems in His hands. To unwind, I focus in prayer on God's mighty power, which is capable of anything; on His goodness and love, which are always at work in my life; on His perfect plan—a plan that I am a part of—which can't be thwarted. God is much bigger and more powerful than any problem. Nothing takes Him by surprise, and He can put every obstacle in perspective. As I focus on Him, I'm reminded everything doesn't depend on me.

Our Wonderful Counselor, Everlasting Father and Prince of Peace, who created each amazing detail in our body, offers His assistance in every detail of our life, too. And the most stress-reducing help can come from just recalling who He is and all He is capable of accomplishing *without* us.

As the writer of Lamentations reminds us, the Lord's compassions never fail. "They are new every morning; great is Your faithfulness." Praising

God for His awesome qualities takes time and focus, but it builds faith and banishes stress. Just like with ongoing rehabilitation, hope is always there when we relax in the hands of our Therapist.

SOUL THERAPY

My loving Prince of Peace,
I'm concerned and preoccupied with so much.
And I can feel the tension creeping in,
Especially when I can't do all I need or want to do,
Or when I feel as if I'm failing to live up to my own
Or others' expectations.
Please help me to relax in Your capable hands
And trust You to provide all I need to overcome obstacles.

WORK OUT

To practice a relaxation technique, lie on your back with your eyes closed and your hands on the side of your ribs. Take a deep breath, inhaling through your nose, until you feel your ribs have expanded as far as they can. Hold it a second. Then force a slow exhale through pursed lips as you allow your body to sink into the floor (or bed). To remember the process, think: "Smell the flowers and blow out the candles." Then, as you breathe deeply, visualize a peaceful place like heaven or God's arms and imagine the sounds and sights around—such as beautiful music from the heavenly choir, smiling faces of loved ones—and as your imagination helps you unwind, take at least ten deep breaths.

JOURNAL

Describe your imagined place and why it helped you to relax.

Dreams

BODY BASIC
We "see" pictures in our dreams, even though our eyes are closed in sleep. That's because although we see with our eyes, we see in our brain through its optical center. If the optical center is destroyed, permanent blindness results.

SPIRITUAL SPECIFIC
"This was the dream, and now we will interpret it to the king." (DANIEL 2:36)

Dreams played an important role in scripture. Because Daniel, a Jewish captive in Babylon, correctly interpreted King Nebuchadnezzar's dream, Daniel saved the clueless wise men of Babylon from execution. He was rewarded with a high position and lavish gifts, and he served as a godly example to others.

Another believer, Joseph, interpreted Pharaoh's dreams, which catapulted Joseph from prison rags to royal robes in Egypt and helped to save thousands from starvation. Joseph's brothers, who had sold him into slavery in the first place, were reunited with him when they traveled to Egypt to ask for grain during a famine. That event fulfilled Joseph's dream from many years before that his brothers would bow down to him.

In the New Testament, the Lord or an angel of the Lord often appeared in dreams. The Lord told Joseph to take pregnant Mary home as his wife instead of divorcing her quietly. A later dream instructed Joseph to flee to Egypt with the Child. The Magi were warned in a dream not to return to Herod after finding Jesus. Pilate's wife sent him a message during Jesus' trial: "Don't have anything to do with that innocent man, for I have suffered a great deal today in a dream because of Him."

Although we rarely hear of prophetic dreams today, all of us have daydreams—our hopes of what our future may hold. When those dreams are dashed by disability, injury or poor health, by a failed business or marriage, by severed relationships or a death, it's hard to dream again. But when we put our dreams in line with God's will, they are attainable. And Christ invites us to hope in Him.

A church friend of mine, David, has Muscular Dystrophy, but he has never let it get in the way of his dreams. "I had never looked at myself as being at a disadvantage because of my disability until recently, when I started interviewing for jobs," he told me. His dream has been to "help develop the next generation by being a teacher and a coach who is also a good role model. But the schools I applied to have not called back. So I just keep praying that God will lead me in the direction He wants me to go. I know He has a job where my abilities are needed. In the meantime, I'm going to further my education, and that accomplishment will help keep my mind off the frustration of not being hired—yet.

"I've learned that no matter what hardships or difficulties one may have in life, God still provides many blessings to those with disabilities and adversities," he continued. "I also know God has a plan for me. Although I don't know His *full* plan, I know I was put here to teach and help people. I also know that God's gift of eternal life through Christ is more important than any earthly position, or being able to walk or having millions of dollars." David's dream stays alive because he's given it to God.

SOUL THERAPY

Creator of dreams,
Let mine be in line with what You want for me.
Help me overcome my disappointment from _____,
And show me a new way, Your way.
When I'm discouraged, remind me
That You hold my future,
That Your plans are best,
And that You alone can make all things possible.

WORK OUT
*Read Genesis 41 to learn about
Pharaoh's dream.*

JOURNAL
*Make a list of dreams you can share
with God. (For instance, Christ
instructed His people to take His
good news to others. Is that a goal
you share?) God's goal for our gifts
is His glory. Write down ways you
can use your gifts to that end.*

A Firm Foundation

BODY BASIC
The foot, including the ankle, has twenty-six bones—one eighth of all the bones in the body—and more than 100 muscles, tendons and ligaments which work together to provide support, balance and mobility to the body. The big toe is the foot's primary weight-bearer.

SPIRITUAL SPECIFIC
"He will guard the feet of His saints..." (1 SAMUEL 2:9)

*F*eet get plenty of mention in the Bible. People fell in subjection at the feet of an important person, and foot washing—servant's work— was a common ritual of hospitality. Moses was commanded to take the sandals off his feet, because he was on holy ground. Ruth uncovered the feet of Boaz, her kinsman/redeemer, in a peculiar Jewish ritual. Two different Marys anointed Jesus' feet. Jesus himself washed the disciples' feet before His own were pierced by nails as He was hanged upon the cross. Paul and Silas as well as other disciples often had their feet put in chains or stocks for professing their faith.

Ruth's ritual of uncovering Boaz' feet eventually led to her marrying him, and they became the ancestors of Christ. In prison, a violent earthquake loosed Paul and Silas' chains on their feet and ankles and opened the prison doors as the men prayed and sang hymns. They didn't try to escape, and as a result, their jailer and his family became believers.

Our feet as well as our faith in God's truth form a firm foundation for us. No matter what happens in our life, we can stand on God's word and His love. The Bible says, "He makes my feet like the feet of a deer. He enables me to stand on the heights."(2 Samuel 22:34)

Dora, a diabetic friend of mine who is a nurse, spent a lot of time standing. But just before her wedding, she began suffering with painful feet. A doctor misdiagnosed her condition and thought nothing could be done. "So I tried to live with it. I got married and limped through my honeymoon," Dora said. When she returned home with worse inflammation, she changed doctors. "I had an X-ray, and found out I'd been walking all that time on a broken foot. My joints were crumbling (charcott joints), which can happen with diabetics."

The break healed, but Dora's foot problems grew worse. She had several operations and was in a wheelchair for months. She was given nursing desk duty. "I was on everyone's prayer list," she said. "My circulation was so bad that I had almost none in my feet. Some of my toes turned black. My doctors said they'd have to amputate my leg below the knee. I just made up my mind to do it, get the prosthesis and go on. Even though I knew God was in control, and I knew He was with me, I was very frightened."

Two days before her scheduled surgery, Dora had a heart attack. That set-back added to her difficult, dispiriting situation. But she soon discovered God was working even in that. "They had to put off the amputation because of my heart. But the great news is that the stents they put in my heart re-established the circulation in my leg. The black skin came off my toes, and underneath they were pink!"

Although she recovered, Dora still can't be on her feet much, so she retired after 34 years of nursing. "I miss being able to help people," she said. Diabetes continually complicates her life, and she is now on dialysis. But she steadfastly looks for and finds many things she can still enjoy, among them Bible study and putting together her church's bulletin.

"Getting into the Bible has really enriched my life," she says. "God has been revealing many things to me. And one time when I was worried sick about a health problem, He focused my eyes on the verse, 'Don't worry about anything, but in everything, by prayer and petition, with thanksgiving, present your requests to God.'(Phil 4:6) I do that every day. And God gives me the strength to keep going."

SOUL THERAPY

Dear God,
Even when my faith falters,
You are my Sure Foundation.
When I'm frightened, threatened or confused,
Please help me to stand firm
On the bedrock truths of Your word.
Truths that assure me that when I walk with You,
You'll guide and help me.
Please keep me from stumbling,
And let my every footstep draw me closer to You.

WORK OUT
While sitting in a chair, write out the alphabet in the air first with one foot, then the other. Try to think of an attribute of God to go with each letter.

JOURNAL
Jot down those alphabetical attributes to refer to when you need encouragement.

Weeping

BODY BASIC
Tears can be defensive weapons, creating a "surface barrier" to defend the eyeball's exposed surface from harmful organisms. Continually cleansing the eye, tears are drained through tear ducts into the nasal cavity. When a person weeps, excess tears not only overflow the eyes, but also rush into the nasal cavity, causing the nose to run, too.

SPIRITUAL SPECIFIC
"Blessed are you who weep now, for you will laugh."
(LUKE 6:21)

*A*s a result of *miscommunication between* my mother's neurosurgeon and the recovery room staff, the hospital was "all out" of the pain-killing drugs ordered for Mom after her back surgery. And nurses were not authorized to substitute any other medication! So as we waited for the pain-killers to arrive from the drugstore, my eighty-five-year-old mother turned to me in agony and said, "Can I just cry?"

I replied, "Of course!" As I held her hand, for the first time in my life I saw my mother weep with pain. I shed a few tears, too, in empathy. Then Mom stopped crying abruptly and said with determination, "Well, that didn't help. I'm not going to do that again." Even though it didn't ease her pain, that brief tear-letting moment let off some frustration and later, the drugs arrived.

Jesus cried during His lifetime, too. The two words, "Jesus wept" make up the shortest verse in the Bible, but they show us much about God. When Mary and Martha's brother Lazarus died, Jesus wasn't there. In fact, when Lazarus' sisters sent word to Jesus that Lazarus was sick, He didn't rush to His friend's side. It seemed He deliberately tarried, giving Lazarus time to die. In that interval, Jesus prophesied to His disciples that He was going to raise Lazarus. He knew there was to be a glorious outcome following the four days of grief His friends had endured by the time He finally arrived in Bethany. Yet, when He saw Mary and Martha and their friends weeping, He wept, too. Why? Because He saw his friends' grief and empathized. "He was deeply moved in spirit and troubled."

I like the idea that God hurts when we hurt. He weeps even though He knows the future of His believing people and knows it's greater than anything we can imagine—whether it happens on earth or in heaven.

He also knows the future of His *unbelieving* people, and that made Jesus weep, too. He shed tears over Jerusalem, as He approached it riding on a donkey and being hailed as a king by people who would soon turn on Him and crucify Him. Jesus cried about His unbelieving loved ones saying, "If you, even you, had only known on this day what would bring you peace..." And He prophesied the coming destruction of Jerusalem and its temple, which happened in 70 A.D. He foretold that the enemy, "will not leave one stone on another, because you did not recognize the time of God's coming to you."

God's heart is broken over the brokenness of all His people—the ones who believe in Him and the ones who don't. Jesus has come to us so that we'll know that God is not "somewhere out there," watching. He is present with us. Jesus came to earth—moved into the neighborhood—to show us God's love and empathy, and give us the invitation to believe and have a relationship with Him.

Once we accept His invitation, we are His forever. "I will never leave you nor forsake you," He promises. And in heaven, He'll dry every tear.

SOUL THERAPY

Jesus, I don't know all that was behind Your tears,
But I know You wept for Your friends,
For Your enemies,
And even cried in anguished prayer
In the Garden before Your sacrifice.
You showed Your humanity,
Your vulnerability,
And Your great love for each of us with those tears.
Thank You for being my Friend,
As well as my Savior and my God.

WORK OUT

Crying reduces stress and so does exercise. For this activity, lie on your left side, supporting your head in your left hand. Bend the left knee as it lies on the floor and straighten the right leg. Lift the right leg up toward the ceiling and slowly lower it back down. Repeat ten to fifteen times. Then roll to the other side and do the same thing. Keep changing sides until you've repeated the set of lifts three times on each side.

JOURNAL

Write down what is saddening or grieving you, and let the tears flow if you want to. Give each unhappy event or feeling to God and ask Him to replace your grief with His peace and healing.

Hope

BODY BASIC
Research has found that optimism may lessen the risk of health problems and may help a person recover from a traumatic experience like the death of a family member. Psychologists have shown, too, that the physical body responds to hope.

SPIRITUAL SPECIFIC
"Hope deferred makes the heart sick." (PROVERBS 13:12)

*I*t's easy to begin losing hope when we feel hammered by life, when chronic pain badgers us, or when various illnesses or crises strike, one after another. David, who had many times of feeling trapped and despairing during his years of fleeing King Saul and his murderous men, gave himself a pep talk in Psalms. "Why are you downcast, O my soul? Why so disturbed within me? Put your hope in God..." David knew God was his Hope and Strength. And he was reminding himself that when every earthly thing looks hopeless, God is nevertheless in charge. Our sovereign Lord can turn things around in any instant. David prayed, waited and hoped in the Lord, His word and His mercy.

David was waiting for God to fulfill His promise to him of making him king. And the wait—which also involved running and hiding, because David refused to kill Saul without God's order—was more than fifteen years long. Like David, we may feel trapped by circumstances, and the longer the situation lasts, the more frustration, disappointment and fear chip away at hope. But God can build it back. And when we pray, we join Him in reconstructing our hope. David's psalms record some of his prayers, and we can see how his optimism grows as he focuses on God and His unfailing love.

Hope is more than positive thinking, optimism or something we can conjure up by our own efforts; it is God's legacy to us. Our faithful God is the God of all hope, Jesus is our "Living Hope," and His gift to us is "eternal encouragement and good hope." (2 Thessalonians 2:16) Paul says, "May the God of hope fill you with all joy and peace as you trust in Him, so that you may overflow with hope by the power of the Holy Spirit." (Romans 15:13)

As we're going through trials, we have to take *hold* of hope by trusting our Creator's promise that He has a plan for each of us that can't be hindered by anything on earth. No matter what your physical condition, if you're still alive, you still have purpose in God's plan—even if you can't imagine what it is!

One of the best books I've ever read, *The Hiding Place*, was by Corrie ten Boom, a Dutch Christian who, along with her family, secretly opened their home to Jews and other fugitives from the Nazi regime. Her family was found out, arrested and imprisoned. In a Nazi concentration camp, with a Bible that they miraculously sneaked past the guards, Corrie and her sister gave fellow death camp prisoners hope, telling them about *life* through Christ. Although Corrie's sister died in the camp, Corrie survived and was later released. She began a worldwide ministry traveling to sixty countries telling of God's love. "There is no pit so deep that God's love is not deeper still," she said. She inspired thousands with her writings.

In her final years, however, Corrie had a series of strokes that left her helpless and unable to communicate except through gestures. Confined, with no chance of recovery, Corrie found purpose in life through being a prayer warrior. She prayed for others faithfully until her final hope for herself became a reality on her ninety-first birthday—she entered eternity where "there is no more pain or sorrow..."

On a bad day, a future in heaven can seem light years away. But the One who suffered for us is with us, giving us His hope to defeat despair.

SOUL THERAPY

Father, I know You tell us so often in Your word,
"Be not discouraged."
But it's hard not to be,
When tough times seem endless.
Please push despondency out of my troubled heart
And fill it instead with Jesus,
My "anchor for the soul, firm and secure."

WORK OUT
Thumb through Romans and find verses on hope. Begin memorizing a favorite one as you take a twenty-minute walk today and reflect on ways God has been your hope during hard times.

JOURNAL
Write down hope verses to read and share.

Scars

BODY BASIC
Scars are areas of fibrous tissue that form over a wound when it has healed. Because the body can't rebuild the tissue exactly as it was, scar tissue has a different texture and quality than the normal surrounding tissue, and does not have sweat glands or hair follicles. The word scar is from the Greek word eschara, meaning "place of fire."

SPIRITUAL SPECIFIC
"By His wounds, you have been healed." (1 PETER 2: 24)

*M*ost of us bear scars of one kind or another—inward or outward. Although a scar itself usually isn't painful after it's fully healed, it reminds us of a hurt, perhaps some "trial by fire" we've gone through. Jesus came to heal His people's hurts—physical and spiritual—and He was wounded and killed so that our fire of affliction would not be eternal.

When Jesus was brought to Pilate to be condemned to die, Pilate had Him flogged. Jesus' flesh was ripped with whips that had pieces of metal, glass and bone in them. Then at the crucifixion, heavy nails were hammered through His hands and feet to attach Him to the cross. After He died, a sword was thrust into His side. When Jesus rose from the dead, He could have risen with a healed body, but He chose for His glorified body to retain the wounds and scars. He used them to help Thomas believe. Jesus' resurrection proved He was who He said He was. He kept His scars in place to remind us how much He loves us and what that love cost Him.

In World War II, my young, athletic father, a pilot, was severely burned in a plane crash and was not expected to live. He pulled through, however, spending an agonizing year and a half in the hospital. All his life he bore terrible scars. Twice a day for fifty-four years, he "dressed" his legs and one foot with special medications and bandages to keep his burned and grafted skin protected. Yet even a slight bump would open a wound.

He limped on a stiff ankle that had been crushed and then fused. He couldn't run, because it wouldn't bend. But he never complained. By his example, he taught my brothers and me to be grateful for life and everything in it. His scars and limping foot reminded him that God had preserved his life, and he rejoiced in that life. He served God with it, too.

Jesus' scars remind us that He overcame sin and death to preserve *our* life. He promises to help *us* overcome, too.

SOUL THERAPY

Scars can be ugly, Lord.
Sometimes they make me feel disfigured.
When I'm self-conscious or sad about them,
Remind me of inner beauty which comes from You.
And if the marks remind me of a fiery trial,
One I would rather forget,
Please encourage and comfort me.
Heal me, too, my Great Physician, from invisible injuries –
The deep wounds of hurt in my heart.
Dress them with the soothing, protecting bandage of Your love.

WORK OUT

Wherever you find a scar on your body, think about the experience that caused it. Do you need to forgive someone who hurt you? Does it remind you to be grateful that you are still alive? How about those unseen inner scars?

JOURNAL

Write out your thoughts and compose a prayer asking God to give you His forgiveness for anyone who has wounded you. If the scar reminds you to give thanks, express that in your journal, too. Whether you repent of a past deed or learn from a mistake, let your scars draw you closer to God.

Disruption

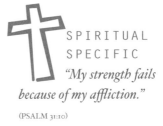

BODY BASIC
During a stroke, the brain's supply of blood is suddenly disrupted and the brain cells are left without essential oxygen and nutrients. Any part of the body can be damaged by a stroke, which can temporarily or permanently cause paralysis and problems with speaking, thinking, emotions and even perception—an affected person may even lose the ability to distinguish between vertical and horizontal.

SPIRITUAL SPECIFIC
"My strength fails because of my affliction."
(PSALM 31:10)

*M*y older friend Ruthie was married to a tall, tough Texan named John, a businessman and rancher who worked hard. He remained rugged even into his early seventies. Then a stroke felled him.

John was so completely incapacitated, that Ruthie had no alternative but to put him into a rest home. I often visited there, where Ruthie spent most of each day reading aloud, keeping John company and trying to keep her own spirits from flagging. Her faith was strong, she told me, but she felt like something had disrupted her closeness to God.

"I felt incomplete somehow," Ruthie later said. "I needed strength. I needed to be closer to God. But how do you get closer to your Lord? I wondered, does anyone ever write a letter to God? "

She discovered the answer is yes. Psalms are writings—prayers, praises and musical letters to God. So Ruthie began composing her own. As she expressed her feelings, she arrived at a place where she could newly appreciate the fact that, despite being surrounded by illness and age, "God had placed eternity in my soul." In one psalm, she anticipated a heavenly future when "there will be no room for black shadows."

Ruthie found her own perception of life becoming more vertical as she turned her eyes heavenward more often. The more she wrote, the closer she felt to God, and the more praise began filling her prose. Her psalms encouraged John, as well.

Although that time of black shadows was not removed, Ruthie's focus on God allowed her to find periods of peace-dappled, God-given grace which restored her soul.

Like Ruthie, King David was familiar with life's depths and heights, and he didn't hold back his feelings about either one. In most of his Psalms, he penned his way from the darkness of despair to the light of his eternal hope. In one of his Psalms David wrote, "Be merciful to me, O Lord, for I am in distress; my eyes grow weak with sorrow, my soul and my body with grief. My life is consumed with anguish and my years by groaning; my strength fails because of my affliction, and my bones grow weak. (31:9-11) Because of his enemies, David was even the contempt of his neighbors and a dread to his friends! He was in a *miserable* place in life!

Yet as he continued to write, David turned a corner and proclaimed, "But I trust in You, O Lord; I say, 'You are my God.' My times are in Your hands; deliver me from my enemies... Let Your face shine on Your servant; save me in Your unfailing love. Let me not be put to shame, O Lord, for I have cried out to You." (31:14-17)

David trusted God, who never failed to restore his soul. David also prayed for everyone who would come after him: "Let all who take refuge in You be glad; let them ever sing for joy. Spread Your protection over them, that those who love Your name may rejoice in You." (Psalm 5:11)

Thousands of years later, Ruthie and John were recipients of David's encouragement through his prayer letter. And by following David's example, Ruthie rediscovered her close relationship with God.

SOUL THERAPY

Dear God, You are my lifeline,
But sometimes my way to You seems obstructed.
When I feel far from You,
Please demonstrate Your loving kindness.
When darkness surrounds me,
Unlock the way for me and my loved ones into Your light.
When I'm paralyzed by grief,
Please deliver Your consolation and restore my soul.
Psalm 29 says "The Lord gives strength to His people."
I claim that promise, Father. I need Your strength!

WORK OUT
Learn the signs of a stroke, because timely treatment is essential. Symptoms of a stroke include sudden numbness or weakness of the face, arm or leg, especially on one side of the body; sudden confusion or difficulty speaking or understanding speech; sudden trouble with vision in one or both eyes; sudden trouble walking, loss of balance or coordination; dizziness; sudden severe headache with no known cause.

JOURNAL
Write a Psalm to God, and don't hold back. Express all your feelings to Him. End it with a sentence or two about what God is capable of doing for you.

Opposing Action

BODY BASIC
*To minimize fatigue,
muscles need opposing
action—stretching out/pulling back,
bending/straightening.*

SPIRITUAL SPECIFIC
"...we rise up and stand firm." (PSALM 20:8)

Staying in one position too long, such as bending forward all day at a computer, causes muscle fatigue that can become very painful. The weariness of bending forward is reduced if you make the opposite move, stretching the shoulders backward and pushing out the chest. By intentionally working opposing muscles equally throughout the day, we gain the muscle balance that reduces strain.

Spiritual muscle needs opposing action too: receiving as well as giving; resting as well as working; being spiritually fed and feeding others; following and leading; times of solitude and times of community; fasting and feasting. Jesus did all these. He allowed Mary to anoint him, Martha to serve Him, John to baptize Him, His disciples to serve the multitudes. He withdrew to quiet places by Himself, but also preached to crowds. He drew people to Him and cast out demons. He asked questions of those who thought they knew all the answers, and gave life answers to those who asked honest questions. And no matter what He did, Jesus preceded it all with prayer.

No matter what position life launches us into, our "muscle balance" is Jesus. He lifts those who are cast down. He exalts those who are humbled. He shares heavy yokes, so that we're not bent too long by the weight of life. He searches and intimately knows us and our every moment: "You know when I sit and when I rise...You discern my going out and my lying down..." (Psalm 139:2-3) And whatever our place – whether we go up to the heavens or make our bed in the depths – "even there Your hand will guide me, Your right hand will hold me fast." (v.10)

Jesus was often a comfortable center of conversation when my husband and I went out with our friends Dennis, a minister, and his wife Linda. We were planning a trip to Alaska together when Dennis and Linda received devastating news—their tender-hearted, twenty-six-year-old musician son, Aaron, had been found dead from an accidental drug overdose. They were in the depths of grief, living with hearts so heavy they could hardly bear it. And even though they could find little relief from the pain, God held them fast. They trusted Him to eventually lift them out of their deep sorrow. And as they grieved and prayed with us and other friends, they decided to do the opposite of what their exhausted emotions tried to dictate.

Rather than isolating themselves from any more pain, they began reaching out to others, forming a support group for parents who'd lost children. In Aaron's memory, they also teamed up with their son's friends to raise money to do something Aaron would have done for the handicapped children he ministered to—build a playground for them. And those things helped them in the healing process.

When our hearts are burdened, when all we can do is just "go through the motions" of getting on with life, God offers His strength for every move. He encourages us to reach up to Him in prayer, to turn inward and tap into His power which lives within us, to stretch outward to take advantage of the support systems available to us. And then, when we're strong enough, He advises us to extend a hand to someone else in need. Most good causes—bike rides and walks to raise money for medical research, Mothers Against Drunk Drivers, memorial parks and personal ministries resulted from someone's tragedy.

God is the Master of creating something positive from the negative, something healing from the pain, something everlasting from the temporary. With His help, we can do it, too.

SOUL THERAPY

Lover of my soul,
You know when I'm stretched to the breaking point
With grief,
When my emotions and energy are strained
To the limit with hardships and sorrow.
You've promised to carry my heavy burdens with me.
And I need Your broad shoulders, Father!
Strengthen me through every give and take of life.
Prevent me from pulling away from You.
Help me press close instead.
Then strengthen me to reach out to others.

WORK OUT

If you've been bent forward reading, make the opposite moves. Stand up, place your hands in the small of your back and gently lean backward ten times, holding the position for five seconds each time. Standing straight lift your arms slightly from your side (elbows out like a bird's wing) and squeeze your shoulder blades together. Hold for five seconds, ten times.

JOURNAL

Describe how you can use Jesus as your "muscle balance" today and ask for His help as you reach in a new direction for Him.

Unimpaired Prayer

BODY BASIC
Each type of cell in the body is programmed to divide on a certain schedule. If that programming is impaired, the affected cell can become the abnormal seed from which cancer begins, producing other "outlaw" descendants that also divide outside normal controls and spread the disease.

SPIRITUAL SPECIFIC
"Is any of you in trouble? He should pray. Is any one of you sick? He should call the elders of the church to pray over him...Therefore...pray for each other so that you may be healed. The prayer of a righteous man is powerful and effective."

(JAMES 5:13,14,16)

*G*od programmed the body perfectly to work without impairment, but when man became an "outlaw" by disobeying God, all human and earthly flawlessness was destroyed. Disease and trouble of every kind entered the picture. However, God in His mercy provides a prescription to help us through adversity: prayer. And He promises that a repentant believer's prayer is powerful and effective. We may not know all of our prayers' results until we reach heaven, but God assures us He is listening.

My childhood friend Karen and I grew up in the same church and re-cited many of the same prayers. But Karen discovered more about prayer as an adult, when she received a frightening diagnosis: she had cancer, a disease that had taken both her father's and her brother's life at a young age. Terrified and dreading the upcoming mastectomy, Karen prayed with her husband and held tight to her faith. Her priest, church members and friends began praying, too. Yet, suddenly Karen found herself asking many questions about intercessory prayer.

"I never said it out loud, but I wanted to challenge anyone who said, 'I'm praying for you,'" she related. "Because I wondered, does that mean the surgeon will do a better job because I am being prayed for? Are fifty people praying as good as 100? Should I get 150? Does God hand out mercy and healing only because of prayer? I don't think that's the way God works. But no one could really explain it. I do know intercessory prayer pleases God; I just wasn't sure how it might help *me*."

She continued, "I was looking for neat and tidy answers—some for-mula like X number of prayers equals no surgery. X-plus prayers equals no chemo—silly things like that. But there are no tidy answers, and we don't get to control things. Even though I'm still puzzled, I know God doesn't require X number of Karen-prayers to work in my behalf."

As she struggled and prayed about her questions, an image came to her. "I thought about what it's like at a rock concert when the crowd lifts someone up and passes him overhead across the auditorium. It was as if I were being uplifted by prayers the way someone might be lifted at a Tina Turner concert. God, with His sense of humor, had already inspired me to name my tumor Tina Tumor, so the mosh pit imagery seemed to fit right in. I decided just to enjoy being uplifted by the faith com-munity. My friends were investing in something God cherishes, and it was precious to me that they were offering to do that. But I still kept seeking answers."

Karen and her husband grew more and more dependent on prayer as well as humor when Karen's mastectomy was followed by thirty months of setbacks and frustration. She endured chemotherapy, three incidences of cancer recurrence, four more surgeries, two rounds of radiation and more chemo. "Each time something new or unknown occurred, I was fearful," she admitted. "But I always wanted a faith-centered take on what was happening—I wanted to see goodness and see God even in those tough things."

So she decided to begin watching for "serendipity things"—ways God sent her comfort in her continuing struggle—and she found one of the primary ways was through other people. The outpouring of support from friends and neighbors flattered and sometimes stunned her. "And I realized they were really a manifestation of God's love. When we reach out to help someone, we might secretly take credit for being a nice person, but it's more than that. We're responding to the Holy Spirit's nudge to take action. When we call someone or send a card or make a meal, our hands are God's hands. For me, it was an awesome thing to realize."

Karen doesn't mind being mystified by prayer or by God. She said, "I actually enjoyed the churning of questions and looking at different perspectives about illness and healing, because it helped me keep my 'spiritual sunglasses' on when I was viewing things."

She has now been cancer-free for five years. I saw her at our fortieth high school reunion, and she was the picture of health. She told me she is surprised how many women with breast cancer have sought her out. "They seem to need someone to talk to who's been through it, and I'm glad to listen. I like being an encourager and helping any way I can." And she takes pleasure in praying for them, too.

SOUL THERAPY

I have so many questions, Lord,
Which remain unanswered in this life.
Please keep me faithful in prayer,
Even if I don't sense Your nearness,
Even if I don't see the results I'm requesting,
Even when I feel disappointed and confused.
Help me to trust You
And rest in the knowledge
That coming to You in prayer does—
In some mysterious way—

Make a difference.

Please open my eyes to every one of Your answers.

WORK OUT

If you don't have a place where you pray each day, find one and converse with God. If you are going through a challenging time, and you don't have someone praying for you, ask God to reveal to you someone who would be faithful to lift you up. Then ask that person if he or she would be willing to do that.

JOURNAL

Express why you think prayer is important. Why do you think it pleases God?

Pity Party Pitfall

BODY BASIC
Research indicates that although the cheeriness of our disposition is influenced by our genes, our coping ability can be developed. Psychological strategies for getting through tough times include striving to remain involved rather than withdrawing; working to influence outcomes rather than remain powerless; and viewing positive or negative changes as opportunities for learning.

SPIRITUAL SPECIFIC
"Be joyful in hope, patient in affliction, faithful in prayer." (ROMANS 12:12)

How could just shrugging my shoulders hurt? As a result of two bulging discs, this simple exercise in the pool was painful. It was my first day of physical therapy, and in my thoughts, I began having a pity party, listing my grievances: Giving up an hour and a half, four times a week for therapy would make my already full schedule way too rushed and tight. I hated missing my usual walks with my friend Rhonda. My neck pain kept me from writing at my computer desk, where I did freelance work. And I couldn't really enjoy social events either, because of the unrelenting discomfort.

As I miserably counted repetitions, I began observing the other people arriving for therapy. Using a walker, an older woman, bent almost in half with osteoporosis, struggled into the pool area. A stroke victim flashed a lopsided smile at his therapist as he walked down the pool ramp into the water, steadying his wobbly body using the ramp's side rails. A beautiful child with a spinal deformity happily gave up her leg braces to become buoyant in the water for awhile.

My admiration for them instantly erased my self-pity. My problem was so minor! As I exercised beside them, I grinned at each one, and they smiled back. We passed each other in the water, paddling, kicking, pushing weights or just walking or being floated across the pool by a therapist. It seemed we were instantly bonded by our different degrees of affliction and by a determination to get better. The physical therapists were our coaches and cheerleaders.

I wanted to reach out to those people, encourage them, learn their names. I wondered if this is how it was with the people lying by the pool at Bethesda, waiting to enter the healing waters. At Bethesda's pool, when the waters mysteriously stirred, the blind, lame and disabled people who had been waiting beside the pool rushed into it for healing. One invalid man had lain near the edge of the water for thirty-eight years, unable to get in fast enough to take advantage of the cure before he was crowded out. Jesus came upon the man, asked if he wanted to get well, and then instantly healed him.

We don't know if the man and the others had become friends as they waited for the waters to stir. We don't know if they shared their emotions of hope or disappointment. And we don't know if faith in Jesus, the Eternal Cure, was aroused within them all as they saw the invalid pick up his mat at Jesus' command and walk away, strong.

But we do know that Jesus' healing pointed to a fact: He wants us well, and immersing ourselves into His "living water" requires no race or competition. There is room for all.

Like the man in the ancient story, my part as a modern-day "invalid" in this pool was not only to try my best, but also to accept Jesus' help.

Whether or not I get well in this life, my job is to make use of every opportunity to improve.

That first day, I found that simply persisting along with an inspiring group of strugglers was therapeutic. And over time, we have become friends, sympathizing with and encouraging each other as we press on. (Some of their stories are in this book.) It is much more fun than having a pity-party!

SOUL THERAPY

Sweet Savior,
Even as You suffered on the cross,
You were concerned for others—
For your disciples, Your mother, even the thief beside You.
Help me to avoid self-pity
By sharing with Your people in need.
Please give me Your heart for others
And Your hope that springs eternal.

WORK OUT

As an exercise, you can clap for the people who inspire you. Stand up, and with arms straight and hands low, clap once in front, then in back, and repeat the forward and back clapping thirty times. You can bend your elbows slightly and clap at different levels. Then, lift your knees high as if you were marching while continuing the front and back clapping for thirty knee lifts.

JOURNAL

List the names of people you thought of as you clapped and what you admire about them. Who needs to get a note of thanks or encouragement? Hearing from you will be therapy for them as well as for you.

Hidden Inside

BODY BASIC
The soft organs most vital to life are hidden from view, protected and organized inside four major internal body cavities.

SPIRITUAL SPECIFIC
"The secret things belong to the Lord our God, but the things revealed belong to us and to our children forever..."
(DEUTERONOMY 29:29)

*D*o *you ever feel like God doesn't divulge enough* "inside information?" You pray that He will reveal His purpose to you about some matter, yet you're still searching? You seek His direction, but still feel confused? God's ways and timing are so different from our own, that they often seem hidden like secret things. But nothing is hidden from Him. Our life, traumas and troubles are all seen and understood by our all-knowing God. And He's involved with us in them, even though we may not see His workings.

During one of Israel's times of distress, Isaiah said, "Why do you say, O Jacob, and complain, O Israel, 'my way is hidden from the Lord; my cause is disregarded by my God?' Do you not know? Have you not heard? The Lord is the everlasting God, the Creator of the ends of the earth. He will not grow tired or weary, and His understanding no one can fathom. He gives strength to the weary and increases the power of the weak." (Isaiah 40: 27-29)

We can't discern all God's secrets. But, through scripture, we *can* know what He reveals to us about Himself and His unfailing faithfulness and love toward us. Those things belong to us.

Joanie, a paratrooper whom I met in the therapy pool, discovered much about God after two near-fatal mishaps landed her in a wheelchair. She told me that her first accident occurred during a jump when a parachute problem caused her to miss the drop zone. She landed in a small lake, unaware of a dead tree limb just under the surface. As she hit, it impaled her, rupturing vital organs. It took seven operations to keep her alive.

In an experimental procedure, her pancreas was replaced with a pig pancreas. It worked, but resulted in diabetes and later bone density problems. Joanie struggled, but was able to lead a full life. Then she fell down twenty cement steps. "My bones were so brittle that they shattered into cracker crumbs," she said. An open skull fracture left her fighting to hang onto life.

Joanie felt guilty for being angry at God. Yet she was. "I felt like I'd been crucified more than once. And I thought God hated me," she said.

Nevertheless, partially paralyzed on her right side, "I had so much idle time on my hands that I started reading the Bible. As I read it, I began to feel loved. Nothing before had ever brought me this close to Christ. I thought, 'There's still hope for me.' After I started reading the Bible, I felt a greater determination to make myself better physically, no matter what." She experienced overwhelming pain in the therapy pool and shed many tears, but she kept saying to herself, "I can't come up short. I'm a paratrooper."

After many months of therapy and hard work, much to her doctors' amazement, Joanie began walking with only a cane. "I guess what I would tell others is this: do what you've got to do, and know that you are not alone." As a paratrooper, Joanie earned her wings, but through an accident that led her to Scripture, she says, "I found my heart."

SOUL THERAPY

God, Your ways are so often hidden from me.
And when I feel battered and bewildered,
I confess that I accuse You of seeming uncaring.
Please forgive me.
Thank you that Your word is not hidden,
And it expresses Your love—
Love which endures forever,
Demonstrated to me through Jesus.
Fill my heart now, Lord Jesus,
And give strength to my weary soul.

WORK OUT

Hidden inside is our internal girdle of supportive muscles. To build those, lie on your back with your knees bent. Keeping your head, neck and shoulders on the bed, lift your buttocks up toward the ceiling. Repeat twenty times.

JOURNAL

Read Psalm 103:11-18. What are some things about Himself that God reveals there? Record them and what they mean to you.

Shaken

BODY BASIC
Shaking or tremor symptoms can be caused by many things, including stress, fatigue, excitement or any one of more than 700 medical conditions.

SPIRITUAL SPECIFIC
Therefore, since we are receiving a kingdom that cannot be shaken, let us be thankful and so worship God acceptably with reverence and awe..."

(HEBREWS 12:28)

I lay on the hotel room bed, fully dressed, too shaky to get up. My whole body felt as if it were trembling from the inside out. I had exercised and showered, eaten some cold peas out of the can, because I thought the "carbs" would improve my flagging energy, and was trying to get downstairs to meet my husband, Joe, and friends for lunch. But I couldn't do it. Frightened, I lay there praying for God's help as I had for months when this "mysterious illness," which had plagued me off and on, returned. Joe came up to the room to check on me. Although medical tests had not shown anything wrong with me, something obviously *was* wrong, and he was concerned. He sat with me until the episode finally passed, as it usually did, and I was able to get up and join him downstairs.

"I'll bet you've got hypoglycemia – low blood sugar," my cowboy friend told me at lunch. "I've got it, too. I used to feel so terrible, I'd have to get off my horse and lie on the ground until it passed. And the fact that you ate peas out of the can just made it worse—that's a quick-burning carbohydrate that will raise your blood sugar temporarily, and then make it plummet suddenly."

Sure enough, a blood test proved hypoglycemia to be my problem. God had solved my "mystery" through a friend I rarely see. I learned lots of things about slow-burning and fast-burning sugars and carbohydrates in foods, adjusted my diet, and felt great.

Those bouts of exhaustion and trembling over a long period had shaken me. But the problem had also led me to learn new things about God. It had built within me more of what is *unshakable*—a first-hand experience of His strength, love and sustaining encouragement. I had depended on Him daily during that time, and He'd faithfully gotten me through it until He was ready to reveal the cause.

When God shakes up our lives, He also demonstrates His power. He shook the ground at the foot of the burning Mount Sinai when Moses went up to receive His law, and His terrifying display of might, which included a great thunder and lightning storm, even frightened Moses. (Exodus 19) God's earth-shaking was meant to strengthen the Israelites' faith in His power over all things, so that they would be encouraged to trust Him as they entered the enemy-filled Promised Land.

God tells us that during the earth's end times, "Once more I will shake not only the earth, but also the heavens." The writer of Hebrews (12: 26-28) says, "The words 'once more' indicate the removing of what can be shaken—that is, created things—so that what cannot be shaken may remain. Therefore, since we are receiving a kingdom that cannot be shaken, let us be thankful, and so worship God..."

When we feel shaken to the core, our Unshakable God upholds us, sustains us and even blesses us in the experience, even though we may not recognize the blessing at the time. It's not just on the mountain that we encounter God. It's in the valleys, too. His love is in every circumstance— a deep, eternal, abiding love for you.

SOUL THERAPY

Father, when I'm shaking in fear,
With illness or uncertainty,
Please steady me with Your unwavering love.
Bind me to You,
As You build the unshakable within me.

WORK OUT

Try not to wobble as you do a yoga "tree pose." Tighten your core and stand on one leg, placing the bottom of your other foot on your standing leg, like you're forming the number 4. Once you've balanced, place your hands together as if praying and lift them over your head. Hold for 20 seconds. Repeat three times on each leg.

JOURNAL

Record your thoughts: is everything about God unshakable? List some of the ways He is unwavering.

A Sensual Prison

BODY BASIC
Some forms of sensual stimulation can become addictive. For instance, when a person becomes compulsively dependent on the visual sexual stimulation of pornography to the point that it becomes the central focus of his or her life, it is considered by professionals to be an addiction.

SPIRITUAL SPECIFIC
"So let us put aside the deeds of darkness and put on the armor of light...clothe yourselves with the Lord Jesus Christ, and do not think about how to gratify the desires of the sinful nature." (ROMANS 14:12-14)

King Solomon was known for his wisdom and riches during much of his reign. But he indulged in many forbidden sensual pleasures later in his life, which led him away from God. Some of his proverbs of wisdom may have been hard-learned lessons from his own life. He is thought to be the likely author of Ecclesiastes, which teaches that a life which is not centered on God is meaningless and without purpose.

The world still offers dark, sensual pleasures, which can imprison a person's mind and heart and shut him off from God's better plan. We can be trapped, too, by our resentments, fears, secrets, addictions and hurts. However, no matter what holds us captive, the key for release is Jesus, who came to "set the prisoner free." Jesus shines His light into any darkness, revealing and healing the shadowy places within His repentant people. In scripture, He rescued souls with forgiveness and repaired bodies with divine power. But, He reminds us, without Him we can't be set free. It's "impossible for man." However, with His power, which He shares with believers, "all things are possible." (Matthew 19:26)

A family friend, Larry, was a prisoner of darkness, and he couldn't conceive of being freed from his addiction to pornography. As a young teen, he'd secretly explored pornography, and by the time he was an adult, he depended on getting a daily "fix" at an adult bookstore. He became a Christian at age thirty-six, and at forty, he married for the first time.

"I guess I thought that becoming a Christian and marrying a Christian girl would solve my problem. Wrong!" he told me. "My wife knew I had a wild past, but didn't know the extent of my addiction. After we were married, I still couldn't leave porn alone, but I kept it a secret. The addiction took me farther away from her; I didn't want to be intimate with her, because I was so into the porn. I knew it was wrong, and I felt guilty. But I couldn't stop."

When his wife caught him one day, he finally realized he had to do something. "I knew our church had a recovery group for sex addiction, but I never would go," he said. "When I realized I had to get help in order to save my marriage, I went. It didn't come easy, but after three or four years of attending the Bible-based weekly sessions, things really got better. Without God, I could not have done it. I had no strength on my own. But as of now, I have been free for over three years, and my marriage is better than ever. I now know that when anyone is trapped by something, we need to admit the problem and seek help and accountability with other Christians and with God. I can truly say my recovery is a miracle. God has answered my prayers."

SOUL THERAPY

You alone know what's in my heart, Lord—
The sins I've tried to ignore,
The hurtful memories I've buried and would rather not dig up,
The unforgiveness I carry for myself and others.
Please, shine Your light inside,
Empower me to acknowledge and confess my sins,
And then to let them go.
Please heal me and set me free.

WORK OUT

Accountability with others helps not only in overcoming addictions but is good for other things as well—such as following through with an exercise routine. If you're physically able, make a commitment with a friend to walk or ride a bicycle for five to twenty minutes, three times this week. Then repeat your routine every week.

JOURNAL

Write out whatever things have imprisoned you mentally, emotionally or physically. Prayerfully give them to Jesus. If you need a support group, ask Him to lead you to the right one. The Bible Study video and workbook, "Breaking Free" by Beth Moore, is helpful, too.

Waiting For Dawn

BODY BASIC
During darkness, the body increases production of melatonin, the hormone which helps us get drowsy. And the resulting sleep is all-important because during various phases of it, the body rejuvenates itself. During the first phase, our system goes through a process of protein synthesis, which rebuilds and repairs organs and skin. During other phases, essential metabolic work takes place for body repair.

SPIRITUAL SPECIFIC
"The Lord turns my darkness into light."

(2 SAMUEL 22:29)

Sleep makes good use of night's darkness. But nights can seem extra long and lonely when you lie awake in pain, ill health or anxiety. Dawn may not bring physical relief, but daylight's activities distract us from our discomfort. Basking in sunlight is a spirit-lifter, whereas lying awake in darkness seems to amplify our troubles.

At creation, when "darkness was over the surface of the deep," the first thing God called into being was light. Then He separated light and darkness, calling them "day" and "night." But God didn't leave us without a night light! The moon and stars draw our eyes heavenward, reminding us that He who never sleeps, has an ever-burning love for us.

Darkness often is equated with doom and gloom, and in scripture, too, it usually has a negative connotation. It is associated with wickedness and falsehood. One of the plagues God sent to Egypt was three days of blackness, and the darkness could be *felt*. (Exodus 10:21-22) When Christ, the "Light of the world," was crucified, midday darkness fell over the land.

Now, however, the risen Christ's light, which is identified with all that is true and good and holy, cannot be snuffed out. And it has been given to all believers. "For you were once darkness, but now you are light in the Lord. Live as children of light...and find out what pleases the Lord." (Ephesians 5:8)

My friend Cecille felt that her light was being dimmed by her fatigue from insomnia. She had to drop out of our Bible study because of it. As the insomnia continued, she told me that her frustration became desperation. "Lying in the dark, I felt abandoned. I had to keep reminding myself God was there, even though I couldn't feel Him," she said. "Insomnia is miserable. I complained and railed at God. But, finally I asked Him to make me open up to what He was teaching me through it. And I learned a lot. One thing God showed me is that I always buzzed around with too many activities, and I put Him last on my list. Insomnia gave me a forced quiet time. And having to drop out of activities because of fatigue, I didn't have any more excuses to put God last. I had time to be quiet and still, praying, reading scripture and devotionals. And I've been growing.

"I am also learning humility," she continued. "I'm a pretty willful, tough old gal, and I've always taken pride in my health and strength. I didn't want to subject my will to the doctor's, especially when he said I needed an anti-depressant. I thought lack of sleep was making me depressed, not that I had depression that was causing my insomnia. I fought it. It was a pride thing— no one in my family had to take medicines, so why should I? But I finally quit questioning, and submitted to the doctor's advice. And I'm sleeping!

"I've discovered I'm not supposed to be able to do it all on my own— that's not what God wants. He wants me to lean on Him, and to let others see me leaning on Him as well as on the wise helpers He puts in my life. I'm learning to listen more and look for God's way instead of my own. I'm glad that dark time is behind me, but I feel like it led me to the right place with my attitude."

No matter how difficult the night is, He who "turns blackness into dawn" is listening to your prayers. As Ken Gire says in *The North Face of God*, "Our prayers [in the night] may not hurry the sun, but they will heighten our awareness to what is happening in the darkness. As incongruous as it seems, sacred things happen there. God is at work."

SOUL THERAPY

Creator of the dawn, Bright Morning Star,
Please comfort me in the darkness.
Help me, like David in his Psalm,
To remember You on my bed
And "think of You through the watches of the night."
Remind me that because You are my help,
I can "sing in the shadow of Your wings."
Please wrap those gentle wings around me and help me sleep.
And when all is not well,
Let me still rest in You.

WORK OUT
As you lie in bed at night, practice relaxing your body. Imagine it sinking into the bed, starting with your feet and working your way up. Then envision the Holy Spirit's light within you chasing away loneliness and any darkness in your soul.

JOURNAL
Share some lessons you have learned through dark times.

Facing It

BODY BASIC
Our flexible face, which is home to most of our sensory organs, consists of a layer of skin cells one one-hundredth of an inch deep, stretched over fourteen facial bones with many underlying muscles and a high concentration of capillaries. The facial skin is some of the most vulnerable on the body.

SPIRITUAL SPECIFIC
"My heart says of You, 'Seek His face!' Your face, Lord, I will seek....You have been my helper." (PSALM 27:8-9)

*I*n many psalms as David faced enemies who conspired to bring him down, he sought the face of his Helper and Shield. Thousands of years later, during World War II, another David, my friend David W., sought the same refuge as his forefather.

When he was shipped off to the Philippines with his Army unit, David W. knew he would be surrounded by danger. To face the enemy, he counted on his military training, his fellow soldiers and the Lord as his shields of protection. But he told me that nothing fully prepared him for becoming part of Texas' "Lost Battalion" and spending three-and-a-half years as a Japanese prisoner of war. Nothing completely readied him for the panic of working deep in a coal mine and feeling the earth shake and the mine begin collapsing on him and fellow prisoners. And he never anticipated the shock of what he would see when he and others finally were able to dig their way out of the mine into the daylight.

"Everywhere you looked, there was nothing. Not a scrap of anything!" he recalled of that sight. The atomic bomb had been dropped on Nagasaki. And David's POW camp there had been obliterated, along with everything else.

The mine had been a temporary earthly shield, but David had depended on an eternal heavenly Shield throughout his days in combat as well as his prison time. "I did a lot of praying and a lot of depending on God. And I believe He sent me an angel. My guardian angel helped me throughout the whole war," he related. "My wife calls Him the Holy Spirit; I call Him my guardian angel. In combat, when it was almost a life-or-death decision which direction to turn, my unseen angel would direct me. And I never made a mistake. Even my captain noticed. He suggested that everyone 'follow Dave and his guardian angel.'"

Although Dave's Protector kept him safe through fierce battles, the Dutch unit his battalion was with at Java surrendered the island, so they had to surrender, too. "Then we were taken to a POW camp in Japan," he said. "The Lord and I talked all day every day for the next three-and-a-half years. I went to work in the ship factories along the coast. I was weak from very little food, but the Lord and I discussed how best to get things accomplished as I helped build boilers for Japanese ships. He was my Friend, and I tried to be a good friend to Him and be a Christian example for others."

However, as Dave's six-foot frame was starved to one hundred pounds, anger, hopelessness and fear became cruel foes against which he had to fight hard. "But I depended on the Lord to help me fight those battles, too," he said. "It was a dark, hellish time, but miraculously, I felt very close to God. With my Savior's help, I learned to live with the brutal conditions. And I was also spared many beatings, because of an arm band that qualified me for ship building.

"One day, when we ran out of coal for our boilers, I suggested that our captors take us to the Oreo coal mines to dig more. They agreed. Just days later, 100 of us were ten levels underground when the atom bomb hit." For years after that POW experience, nightmares plagued David.

Sixty years later, I interviewed David as he lay dying on a hospital bed set up in his living room. Most of the left cheek of his face has been eaten away by a rare form of cancer, probably caused from exposure to radiation when he and his fellow soldiers went into Nagasaki. He has lost his sight and hearing on that side. But, even with the obvious, gaping cavity where his cheek should be, David finds the strength to smile cheerfully.

He said, "I'm being watched over by my loving family and my same Friend. My days as a POW taught me perseverance. Whatever bad things happen, I just keep singing to myself the words of the old song—'Keep a smile on your face and a song in your heart.'"

And David keeps a prayer in his heart, too, to his Friend who stays by his side in every struggle, to his Shelter which can never be destroyed.

SOUL THERAPY

My Refuge,
Thank You that my face is always before You,
And You are my constant Spirit-Shield.
Please calm me in every calamity.
Thank You for promising that in Your eternal dwelling place,
Each of us will have an indestructible body,
And there we will have the blessed bliss
Of at last gazing into *Your* wonderful face!

WORK OUT
Check out Psalms 3:3, 7:10, 28:7,
33:20, 84:11, or 91:4 and read about
God as a shield.

JOURNAL
Write your reflections on the verses.

Breath Of Life

BODY BASIC
Oxygen, the single most important substance taken into the body, is necessary for every important chemical reaction within us. With each breath, the lungs' capillaries—tiny blood vessels—act as a doorway for oxygen to enter the body. Without oxygen, biological death begins to occur within three minutes.

SPIRITUAL SPECIFIC
"...the Lord God formed the man from the dust of the ground and breathed into his nostrils the breath of life, and the man became a living being."
(GENESIS 2: 7)

*B**reathing is an automatic action.* Since we don't have to think about it, breathing is easy to ignore and take for granted. But when we're laboring for breath, that struggle becomes the center of our focus. Any battle—for breath or life or with daily tasks—can stagger us, making us feel isolated and even panicky. But we are never alone or without a Helper. Even when emotions tell us otherwise, God, our Sustainer, is near. "He Himself gives all men life and breath and everything else." (Acts 17:25) He is involved with us every moment of our life; if He ever withdrew, we would immediately perish.

The late A.W. Tozer, minister and author, wrote, "God is always nearer than you imagine Him to be. God is so near that your thoughts are not as near as God; your breath is not as near as God; your very soul is not as near to you as God is."

Focusing on God's nearness is the only way my church friend Marion can endure her days with a suffocating lung disease. She is on oxygen, and feels "like I'm going through hell on earth," she admits. "But then when I ask God to grant me the peace that passes understanding, I experience it, even if I'm still laboring for breath."

Marion, along with each of us, has a specific promise from Jesus, the Prince of Peace, to claim: "Peace I leave with you. My peace I give you. I do not give to you as the world gives. Do not let your hearts be troubled and do not be afraid." (John 14:27) When Jesus gives His peace, which is inseparable from Himself, He's promising His presence.

Marion begins each day by tapping into God's intimacy through prayer. "First thing in the morning, I start off with giving thanks for my blessings, because I still have many. Then I ask God to help me through each moment and put joy into my life. I'll pray specifically and say, 'Let me find two joyful things. Let me accomplish three tasks. Help me not to be self-absorbed.' It's hard. But 'Jesus loves me, this I know.' Those are not just words to a childhood song; it's a truth. And I cling to it."

God knows we tend to doubt what we can't see or feel, so He's preserved His written word to communicate His nearness. Scripture itself is described as "God-breathed." Just as God breathed life into Adam, He breathes life into our spirits through His word. "The word is very near you; it is in your mouth and in your heart so you may obey it." (Deuteronomy 30:14) The Word made flesh, Jesus, when He appeared at the resurrection, breathed on His disciples and said, "Receive the Holy Spirit."(John 20:22) That same Holy Spirit dwells within you as a believer and makes God not only near, but also a part of you.

Scriptures along with prayer are Marion's mainstays. She refuses to let her physical suffering suffocate her faith. As her dependence on God has grown, so has her trust. Focusing on God's presence, Marion clings to Him.

SOUL THERAPY

Giver of Life,
Be as near as my breath.
And when I'm struggling,
Please permeate my life with Your presence.
Let Your unexplainable peace settle on me.
Thank You for the assurance
That when I finally come home to You,
I'll never again have to gasp for breath or grasp for life—
It will be mine forever.

WORK OUT

Lie down and (if you are able) take slow, deep breaths, not just expanding your chest, but also the abdomen/diaphragm. With each breath, ask God to fill you with His presence and peace. With each exhale, prayerfully give Him your problems. As you exhale, let out all the air you think you can, then purse your lips, and see if more flows out. (It will.) Repeat the deep inhale-and-exhale several times. Even if you can't breathe deeply, you can pray with each breath.

JOURNAL

Reflect on God being as near as your very breath. What does that mean to you?

Stature

BODY BASIC
Across the world,
the average height for a man
is approximately 5 feet 9 inches, and for
a woman, it is 5 feet 4 inches.

SPIRITUAL
SPECIFIC
"Who of you by
worrying can add a single cubit
to his height?" (MATTHEW 6:27)

*M*ost of us prefer to be above average, whether in stature or in life. We'd rather not be defined by words that relate to average, such as "ordinary, undistinguished, inconsequential, run-of-the-mill."

But when we are taking care of ourselves or a loved one who is sick, we may feel restricted and confined by dull routine. Days filled with doctors' appointments, physical therapy, measuring out medications, preparing a special diet, etc., can be disheartening when you would like to achieve more. During several months of mysterious fatigue, I was discouraged that my lack of energy prevented me from accomplishing anything other than the boring, run-of-the-mill routine of getting by. My wings had been clipped, and I didn't like it.

But during those slow days, as I read my Bible, I felt God reassuring me that no one in His hands is inconsequential or insignificant. Our significance is in *Him*, and to Him, "average" is an opportunity. For instance, Bethlehem was just an ordinary little town, yet it was Christ's birthplace. Mary, an obscure handmaiden, became the mother of Christ. Joseph, a common carpenter, was chosen to provide for and help raise God's Chosen One. The shepherds, who were "nobodies," were in the midst of their mundane sheep watching, when angelic beings announced Christ's birth to them. They were the first outsiders to hear the good news and to see Jesus. Scripture shows us again and again that God delights in taking the most unlikely person and making him or her into someone significant in His plan. For instance, Rahab the prostitute, who hid the Israelite spies in Jericho, became a believer and an ancestor of Christ.

No matter what fills your days, when God fills your heart you have "the glorious riches of this mystery, which is Christ in you, the hope of glory." (Colossians 1:27) Jesus shares His glory and riches with you. No matter what your physical limitations, your spirit is one with the most powerful, influential Being in the universe, who has chosen you as His own. He can do whatever He wants to do through you, no matter what your restrictions.

As part of a royal priesthood of believers, you are designed to "stand tall" for Him. There's nothing routine or run-of-the-mill about anything God does, and He is working in, through and *for* you!

SOUL THERAPY

Lord, I'm so ordinary,
But I thank You that You are extraordinary,
And You've chosen to dwell in me.
Help me not to worry about "adding an extra cubit"
To my height or my accomplishments,
Because You are in charge of that.
Allow me to seek Your plans,
Depending on Your untiring Spirit
When mine is flagging.

And no matter what my humdrum routine may be,
Help me to perform it with a full and thankful heart.

WORK OUT

Stretch yourself up to your full height. Standing tall, clasp your hands flat together, in a praying position at chest level. Then, breathing in deeply, raise your clasped hands straight over your head, as if you were going to dive. Then open up your arms and hands and slowly lower them (still outstretched) to your side. Breathe out slowly as you lower them. Then bring them into a praying position and begin the motion again, breathing deeply. As you make five to ten repetitions of the motions (folding hands, reaching toward heaven, opening your arms, then bringing hands together again), give your body and life prayerfully to God.

JOURNAL

How do you think God can use you in your current circumstances? Record some thoughts.

Bone Dry

BODY BASIC
Bone tissue is alive and requires nutrients. The adult human body has 206 bones, but a newborn baby has more—305 bones, many of which are soft and pliable and allow the flexibility required during the birth process. As the child grows, his bones will gradually fuse together (into 206) and become harder.

SPIRITUAL SPECIFIC
"So I prophesied as I was commanded. And as I was prophesying, there was a noise, a rattling sound, and the bones came together, bone to bone."
(EZEKIEL 37:7)

If nutrients are cut off from a bone, it will die. Likewise, when life is tough enough for long enough, we may feel as if we've grown as hollow as a dead bone. Our faith may seem dry and brittle, and our prayers lifeless. But we can find encouragement in the unusual story of Ezekiel's vision in the valley of dry bones. The bones were representative of the disobedient House of Israel, which was in exile and whose people said, "Our bones are dried up, and our hope is gone; we are cut off." (Ezekiel 37:11)

In Ezekiel's revelation, God showed him that Israel's bleak situation would not last forever. He commanded His prophet, "Prophesy to these bones and say to them...this is what the Sovereign Lord says...: I will make breath enter you, and you will come to life. I will attach tendons to you and make flesh come upon you and cover you with skin...Then you will know that I am the Lord." Ezekiel obeyed and spoke God's words, and the dry bones came to life and stood up as a vast army, representing the nation of Israel, which would come out of exile. The vision personified God's life-giving power and hope.

When we feel cut off and have a sense of despair, when God seems distant, our days in the "bone heap" seem long. But this story reminds us that God still specializes in bringing new life to His repentant people, no matter how beaten down and bone-dry we feel.

I read a book by a friend's college roommate, Leslie, who felt battered and in need of increased faith after she made a move with her minister husband to help rescue a divided church. She wrote that she'd given up everything she loved in order to make the move and do what she believed God wanted. But despite her efforts, she wound up in a lonely, unhappy situation. Tragic family deaths added to her grief. Leslie spent many wakeful nights "wrestling with God" in prayer. And she heard what she called "a terrifying sound": the silence of God.

Through a long, difficult journey and a "painful process," Leslie wrote that she finally made a discovery: "God in all His wisdom, kept quiet until I finally could hear the high-pitched 'me, me, me, me' in all my prayers. He led me to a sensitive spiritual adviser, who helped me see that silence can be a great purifier, not a denial of love and concern. I was still hanging onto 'my rights' even though I thought I'd given them to God. I had to die to self and let go of trying to control things before I could really be free to live out God's plan. I had to trust Him even when it didn't look like He was in control. Even when it didn't feel as though He was home—or anywhere in the universe! I *had* to have faith in His ways, and know they are always much better than mine."

Looking back, Leslie said she never fully understood God's plan in her situation, except that the move to a new location had put her in a position to help a dying relative. "Who knows?" she wrote. "Sometimes we are seemingly destroyed in order for God to build something more wonderful within. I was just too busy sulking to see it."

Leslie found that like Jacob, who wrestled with God, "we have permission to ask for God's blessing even as we struggle. Whenever I asked for a blessing, God never failed me." Although God didn't change her situation, and He didn't "send a postcard with instructions for the future," Leslie said, "He never failed to give me a nugget of peace, a glimmer of a plan, or a shelf to place my worries on."

When we're faced with impossibilities and find it hard to trust, we may think our faith is too small. But *any* amount faith in God is enough for Him to use. He can accomplish great things within us as easily as He made a vast army out of the bones in Ezekiel's vision. Just as easily as He clothed *Himself* in flesh and bones and came to dwell with us as Jesus Christ. No matter what shape our faith is in, God remains faithful to us, His much-loved children, and He enables us to grow spiritually.

SOUL THERAPY

When I'm in a "valley of dry bones," Lord,
Confused, hurting, and doubting,
Remind me that You are never distant and uninvolved.
Please rebuild my faith.
Refresh me with Your Holy Spirit.
Help me, instead of wrestling for *my* way
To surrender into Your infinitely capable hands,
And when I do, please create something wonderful within me.

WORK OUT

Using weights strengthens bones. Holding weights or a household item that is right for your strength, such as an empty milk bottle filled with however much water produces the right weight, or a five-pound bag of pet food, etc., sit on the edge of a kitchen chair and rise, sit and rise, ten times.

JOURNAL

Describe the condition your faith is in at the moment. How can you, with God's help, build it?

Exam Time

BODY BASIC
A medical examination may detect problems that may not produce noticeable symptoms, such as high blood pressure, high cholesterol and even some early cancers.

SPIRITUAL SPECIFIC
"Examine my heart, O Lord." (PSALM 26:2)

Medical tests are important to good physical health. And our Great Physician, who is always concerned with our spiritual health, advises His people through Paul: "A man ought to examine himself..." (1 Corinthians 11: 28) Once we judge ourselves, recognizing our sins and repenting, God assures us of His forgiveness through Christ, our Healer.

Although the Bible assures us that God's forgiveness is complete when we are penitent, it also says, God "disciplines those He loves..." (Hebrews12:6) His discipline is not intended to produce guilt and condemnation. Instead, it is prescribed for our good—to chisel us more into the likeness of Jesus.

Biblical heroes and heroines' sins and consequences are laid out for all to see. King David repented of his adultery and murder, but he still harbored a hellish household of sons who committed incest, treachery and more murder that David seemed powerless to control. Nevertheless, long after his death, David's line of descendants produced the promised Jesus, fulfilling prophecy and proving God can use imperfect human beings to fulfill His plans.

Moses, who let an outburst of temper get the best of him, lost his chance to lead his people into the Promised Land. Despite that discipline, however, God still rewarded him after his death when, in his spiritual body, he and Elijah stood with a transfigured Jesus on a mountain in the Promised Land.

God is never surprised by our weakness. And He, who gave up His Son to pay for our disobedience and failures, doesn't want us to reject His gift of salvation or hold onto guilt. God's intention for self-examination is to foster repentance, not to make us feel unlovable and unforgivable. It's Satan, the Liar, who takes destructive delight in trying to make us feel unforgivable.

A pastor friend of mine, Dave, allowed his own self-condemnation to overcome him when his wife demanded a divorce. He told me, "Divorce is sin and a death. It's a sin in the way that all broken promises are sins— and marriage vows are the largest of promises. When my wife told me she no longer even believed in God, I blamed myself for that, too. I felt like a failure, a destroyer." And worse, he admitted he felt as if "Jesus died for everyone except me."

He couldn't internalize God's forgiveness. All that enabled him to get through each dark day was God's grace that he absorbed through his congregation, the elders, clergy and friends. "Over me beat the invisible wings," he said. Nevertheless, he continued to berate himself. And, in his darkest hour, his mother's terminal illness and other problems added to his heavy grief; he began crying and couldn't stop. At that moment, his estranged wife called. When she heard his despondency, surprisingly she comforted him. "It seemed strange that the one who was the source of most of my grief was also the one God sent to be the source of my conso-lation. That was a huge manifestation of His grace," Dave said. And it was a turning point.

That unexpected event changed Dave's focus from guilt to grace and enabled him to feel thankful—not only for God's kindness, but for what he had once had. That gratitude "somehow opened a portal" for conscious-ness of the Holy Spirit's forgiveness, and Dave began healing. He was able to start a new life. Later, he remarried and fathered a baby girl, who brings him great joy.

SOUL THERAPY

Examine my heart, my Great Physician,
And reveal to me my sins.
Please forgive me for _____.
And help me, after confessing and repenting,
To forgive myself, learn from my mistakes, and move forward.
When I'm suffering the painful consequences of my actions,
Please give me a large dose of Your undeserved grace to see me through.

WORK OUT
If it's been too long since your last physical examination, set one up. Then, take your life to God in prayer and self-examination.

JOURNAL
Write out some things about your spiritual health that you'd like to improve.

Ins And Outs

BODY BASIC
The brain's wrinkly gray exterior conceals many interior marvels. Our outer body hides its inner workings. Each of our collaborating microscopic cells, too, contains an inner blueprint to direct it in doing its part in building our body and its systems and in helping to maintain life.

SPIRITUAL SPECIFIC
"I pray that out of His glorious riches He may strengthen you with power through His spirit in your inner being." (EPHESIANS 3:16)

*O*ur *body, as well as each of its microscopic cells,* has inner and outer parts. Yet our "inner being" is much more than the physical. God created each person with a unique spirit that exhibits distinctive gifts, resources and characteristics that set him or her apart. God also gives us Christ's Holy Spirit, His divine nature, to help and comfort our spirit. The Bible says in 1 Corinthians 12:4: "Now there are diversities of gifts, but the same Spirit."

When our outer body is damaged, our inner resources are tried as well. It's easy to give in to anger, discouragement and hopelessness. But God tells us how to get through seemingly impossible situations: "Not by might, not by power, but by My Spirit." God's invincible Spirit and several *thousand* of His "great and precious promises," are given to us to lift us supernaturally over any mountain of difficulty.

My church friend and a retired minister, O.C., had often depended on the Holy Spirit and God's promises to strengthen him and to comfort others. He was a widower and in good health at age ninety-one, and when he married an eighty-nine-year-old widow, Joan, our whole congregation was delighted. (The two had become friends riding recumbent bicycles.) They began a ministry together to shut-ins. One Sunday, they were on their way to deliver communion. A speeding driver ran a red light and broadsided them, injuring them severely. They were rushed to the hospital.

Badly battered and with internal injuries, O.C. was helpless to assist his beloved bride who had a broken leg on one side, a broken foot on the other, many painful broken ribs, and an eye injury.

The two chose to go home with nurses rather than stay in the hospital. "We found out later," Joan recounts, "that our nurses and friends didn't expect us to live. But I expected that we *would!*"

At times, each of them needed the other's inner strength as well as his or her own personal faith. O.C. said, "I feel sure if I hadn't had Joan and her strong faith, I wouldn't have made it. What pulled me through was the strength we had together. Being a minister, I could trace back through my years and find lots of inspiration. I had plenty of time for meditation and prayer. But one of God's best provisions was Joan."

Despite being in terrible pain—she couldn't tolerate pain medications—Joan felt the Holy Spirit's constant presence and assurance. Talking about His very real comfort helped Joan to buoy O.C. "With my eye injury, I couldn't even read the Bible," she told me. "But I'd memorized many scriptures, so I focused on them and felt reassured. Prayer helped me, too. God is still the Healer. I just kept on trusting Him."

As their outer bodies slowly healed, O.C. and Joan gained a more intimate knowledge of each other's inner resources and essence as well as the Holy Spirit's personal and supernatural encouragement. Now recovered, they are closer than ever, and they minister with a deeper understanding of suffering.

SOUL THERAPY

Lord, it's so disheartening
To be badly injured,
While I'm right in the middle of doing Your will.
And yet I know there is no safer place for me
Than being in Your will.
So, as I struggle to recover,
Please strengthen my spirit
With Your divine nature.
And thank You for the unique inner gifts
Of my loved ones who, along with You, cheer me on.

WORK OUT

You can stretch your outer body while extending your inner being in prayer as you practice this yoga position. Start on your hands and knees (floor or bed) and use your hands to push yourself back until your arms are fully stretched out in front of you, your forehead is resting on the floor and your buttocks is resting against your heels. Stay in this stretched position, and take a long slow inhale, then exhale. Breathe in and out deeply five times as you pray.

JOURNAL

1 Corinthians 10:13 in The Message's paraphrase says, "No test or temptation that comes your way is beyond the course of what others have had to face. All you need to remember is that God will never let you down: He'll never let you be pushed past your limit; He'll always b e there to help you come through it." How can you apply that scripture when you feel depleted of every inner resource? Write out your thoughts.

Living Water

BODY BASIC

Water constitutes more than half of the human body. Muscle tissue is about seventy-five per cent water; bone is about twenty-two per cent. We can only live a few days without water, which helps carry nutrients and oxygen to different parts of the body and also flushes out toxins and waste.

SPIRITUAL SPECIFIC

"...Jesus stood and said in a loud voice, 'If anyone is thirsty, let him come to me and drink. Whoever believes in me, as the Scripture has said, streams of living water will flow from within him.'"

(JOHN 7:37)

Waters are mentioned from the very beginning of the Bible in Genesis, when "the Spirit of God was hovering over the waters." In creation, God tamed those waters and assigned them to their place, gathering them to form sky and seas, letting dry land appear. Later, in judgment for mankind's wickedness, God covered the world again with those same waters, destroying everyone except the righteous Noah and his family. In various Bible stories, waters were miraculously parted, purified, or plagued. God dried up waters in judgment and sent waters upon the fields as blessing. Water wells were settings for love stories and providential meetings. Water was, and is, used in baptism. And Christ's first miracle involved water becoming wine. Water is such an essential to humans, that Christ called Himself Living Water that will never run dry within us.

Jesus' words are easy for me to picture because water is powerful, vital and teeming with life. Yet it became significant to me in a new way when I began working out in a therapy pool. I experienced two of the ways water helps me grow stronger: its *lift* allows me to move quickly by swimming, building up my heart rate, and its *resistance* increases my strength as I slowly push floating barbells and other equipment through it.

My Lord, my "Living Water," had recently been using lift and resistance in training me spiritually. He had allowed a "mystery illness" to restrain me from my usual busy way of life, yet, during that period of fatigue, weakness and dependence, He also gave me a lift: His presence. I can't explain it, but I *felt* it.

I had desperately wanted to get well in time to help our daughter Joanna with our first grandbaby, who was due by Caesarean section in a few months. But despite fervent prayers, I stayed exhausted, and doctors remained baffled. In that time of dependency on God, I began experiencing Him in a new way. Through my frustration and fear, He showed me how He would provide—an encouraging word here, a thoughtful helper there, a surprise shot of energy, even a day of complete reprieve. Often, He gave me wisdom to realize my stressful agenda wasn't important, and to let it go. He instilled in me a deep trust, and I knew that if I couldn't help Joanna, He would send someone else who could.

It was a difficult time, but it stretched my faith. And by the time Joanna's due date arrived, I had stopped worrying about what I could or couldn't do and trusted God to provide the help that was needed.

Buoyed by B-12 shots, energy foods and many prayers, I traveled with my husband Joe to Joanna's bedside, not knowing whether or not I'd have the stamina to help her through those first days. But God granted me just enough strength to assist her, along with Jayne, Joanna's mother-in-law, who cheerfully took the night shift. It was a joyous time.

Later, my problem was diagnosed as both gluten intolerance and hypoglycemia (low blood sugar). So I learned new eating habits! But more than that, I learned that the Living Water is always working His purposes to strengthen me, whether He slows me down or lifts me up.

SOUL THERAPY

Heavenly Father,

Thank You for the gift of Your Living Water.

Please help me to plunge into Your promises,

Rather than to sink in life's struggles.

Buoy me with Your mercies.

And help me to remember that You use tough times

Not to cast me away,

But to sweep me ever closer to You.

WORK OUT

Leaning back in a deep, warm bath, bend one leg, keeping that foot on the bottom of the tub, and leave the other leg straight. Then, with abdominal muscles tight, lift the straight leg up out of the water until it is about four inches above the water. Then lower it back in. As you begin the lift, notice how light your leg feels while it's in the water, then note how heavy it becomes as it leaves the water. Lift each leg ten times or however many times you comfortably can. Then just relax in the tub, thanking God that He can make the weighty things in our life feel lighter.

JOURNAL

Tell why you think Jesus used the term "Living Water" to describe Himself. In what ways is He Living Water to you?

Behold

BODY BASIC
*The eye is the only organ
with nerve receptors that
respond to light. In a healthy eye,
photoreceptors can respond to a billion
different stimuli per second. However,
with an eye disorder such as glaucoma,
called "the sneak thief of sight," the optic
disc can be damaged and cause loss of
vision or even blindness.*

SPIRITUAL
SPECIFIC
*"Blessed are the eyes
that see what you see."*

(LUKE 10:23)

*J*esus *gave sight to many who were physically blind.* Yet despite
Jesus' frequent miraculous signs, many of the Jews and most of their
leaders refused to believe in Him. Jesus called those people blind; their
spiritual eyes were darkened. Jesus wanted to open people's spiritual eyes
and turn them from darkness to light.

While we are on earth, our spiritual eyes only "see" God dimly. But He
is always eager to teach us something about Himself. Moses asked God to
do that, saying "Teach me Your ways so I may know You and continue to

find favor with You." Then he boldly added, "Show me Your glory."

God only granted Moses a partial glimpse of His glory—His back—but He did agree to reveal His goodness. In Exodus 34:5-7 as God passes by Moses, He describes Himself: "The Lord, the Lord, the compassionate and gracious God, slow to anger, abounding in love and faithfulness, maintaining love to thousands and forgiving wickedness, rebellion and sin. Yet He does not leave the guilty unpunished..." God was true to that self-description—He led Israel and was slow to anger. But they suffered throughout their history for their unbelief.

Others in the Bible had their spiritual eyes opened, too. At Bethel, Jacob had a dream (Genesis 28) and the Lord spoke to him. When he awoke, Jacob said, "Surely the Lord is in this place, and I was not aware of it."

Like Jacob, when we're going through difficulties, we may or may not be aware of God's presence. But surely the Lord is in this place. No matter how disheartening our circumstances may be, God encourages us to always look for Him, saying, "Seek and ye shall find." As Paul counseled, "We fix our eyes not on what is seen, but what is unseen. For what is seen is temporary, but what is unseen is eternal." (2 Corinthians 4:8) Scripture and prayer both help to sharpen our focus so that the eyes of our heart can see God.

When my mother learned she had an unsuspected glaucoma that could destroy her sight, she said, "I was terrified about possibly going blind." She turned to the Bible. "I asked God to let me open my Bible to a word of comfort from Him. When I opened it, a four leaf clover that I had found months before was in that spot, and my eyes were drawn to the phrase, 'Blessed are the eyes that see what you see.' I realized then I had what counted—Jesus, who was speaking to me directly, now. Everything else, even my sight, seemed trivial compared to that. I thought it was amazing God would comfort me so perfectly. It's one of the most immediate, clear answers I've ever gotten to a prayer." Not only that, but after laser procedures and cataract surgery, Mom's eye pressure went down to normal.

SOUL THERAPY

Thank You for the precious gift of sight, Lord.
And even though my physical eyesight dims with age,
I'm grateful that my spiritual vision grows ever sharper.
Please give me the eyes to recognize You
In everything today.
Especially when I feel frightened,
Or overwhelmed by my challenges,
Show me Your glory.
Teach me Your ways.

WORK OUT
Hold your finger about ten inches from your face and focus on it for a couple of seconds. Then move your focus to an object across the room, keeping your eyes on it briefly. Then bring your focus back to your finger. Repeat ten times. Then watch for God in everything that happens today.

JOURNAL
Record any of this coming (or past) week's "God-sightings."

What's The Upside?

BODY BASIC

The brain regulates virtually all human activity, but we only use about two per cent of its capabilities. Weighing about three pounds, the brain contains more than one hundred billion cells and some quadrillion synaptic connections.

SPIRITUAL SPECIFIC

"For He will keep in perfect peace him whose mind is steadfast, because he trusts in You." (ISAIAH 26:3)

A drug overdose stopped the heart and damaged the brain of Carol's twenty-one-year-old son, Daniel, whom I met at my Rehab Center. Daniel would have died, except that he collapsed while carrying his sick girlfriend into the emergency room, and medical personnel saved his life.

Carol told me that she sat by Daniel's bedside, praying, and Daniel remained in a coma for eight weeks. Doctors advised Carol that he would not get better. She said, "They said to think about taking out the feeding tube and letting him go. He wouldn't want to live this way."

"I had to come face to face with what I believed about God," she continued. "And I knew it was not up to me at all whether Daniel lived or died." So she said to the doctors, "God has a reason that he's still alive. However God leaves him, I'll deal with it." She left the feeding tube in.

One of the ways she coped was by quoting Jeremiah 29:11-13 to a comatose Daniel: "For I know the plans I have for you, says the Lord, plans for good and not for evil, to give you a future and a hope." That promise, although given specifically to Jews exiled to Babylon, contains truths for us as well: God, who can work even in calamities for our good, has a plan for each of us. And His plan for every believer is reconciliation to Himself through Christ, giving us a future and a hope.

Carol continued to hope and pray for her son, and finally, miraculously, Daniel woke up from the coma. After much work with his speech therapist, his mom and others, he began repeating a few words four months later. And he finished the scripture his family had quoted to him. Daniel is now walking with a walker, feeding himself, and making jokes. I often pass him in the halls of the rehabilitation center, and I can see him progressing.

But it's tough. And as Carol struggles with him through rehabilitation, caring for his many needs and feeling exhausted, she says, "I depend on the serenity prayer, and I pray it often. I know I can't control this situation. All I can control is my own mind and heart and my own perception of things. I could think sad thoughts—and I have—but God has taught me that there is an upside to everything. So I focus on finding the upside when I'm tired or frustrated. It's really changed me."

Whether you are the caregiver or you require care, a big part of life's battles takes place in the mind. Paul says, "...Be made new in the attitude of your mind." (Ephesians 4:23)

Even though it's often hard to reset our thinking, Paul reminds us that as believers who are one with Christ, we "have the mind of Christ." (1 Corinthians 2:16) Jesus Himself enables us to look for the upside, because He *is* the upside! He gives us the capacity to love God with all of our *mind* as well as all our heart, soul and strength. God has far more power than we can ever take advantage of, just as our brain has far more capabilities than we utilize. As Carol discovered, it's when we depend on God, who is ever-mindful of *us*, that we find the peace, courage and wisdom to see us through.

SOUL THERAPY

God grant me the serenity
To accept the things I cannot change;
Courage to change the things I can;
And wisdom to know the difference.
Living one day at a time;
Enjoying one moment at a time;
Accepting hardships as the pathway to peace;
Taking, as He did, this sinful world
As it is, not as I would have it;
Trusting that He will make all things right
If I surrender to His Will;
That I may be reasonably happy in this life
And supremely happy with Him
Forever in the next. Amen.
— *Reinhold Niebuhr*

WORK OUT
Coordination exercises work the brain. Lie down on your back and tighten your abs for this pattern exercise: start with your right arm, lift it to the ceiling and back to the floor, then lift and lower your left leg to the ceiling/floor, then lift the right leg up and down, then the left arm. Repeat the cycle five times, keeping abs tight. Then switch and start with the left arm, right leg, left leg, right arm. Repeat five times.

JOURNAL
Record any "upside" you can think of about a present challenge you face.

Remember

BODY BASIC
The brain can store 800 memories per second, and it stores information for a lifetime, whether we can consciously recall the information or not. Since the brain itself feels no pain, researchers have performed brain surgery on patients who are awake and discovered that a tiny bit of electrical stimulation to different areas of the brain can cause a person to "see" a long-forgotten face or "hear" a sound or rhyme the person could not have recalled earlier.

SPIRITUAL SPECIFIC
"Remember the Lord who is great and awesome..."
(NEHEMIAH 13:22)

*A**ll through scripture God tells people** to remember His words, His deeds on behalf of His people, His commands, promises, and goodness. After God held back the waters of the flooding Jordan River so the people of Israel could cross on dry ground, He told Joshua to make a stone memorial "as a sign among you. In the future, when your children ask you, 'What do these stones mean?' tell them...He did this so that all the peoples of the earth might know that the hand of the Lord is powerful..." (Joshua 4:6-7, 24)

God's people throughout history have also asked God to remember *them*, along with keeping in mind His promises to them. Nehemiah 13:22 says, "Remember me..., O my God and show mercy to me according to Your great love." David says, "Remember Your word to Your servant, for You have given me hope. My comfort in my suffering is this: Your promise preserves my life." (Psalm 119:49) This mutual recollection helps keep the God-man connection strong.

However, sometimes God's people ask Him **not** to recall something. Isaiah the prophet said, "Do not remember our sins forever." And God, creating a new covenant with His people through Jesus—His promise of forgiveness and eternal life through faith in Christ—answers the prophet's request. "For I will forgive their wickedness and will remember their sins no more." (Hebrews 8:12)

The Bible's heroes and heroines habitually recalled God's kindness to them in the past and recollected His promises to them. They often erected memorials or altars to be physical reminders of God's protection and provision. For example, after God gave the Israelites victory over the Philistines, "Samuel [the prophet] took a stone and set it up between Mizpah and Shen. He named it Ebenezer, saying, "Thus far has the Lord helped us." (1 Samuel 7:12)

When Jesus' disciples worried about not having any bread to eat, Jesus reiterated the importance of memories. "You of little faith," he said, "Why are you talking among yourselves about having no bread? Do you still not understand? Don't you remember the five loaves for the five thousand, and how many basketfuls you gathered? Or the seven loaves for the four thousand, and how many basketfuls you gathered?" (Matthew 16: 8-10)

After Jesus' death and resurrection, His disciples encouraged each other in times of persecution to keep in mind Christ's love and sacrifice, demonstrated through His suffering on the cross. For them and for us, remembering helps build faith and keeps creeping fear at bay.

Although the brain has a great capacity to retain a memory, it can be hindered by many things, such as the mysterious disease of dementia and

Alzheimer's. My mother-in-law, Lou, still enjoys conversation, but the memory of it slips out of her mind instantly. Nevertheless, her love of God remains, no matter what else she forgets. I dropped in for an Easter party at her Alzheimer's facility, and while I was there, she was asked to read to fellow residents from the Bible. One visitor went up to her afterward and told her, "You read with such faith and sincerity. You've always been like that—I remember that same faith when you taught me in Sunday school!" Even though Lou didn't remember teaching him years before, he remembered, and his life had been influenced by her faith.

Whatever else fades away in life, God tells us His love for us and His Word to us endure forever. And in His Word He promises, "I will not forget you." (Isaiah 49:15)

SOUL THERAPY

Lord, as I age,
My attention span and memory both grow shorter.
Please help me not to fear those changes.
Instead, strengthen my recall of Your word and Your love.
Sustain me through all my present problems
With reminders of the ways
You've been faithful and kind to me in the past.

WORK OUT
Memorization is good for the brain. Memorize a scripture. (1 Samuel 2:2 is a good reminder: "There is no one holy like the Lord; there is no one besides You; there is no Rock like our God.")

JOURNAL
How have you seen God's goodness in your life? Write down some of your memories.

Tension Relief

BODY BASIC
Strong emotions tighten muscles. Tensed muscles grow tired and achy. Pain from conditions such as arthritis-related fibromyalgia, which causes generalized muscle pain and fatigue, is intensified by tension.

SPIRITUAL SPECIFIC
"Martha, Martha," the Lord answered, "You are worried and upset about many things, but only one thing is needed. Mary has chosen what is better..."[sitting at the Lord's feet] (LUKE 10:41-42)

My friend Johnelle struggled with the intense stiff muscle pain of fibromyalgia for more than a year. She was in such pain, she rarely left home. "I cried as I faced the thought that life might just pass me by, and I wouldn't be able to keep up with my family," she told me. "I didn't want to drag anyone down; I wanted to get well!" Drugs caused intolerable side effects. She prayed for help and began researching. She discovered that diet, exercise and skilled relaxation techniques were a natural therapy that helped her. "But relaxation helped the most," she said.

After practicing techniques to get her muscles to relax, she discovered that deep, focused prayer achieved much the same physical result. Twice a day for twenty-minute periods, she disconnected the phone, did some deep breathing, then prayed, focusing on God's characteristics and giving thanks. She also shared the burdens of her heart. "Even though I had always studied scripture, I rarely took time to truly meditate on what I read or to just listen for God's voice," she says. "What used to be a disciplined time of Bible reading and prayer now has become the delight of just sitting adoringly at His feet, reflecting on Him and His words. As I relaxed and was still, the verse 'Be still and know that I am God' took on new meaning. Finding that intimate place with God not only gave me a deeper relationship with Him, but as my muscles relaxed, my pain eased. I can honestly thank God for the fibromyalgia, because it led me closer to Him. And it made my prayer life much deeper."

Johnelle carefully continues her prayer and relaxation regime, not just because it has helped her return to a full life by lessening the pain, but also because it makes her life joyfully full.

Jesus wanted His disciples always to pray and never to give up. And to illustrate His point, He told a parable in Luke 18 (2-6) about a widow who persisted in presenting her requests to an uncaring, ungodly judge, even when the odds were stacked against her. Eventually, her perseverance paid off with an answer to her petition. Jesus' story illustrated that if a hard-hearted human judge responds to persistence, how much more is our loving God eager to reward faithful prayer. Jesus showed in the next parable (9-14) *how* He expects us to draw near to Him: humbly, and confessing our sins. And in 15-17, He gave His followers another hint about approaching Him: adults should come as simply and sincerely as the children who climbed into His lap—with dependence, openness and trust.

Christ tells us one way to persevere in prayer is by remembering His words, so that "My words remain in you." Those words, which Johnelle meditated upon as she relaxed and prayed, reflect His grace, love and power. They remind us "what's impossible with man is possible with God." With His encouragement, even drawn-out tribulation can never win over our persistence in coming to Him.

SOUL THERAPY

Heavenly Father,
"You have searched me and You know me."
You know all my anxieties.
And You are the only answer
To release me from the tension
In my mind and body.
Please deepen my prayer life.
Let Your words seep into my soul,
So that I can be still
And know that You are God.

WORK OUT
Read some of Christ's parables
about prayer in Luke 18.

JOURNAL
Jot down what some of those
parables say to you about prayer.

Warfare

BODY BASIC
*The flesh, bones and blood
of our body are each
vulnerable to the environment, where
invading bacteria and/or physical
trauma threaten to destroy us. Our
spirit, too, is in danger of a "destroyer."
Satan uses anything he can, to turn us
away from God and bring our mind
and spirit into despair, fear and distrust.*

SPIRITUAL
SPECIFIC
*"...Be strong in the
Lord and in His mighty power.
Put on the full armor of God
so that you can take your stand
against the devil's schemes.
For our struggle is not against
flesh and blood, but against...
the powers of this dark world
and against the spiritual
forces of evil in the heavenly
realms."* (EPHESIANS 6:10-12)

*O**ur body's defenses can be weakened by many things.** And when
we're in physical or emotional pain—or both—we become more
susceptible to our spiritual enemy, Satan, who tries to defeat us and fill
us with hopelessness. He is "like a roaring lion looking for someone to
devour." (1 Peter: 5:8) Satan often attacks us when we are weakest, and he
assailed Jesus, too, at His most vulnerable time in the wilderness. But the

Bible advises us to do as Jesus did: "Resist him, standing firm in the faith." Sometimes our battle is long. But God always wins. His plans are never frustrated.

Many of the Bible's heroes struggled for years before they saw God's plan for them come to fruition. And there were those who didn't get to see it in their lifetime. Some had God's promise of a future glory or kingdom, but those assurances eluded them as they warred against enemies determined to thwart God's objectives. Moses faced Pharaoh. David was stalked for years by Saul and his army. Joseph suffered from his brothers' treachery and was thrown into slavery and prison for many years. But each of those men emerged from his trials with a deeper faith and stronger character. Each saw God's power at work, and His promises finally delivered.

Joseph, who became Pharaoh's number-one man and saved thousands of people from famine, said to his betraying brothers, "You meant it for evil, but God meant it for good." That's still true.

It may appear that an illness, a person, or a circumstance is "the enemy." But, we're struggling against more than those things. Our real enemy is not flesh and blood, but spirit, according to Ephesians 6. It is Satan. So how do we ready ourselves to battle him, when our human resources aren't enough? By putting on the armor of God which can't be penetrated.

Paul tells the Ephesians (6:14-17) and all believers to wear Christ's salvation like a helmet, which not only was designed to protect a soldier, but also provided an impressive symbol of military victory. Since I frequently fight discouragement from the pain in my arthritic spine, I try to follow Paul's advice each day. And the first piece of armor I mentally put on is that helmet. I ask Jesus to guard my thoughts, to fill my mind with Himself and to push out everything that is negative and hopeless.

Paul also advises us to wear the "breastplate of righteousness." I prayerfully don that in my mind next, claiming Jesus' perfect character and His righteousness, which cover me and protect my heart and emotions. Then, I buckle on the "belt of truth," God's truth, as I read scripture. By knowing His truth, I am supporting my Christian stand, which fits my feet with "readiness that comes from the gospel of peace." In addition, I mentally grasp the only weapon any of us can use to fight a spiritual war: the "sword of the Spirit, which is the word of God." Jesus used that symbolic sword, God's word, to fight every one of Satan's temptations in the desert. Lastly,

I grab hold of the "shield of faith with which you can extinguish all the flaming arrows of the evil one."

Sometimes if I'm fighting fear or melancholy or the desire to give up, I mentally re-dress in the armor several times a day. The process helps me focus on the fact that even though my own defenses are inadequate against the Destroyer, with *God's* power, I am invincible! I praise God out loud for that, too, because praising God also repels Satan.

When the battle is long, grab a sword like God's promise that He will "work in all things for good for those who love the Lord and are called according to His purpose." While you wait and trust, remember God is working. As Chuck Swindoll says, "We focus on the immediate, but God focuses on the ultimate." And ultimately, good *will* result for you.

SOUL THERAPY

All-powerful, all-knowing, all-loving Creator,
My only protection from evil is You.
Sometimes my circumstances
Look so overpowering,
My inner turmoil
Feels so overwhelming,
My own nature is so sinful,
That it seems the battle can't be won.
But You assure me You have already won it for me!
Help me to stand strong in Your armor
Against the enemy's cruel sword of despair
And against any sin that masquerades as relief.
Cover me with Yourself, Mighty Father,
And deliver me from evil.

WORK OUT

Prayerfully "dress" in God's armor. If you want to put a little extra life into the prayer, you can make it physical. Stand up, and as you mentally put on the salvation helmet, place your hands on your head; then move them to your heart for the breastplate of righteousness; place them around your waist as you envision girding yourself with truth, then touch your toes for the shoes. As you pick up your sword and shield, hold them high as if you've won the victory. Thank God out loud that He has won it for you. It'll make you feel like a winner!

JOURNAL

What temptations do you fight most often? What sin tries to master you? Copy the pieces of armor in Ephesians 6:14-17, and write down how you could use each one to protect you from Satan's arrows, which are always aimed directly at your weak spots.

Getting
A Grip

BODY BASIC
*The hand's gripping
strength comes from the
thumb. The simple act of rotating
the thumb requires the brain to send
thousands of messages to various
muscles and tendons, telling each one
when to contract or relax, pull or rest.*

SPIRITUAL
SPECIFIC
*"...hold fast to
Him."* (DEUTERONOMY 11:22)

*A*lthough God tells us in the Bible that He upholds us in His "righteous right hand," we're also instructed to "hold fast to Him," while loving Him and walking in His ways.

Sometimes clinging to God is all we are capable of doing in life's storms. Doubts and fears can swamp us. Grief or pain can devastate us. Depression darkens our soul and sleeplessness exhausts us. When we feel forsaken, and when life-changes overwhelm us, we must tighten our grip on God's promises and hold fast to His hope.

Jim, a family friend and neighboring farmer and rancher, reached for God in desperation after a terrible accident with a hay baling machine.

He was attempting to unclog the baling apparatus when one of his arms got caught in it. As he instinctively reached to free that arm, his other arm was caught, and both were torn off. Although Jim was grateful that God preserved his life, he found coming to grips with his handicap even more trying than his long recovery. "With no arms, I couldn't accomplish *anything*," Jim related. "It was unbelievably frustrating. But I felt hopeful that once I got my prostheses everything would be okay. It wasn't! When I discovered that even with prostheses I was still terribly limited, it was a really dark time. The let-down and discouragement were fierce."

Not only would he never again be able to hold onto things as he always had, Jim also had to face the fact that he must let go of much of his independence. "Before the accident, every time life would flatten me, I would just pull myself up by my bootstraps, dust myself off and get on with business." No more!

He was forced to discover different "bootstraps." The first thing he grabbed hold of was God. "I knew He had some plan. I've never blamed Him for anything—I figure He set up the universe; we're the ones who make the mistakes. Sometimes it seems we get more than our share of hard times, though. So, my constant prayer is that God will reveal what it is He wants me to do. And I decided that through all my daily battles, I would use all the gifts He has given me to cope: my faith in Christ and in the power of prayer, the love of family and my wife's and my faith in each other, as well as humor, which my wife and I use a *lot*! Those things have been central to thriving after the accident."

Jim has a different outlook on life and what's important now. "In my dreams, I always have my arms back," he says. "And I think the real message of my dream imagery is that our bodies may become broken, but our soul is restored by the grace of God. Through prayer, we are whole again. No matter how much our outer shell gets blown up, our inner soul is restored to its original appearance."

As he deals daily with his broken body, Jim continues to improvise new ways to be independent. But he's also found new joy in interdependence with his wife Jill, his friends and prayer partners. He teaches a farm safety course to school children, ranches and farms with Jill's help, and has given his testimony to hundreds, telling of God's faithfulness in upholding him.

Although he still struggles to get more adept at using his prostheses,

Jim is grateful he doesn't need arms or hands to keep a grip on the Lord. His Strength is always at his side, helping him through every trying day.

SOUL THERAPY

God, I never know what life holds,
But I know You hold me.
When I'm disheartened,
Defeated or despairing,
Tighten my grip on You.

WORK OUT
Strengthen your grip: take a wash rag and wring it out by twisting it hard with both hands. Do ten to fifteen repetitions.

JOURNAL
Grasp a pen and list ways you can hold tight to God. Add any of His promises that build your hope.

What Are You Waiting For?

BODY BASIC
Certain body processes "wait" for their cue to kick into action. For instance, the liver stores glycogen until the body signals that it requires sugar. Then the liver converts the stored glycogen into glucose and sends it back into the bloodstream.

SPIRITUAL SPECIFIC
"But as for me, I watch in hope for the Lord, I wait for God my Savior; my God will hear me." (MICAH 7:7)

Parts of the body are created to "wait" until the time is right to kick in to start a chain of events. Those built-in delays don't bother us. But when we're waiting for a job offer, for test results, for recovery or any number of other things, delay can be a frustrating faith-tester.

God's people waited all through the Bible. Noah continued to build for 100 years from the time he began constructing the ark until the rain began. Caleb had to cool his heels for forty-five years from the time Moses gave him God's promise that he would enter the Promised Land until he finally led the people in.

Simeon, who remained ready for an undetermined amount of time to see the Messiah, believed God's promise that he wouldn't die until he'd seen Him. As a very old man, Simeon spent many days in the temple watching for his King. When Mary and Joseph brought the infant Jesus to be dedicated to God at the temple, Simeon recognized the Promised One in their arms. He exclaimed, "Now Lord, you are releasing Your bond-servant to depart in peace, according to Your word; for my eyes have seen Your salvation..." (Luke 2:29-30)

We no longer need to anticipate our salvation—Christ has already accomplished it for us. But other waits, especially frightening and confusing ones, keep us watching for God.

My friend Gayla immediately turned to God when she learned she had cancer of the vena cava, the major vein carrying blood to the heart. Doctors told her that the condition was not only rare but probably inoperable. "When everything inside of you is in a panic, it's easy to ask God for help," Gayla told me. "But it's hard to listen, wait and believe."

She had no idea what to do or where to turn, and many voices offered advice. "It's a struggle to hear God's voice and get His direction. And you're always second guessing about your own thoughts, too—is this me talking or God?"

As Gayla prayed for wisdom and listened, she wondered not only which specialists to contact, but whether or not she should even undergo the life-threatening surgery if someone offered to try it. "When you are confronting something that's probably not going to have a happy ending, you have to face that fact and yield it to God. When I opened myself up to God, He showed me an amazing hope. I knew without a doubt that He would take care of me, whether I had a miracle and was cured or not. I knew I could trust Him and His plan. No matter how it all came out, I had every reason to hope for what was good."

Her panic abated. Over many long days, Gayla continued making phone calls, searching for information and specialists, and asking friends to pray for her. Then amazing connections began happening all at once. She was led to some of the top specialists in the nation who agreed to take her case. As things fell into place, she said, "I knew it was God."

She underwent successful surgery, which, so far, has lengthened her life by five years of exciting opportunities and joy. And although she is still at risk, Gayla says the experience has left her grateful—not only for a miraculous extension of her life, but for the blessings of becoming first-hand-familiar with God's strength, peace and hope at work within her as she waited, and continues to wait, for His plan to unfold.

SOUL THERAPY

Waiting can be so wearying, Lord!
And it's easy to lose hope.
Please build up my confidence that You are working
Even when delays are long.
Prevent me from running ahead,
And help me to follow Your lead in Your time.
Thank You for Your assurance: "The Lord longs to be gracious to you;
He rises to show you compassion.
For the Lord is a God of justice.
Blessed are all who wait for Him."

WORK OUT
With a wall nearby to steady you if you lose your balance, take a long step (like Groucho Marx) bending your knee as your foot lands. Wait in that position, keeping the knee bent for a count of five, then step with the other foot. Keep that leg bent to a count of five. Continue stepping and waiting ten times on each leg.

JOURNAL
Recall a time when you've had to wait for God and record it along with any lessons you learned through the experience.

Fight Or Flight?

BODY BASIC
The core of the adrenal gland gets instant information from the brain. So if a person feels any strong emotion, such as rage or fear, the adrenal core releases hormones that immediately prepare the person for "fight or flight."

SPIRITUAL SPECIFIC
"Be strong and courageous, for I, the Lord your God, am with you wherever you go." (JOSHUA 1:9)

When threatened, our body's adrenaline temporarily gives us "super strength" which we can use either to run away or to stand and fight. It takes courage to fight an enemy.

Many times in the Bible, God admonishes His people to "be not afraid," to "be of good courage," to "be strong," but that kind of courage has nothing to do with adrenalin and everything to do with faith in God's strength. A trivia expert says the Bible exhorts "do not be afraid" or something similar 365 times—one for every day of the year.

When the Assyrians came to besiege Jerusalem, King Hezekiah told his military officers, "Be strong and courageous. Do not be afraid or discouraged because of the king of Assyria and the vast army with him, for there is a greater power with us than with him. With him is only the arm of flesh, but with us is the Lord our God to help us..." (2 Chronicles 32:7-8)

Facing and fighting life's difficulties require boldness, and God can provide it. Courage is not a lack of fear—that is fearlessness—but it is a supernatural gift that enables us to press on despite being afraid. Jesus demonstrated incredible bravery in going to the cross, but He was totally dependent on His Father to give it to Him. He was strengthened to stay the course by the same Father who empowers us.

A friend told me about an older woman named Billie whose courage she admired. When I called Billie, she told me her story (which took place before polio vaccines had been introduced). When she was twenty-two years old, married, and three months pregnant, Billie had been stricken with polio. One arm was paralyzed and the other side was weak. Nevertheless, Billie had managed, with her husband's help, to take care of their baby daughter when she was born, and they joyfully raised her. Billie tackled all life's daunting challenges armed with all she needed—her Lord's help.

Then, many years later, Billie's husband Dan, at age sixty-five, suffered Guillain Barre Syndrome and was paralyzed from the neck down for three months. Just when he was able to move again, he had a brain stem stroke. Now he has a feeding tube, tracheotomy and many other health problems.

"With just one arm, it's hard for me to handle my husband," Billie admitted. "And Dan gets down sometimes. I have my days, too. But we love the Lord. And the way we get back on track is that we start every day with Bible reading, and we memorize scripture. We share things we read that really affect us. Each day I get up, I thank God that I **can** get up. And when I'm feeling so bad for Dan in his condition, I repeat some of my favorite verses like Isaiah 26:3 'You will keep in perfect peace him whose mind is steadfast, because he trusts in You.'

"I also quote Isaiah 41:10," she continues. "'...do not fear, for I am with you. Do not be dismayed, for I am your God. I will strengthen you and help you; I will uphold you with My righteous right hand.'" Billie claims those promises, because "God is our only answer." She and Dan find the courage to press on by pressing close to Him.

SOUL THERAPY

Despite my daunting circumstances,
Great Giver of courage,
Please provide the stoutheartedness I need
Not just to survive,
But to thrive in Your love and sufficiency.
Often I'm tempted to run away from the fight,
To give up or give in.
Please remind me instead to flee to You,
Because You can conquer anything—
Including my fear.

WORK OUT

*Continuing to courageously keep
going is boosted by outer strength
as well as inner strength, and doing
"presses" with weights can help
build your body. Lie on your back
with small weights or cans
in each hand, and push them
upward from the chest twenty
times, either one arm at a time
or both at once, resting between
repetitions. (Be sure to hold the
weights or cans away from your
face in case you drop one.)*

JOURNAL

*What or who is the "enemy" you
face right now? How is God more
powerful than that? Write out your
fears and feelings and ask God to
help you cope without fear. Leave a
spot to record any ways He reaches
out to you in His word or in your
heart as days go by.*

Expectations

BODY BASIC
During a woman's monthly cycle, her hormones fluctuate and coordinate changes so that her uterine lining grows and thickens "in expectation" of a fertilized egg being implanted in it. If that doesn't happen, the uterus sheds that built-up welcoming environment, and a new cycle begins.

SPIRITUAL SPECIFIC
"The people were waiting expectantly and were all wondering in their hearts if John might possibly be the Christ. John answered them all, "I baptize you with water. But one more powerful than I will come, the thongs of whose sandals I am not worthy to untie." (LUKE 3:15,16)

The people of Israel had heard from their last prophet, Malachi, 400 years before John the Baptist appeared. They'd waited all those years for God to break His silence. They were weary, burdened, oppressed and ready for their expected Savior. They'd been disappointed by many false Messiahs. Was John the real Promised One? He was quick to let them know that he was only preparing the way for the true Messiah, Jesus.

Yet Jesus was so unlike what the people anticipated that many rejected

Him. Hadn't scriptures foretold He'd be a king? Where were the royal robes? He was only a carpenter's son from no-good Nazareth, they thought, not royalty from Bethlehem. Why wasn't He freeing them from Roman rule—setting the captives free? The list of reasons to doubt was long.

Like those ancient searching believers, we, too, have expectations and goals in life. A list might include: take care of yourself and enjoy good health; work hard and succeed; love well and stay married; have children and enjoy them; pray and get what you ask for; believe and be happy. And those presumptions are very often crushed, even when we do the right things. We ask, "Why?" And doubt tries to creep in with its false answers to our questions.

When my husband, Joe, and I began trying to have a baby, we went through five long years of infertility. We prayed earnestly for a child. Both of us had surgery to increase our chances, and we tried everything that doctors had to offer in those days. Finally, the situation became emotionally difficult as our hopes were dashed month after month.

Although I asked, "Why?" about the delay and wondered what God's plan might be for us, I wasn't plagued by doubt. I knew that the Giver of Life was in full control, so I finally decided maybe His answer to our prayers for a baby was "no." With a disappointed heart, I tossed out the temperature charts and let go of my striving. It was difficult, but I determined to fully give my dreams of motherhood to God. I knew whatever God wanted for me was best, even if it meant childlessness.

When I let go of my goal and focused instead on God, I experienced surprising relief. I felt myself relaxing more as my attitude changed; I now watched expectantly for God to give birth to His plans in my life. And then, much to my surprise, within six months of my decision to turn it all over to Him, I became pregnant!

Struggles don't always end so in line with our hopes. Nevertheless, living expectantly is important—anticipating a better tomorrow, trusting God to work in your life to replace your goals with His prospects. One thing you can count on completely: God will keep the promises He makes in scripture. It's comforting and powerful to pray His promises back to Him. For instance, I often pray, "Lord, You've promised You are close to the brokenhearted. I'm feeling very alone and confused, so I claim that promise."

The Bible is filled with great expectations of what God in His awesome power will continue to accomplish on this earth. And He intends to do it in partnership with you and me. No matter what we are going through, we can say as the Psalmist did (62:5-6): "Find rest, O my soul, in God alone; my hope comes from Him. He alone is my rock and my salvation...".

SOUL THERAPY

My Hope, when my expectations are dashed,
When my best efforts fail,
When my plans crumble,
When my health gives way,
When I wrestle with doubt,
Increase my faith.
Build in me what can never be destroyed—
The works of Your Holy Spirit.
Protect me from the demon of discouragement,
And keep a joyous anticipation alive in me
Until my hope becomes reality in heaven with You.

WORK OUT

If you can ride a bicycle and have one, go on a prayerful, exploratory ride, expecting to see something unique in God's creation. As you pray, think of ways God has met your expectations in life and thank Him for the fact that He's always at work, even in unexpected circumstances. (If you can't bicycle, perhaps you can visualize a ride from your childhood or a walk in the woods.)

JOURNAL

Recount some joys and some letdowns in your life. Do you have an overwhelming disappointment that you are dealing with? Ask God to show you how to build new expectations that are in line with His.

Battleground Of The Mind

BODY BASIC
*Both thinking (cognition)
and feeling (emotion) are
involved in the forming of attitude.
Attitude affects behavior, but can
be changed through experience or
persuasion.*

SPIRITUAL
SPECIFIC
*"...Be transformed by
the renewing of your mind."*
(ROMANS 12:2)

*T*he mind is a battlefield where good and evil, victory and defeat, hope and hopelessness wage war. Our thoughts and feelings, which form our attitude, often may seem as impossible to change as our circumstances. The key to victory—to having a transformed, renewed mind—is setting our thoughts on our always victorious God. "You will keep in perfect peace him whose mind is steadfast, because he trusts in You," says Isaiah (26:3). God is the ultimate attitude-adjuster.

One of my physical therapists, who encourages a good attitude in each client, showed me a video about a man named Nick, an inspirational speaker, who was born with no limbs. Nick had only a small foot with two toes protruding from his left thigh. After seeing Nick's amazing video, I read his testimony and called his non-profit organization, which gave me permission to share his story.

At age eight, bullied at school and beat-down by frustration, Nick felt hopeless, broken and alone, with no point to his life. "I felt cold, bitter. I contemplated suicide," he said.

He and his devoutly Christian parents prayed for arms and legs for him, but God's answer was no. Instead, over time and through prayer, "God gave me something better," Nick said. "He changed my attitude and strengthened my heart. He began showing me that the single most effective factor in overcoming my struggles was my attitude." In the middle of circumstances that still didn't make sense, "God gave me grace, comfort, peace, purpose and joy. I began being grateful I was alive."

God also revealed His purpose for Nick—a purpose He had perfectly equipped him for—"demonstrating to others that His strength is made perfect in my weakness."

Fueled with God's fire, Nick learned to write and use a computer with his two toes. He graduated from high school and college, and invented ways to be self-sufficient. He even swims and can accurately putt golf balls with a club between his neck and shoulder. He began a non-profit organization called "Life Without Limbs," and he travels the world as an inspirational speaker. His message is *attitude* is *altitude*.

"When people see me, they think, 'There's something more to life than meets the eye if a guy without arms and legs is living a fuller life than I am.' And that opens the way for me to tell them about God's grace and goodness. God took my life, which others might regard as having no significance, and has filled it with the joy of moving hearts and lives toward Him."

Even though frustration will always be a part of his daily life, and he still wishes for arms and legs, Nick said, "I'm happy. Content. Struggles are opportunities to grow and reach out, to persist rather than get paralyzed. I tell audiences that they are precious to God, and when we're in the fire, there is always a purpose. There is always hope. Nothing is impossible with God."

SOUL THERAPY

Loving Creator,
Life is so full of hardship, heartache,
And unfair things that will never make sense to me!
Only You can see Your divine design
And Your unfailingly good purposes.
Since the only thing I can control
Is my attitude,
Please give me one that gladdens You.
Bless me with perseverance, purpose,
Your strength,
And tireless trust in Your goodness.

WORK OUT

Attitude is important in all areas of life, including exercise—because if we don't want to exert ourselves, we won't. When we don't feel like exercising, one way to change how we feel is to make the activity fun. You can window shop as you mall walk, or call a friend and talk together as you enjoy an outdoor stroll. Any movement is beneficial.

JOURNAL

Buoy your attitude by reading Romans 8:35-39 and put your name in place of the "we" and "us." (For instance, "in all these things Marjorie is more than a conqueror, through Him who loved her...")

Describe how you can make some obstacle in your life into an opportunity.

Resting

BODY BASIC
Building muscle requires rest as well as exercise. When you're gaining muscle by lifting weights, you are actually developing small micro-tears in the muscle. During rest, proteins mend the muscles' tears, and that repair work creates more muscle.

SPIRITUAL SPECIFIC
"There remains then a Sabbath-rest for the people of God; for anyone who enters God's rest also rests from his own work, just as God did from His. Let us, therefore, make every effort to enter that rest..."
(HEBREWS 4:10-11)

Whether or not you are building muscle, rest is so important that God commanded a day of it each week (Exodus 20:8). Our bodies require time out, especially if we're ill or taking care of someone who is. Illness usually forces a rest. But steady caregivers of loved ones in need often deny themselves needed respite. And that can cause stress-related health problems in the caregiver. Although sometimes it's hard to give ourselves permission to take a break, God says a time to cease laboring is essential. And He commands us to keep that respite holy, or whole.

A whole rest always includes God—because He is where real refreshment and strength are found.

Jesus says, "Come to me all you who are weary and heavy-laden, and I will give you rest." *Intentionally* creating refreshing "alone moments," taking time to lie down, breathe deeply, and pray helps a person enter both physical and spiritual rest. The writer of Psalm 116:7 took a breather by recalling God's compassionate help in the past, saying, "Be at rest once more, O my soul, for the Lord has been good to you."

God intended the Promised Land as a place of repose for the Israelites. Yet when He presented it to them, they refused to go in, for fear of giants. Even after they'd witnessed numerous miracles from God, they wouldn't listen to or trust Him when He told them He'd lead them to victory. So God declared in His anger, "They shall never enter my rest." (Psalm 95:11), and they wandered in the wearying wilderness for forty years. An entire unbelieving generation died there.

When we're thrust into a situation where the demands of caregiving feel like overwhelming giants, it's hard to take advantage of God's rest. Attending to another person while taking care of ourselves is tricky, but our all-wise God can show us how.

I admire a caregiving friend of mine, Donna, who willingly opened her home to her handicapped brother and their aging mother, who developed cancer. A hard worker, Donna still found that the caretaking quickly became overwhelming. "I'm always going full throttle," she admits. "I can be up eighteen hours and still not find a place to stop. Sometimes my husband just grabs my shirttail and says, 'Whoa!'"

"Even when I try to sleep, my mind often keeps spinning," she continues. "One morning in desperation, I got up early and opened my Bible, seeking the comfort I nearly always find in the word of God. That morning, I turned to Psalm 42:5, and it was as if it rose up off the page to command my attention. It said, 'Why are you downcast, O my soul? Why so disturbed within me? Put your hope in God, for I will yet praise Him, my Savior and my God.' It was like the Lord was assuring me that I don't need to be fretful, trying to do so much—He's the One in control, not me. He provides Himself to lean on and others to call on. Just that assurance from Him made my burden feel lighter."

She now "forces" herself to get some physical rest by regularly allowing family and other helpers to take over. And sometimes God sends her another kind of boost. "One day a friend asked how Mom was, and when I tried to say, 'She has cancer,' all that would come out was a trembling lip! She grabbed me and hugged me and just held me, praying in my ear for God to strengthen me. And it was such a comfort! I came away stronger."

SOUL THERAPY

Generous Provider,
Sometimes I feel as if everything depends on me.
But it doesn't.
You have offered Your divine assistance
And supplied other helpers, too.
Your word instructs me more than 600 times to rest,
So, please show me how.
Whether I'm struggling with my own challenges
Or providing care for someone else,
Help me to take time to rest in You.

WORK OUT
Let your workout be a time out today. Use it to rest and pray.

JOURNAL
Copy down Jesus' promise about giving us rest in Matthew 11:28 and claim it. Then watch expectantly for how He will do it.

Surprise?

BODY BASIC
The body's own healing processes can often be aided by medication, and many scientific investigations are carried out to discover medical remedies and life-saving techniques. But not all research produces the desired results; sometimes it leads to surprise findings, unrelated to the study. Nevertheless, researchers put the unexpected to good use. For instance, some chemotherapy drugs and anti-depressants, the X-ray, and the PAP smear were all discovered by chance. So was a life-saving medication stumbled upon by Sir Alexander Fleming. When cultivating bacteria in a glass dish in his lab, Fleming found mold growing on the dish that appeared to kill the bacteria. He named it Penicillin.

SPIRITUAL SPECIFIC
"Dear friends, do not be surprised at the painful trial you are suffering, as though something strange were happening to you." (1 PETER 4: 12)

*T**he Bible is full of surprises, some good,* some bad, and many both positive and negative. For instance, the ordinary young shepherd David was astounded when he was brought in from the pasture one day and anointed by the prophet Samuel to be the next King of Israel. That surprise honor, however, also required years of waiting, deprivation and loneliness.

Suddenly visible angels astonished many of God's servants with happy messages from heaven. But some tidings, particularly Gabriel's good news to the Virgin Mary, also carried a sword-to-the-soul type of grief for the future. And Jesus' unexpected (but prophesied) resurrection—although an eternal kind of Good News—resulted in terrible persecution and even death for the disciples sharing it with the world.

As they followed Jesus, the disciples learned an important life lesson: a furious squall can blow in from nowhere, and waves can nearly swamp the boat, even when Jesus is in it. "Lord, don't you care if we drown?" they cried, waking Jesus from sleep in the boat's stern. Jesus rebuked the storm, and it instantly subsided. (Matthew 4:35-41)

Like the disciples, we, too, face fearsome tempests in our life, and sometimes we ask the Lord, "Don't you care?" He says He does. Nevertheless, He allows plenty of life-storms to suddenly assail us, and He rarely makes them instantly subside. Peter guaranteed we'd have trials, and said we shouldn't be surprised at them. He simply advises that "those who suffer according to God's will should commit themselves to their faithful Creator and continue to do good." (1 Peter 4: 19)

Lynn, a twenty-seven-year-old Texas cowboy who is now a neighbor of ours, had always made helping others a part of his life. He often competed in ranch rodeos to benefit a local rehabilitation center, which provides free help to patients who can't afford treatment. He never thought he might need that same facility one day.

As Lynn rode alone one morning checking ranch windmills, his galloping horse stumbled and fell, rolling over on Lynn before he could react. Lynn's windpipe was damaged. He lay barely breathing in the hot sun for seven hours before someone found him. He was not expected to live.

His mother, grandmother and others prayed over him as he lay in a coma for 28 days, then remained in the hospital for more than a year, with partial paralysis on his left side and an uncontrollable right side. Brain surgery stopped the tremors in his right side, but his speech was permanently affected. His young wife left him and took their two girls with her. His life had fallen apart.

"But God had saved my life," he told me. "And I knew He was with me, helping me. I didn't just believe it, I *knew* it. The accident made my faith much deeper and stronger. It's been 17 years since the accident, and even though I still can't do what I used to, I'm getting better every day. And God's still helping."

Lynn recounts many of God's kind surprises along the way. The insurance company paid an unheard-of amount, not only for a long rehabilitation, but also a second, third and fourth round of therapy. "And God worked good even through my divorce," Lynn says now, "Because it forced me to live alone—which doctors said I could never do—and I got stronger."

Lynn's fifteen-year-long prayer was that "God would send me a wife who would never leave me." And at the grocery store one day, God surprised him with an old friend from high school, who became his bride a few months later. He still laughs about his marriage proposal to Regina. "I was pretty awkward getting down on one knee to propose. Regina thought I had fallen and kept trying to pull me up!"

With a daily dependence on God, Lynn continues to make progress, and he's even riding his horse again. "God has amazed me many times," he says. "But the best gift He's given me is Regina."

SOUL THERAPY

Lord of life,
I'm grateful that no matter what I do
Or what happens to me,
You are never taken by surprise.
You are never out of control.
And You are always present with me,
Through every painful ordeal,
Caring, providing, and bestowing small and large gifts of grace.

WORK OUT

Surprise someone today with an unexpected kindness—and remember, you are acting as God's hands and feet when you do.

JOURNAL

Has God ever surprised you? How did you feel about it?

Wrapped Up

BODY BASIC
Our entire body is under wraps. The skull, the brain's protective case, is made of twenty-nine bones, many of which fuse together as we grow older. It is one-fourth of an inch thick at the top, and even thicker at the base. Our all-over cover, the skin, shields us from the invasion of deadly bacteria along with serving many other functions.

SPIRITUAL SPECIFIC
"Meanwhile we groan, longing to be clothed with our heavenly dwelling...For while we are in this tent [body], we groan and are burdened..."

(2 CORINTHIANS 5:2-4)

God created mankind with sturdy body-wrappings that provided plenty of protection in His perfect garden. However, after Adam and Eve sinned by disobeying God, He banished them from the garden. Then, He outfitted them with something more—garments of animal skin to help shield them in the harsh and thorny world they would enter. Their own skin was no longer enough, and their self-made fig leaf covering was worthless.

Paul says our "earthly tent" is easily destroyed. In it, "we groan and are burdened." However, God has provided a permanent "garment" to shield us from an eternal groaning: Christ. He clothes believers "with garments of salvation" and "a robe of righteousness...". (Isaiah 62:10a) Those clothes, freely provided by our Great Designer, are ours forever.

One of the most dynamic, energetic people I know, Dana, had always been served well by her "earthly tent," until a bout with what she thought was food poisoning sent her on a downward health spiral. A speaker, mom and educator who always went "100 miles per hour," Dana thought she had recovered from the worst of the food poisoning. But, as time went on, she became exhausted and developed memory problems. Her hair fell out and her skin thinned, bruising and tearing easily. For five years she went to various doctors searching for a diagnosis. She underwent ten stomach biopsies and a wrong cancer diagnosis, took medicines that permanently damaged her system, and was told by a puzzled physician that maybe she was depressed and needed counseling.

"I knew that wasn't my problem, so I kept praying," she told me. "I knew in the midst of my illness that I needed to focus on eternity and the things that I needed to value. But it was a battle. My body wasn't working right, and it was easier to get focused on myself, to get consumed by the management of my health. But I didn't want that!

"It's always a steep learning curve when God teaches me something," she continued. "He kept reminding me that the body is only temporary and that all that I am comes from Him. I learned that the hard way. I was forced to rely on His strength as I dragged through each day. Finally, He led me to a wonderful endocrinologist who saved my life by discovering I had picked up a bacteria, probably in a restaurant, that had destroyed my ability to digest food."

With the specialist's help, Dana found foods she can eat and medicine that helps move the food through her system. But the medicine's side effect is that when she takes it, she loses her voice. "I can't make a sound, not even a whisper," she said. "And I speak for a living! But I have to take the medicine when I'm under the stress of traveling to speaking engagements. So, since God had been teaching me that He was my strength, I specifically asked Him to help me speak even after taking the medication. It's a miracle—I can wake up without a voice, step up to the microphone and be able to teach and talk all day. Then my voice will disappear until the next day."

Dana discovered that even though she can't count on her "earthly tent," she can count on God. "Especially when going through trials," she said, "We must never lose sight of the fact that God is trustworthy, even when it's hard to figure Him out."

SOUL THERAPY
"Lord, help me see
That the hard mercies of adversity
Are not stones thrown to hurt me,
But stones that serve to get my attention—
To tap on the window of my comfortable estate
And remind me that this is not my home.
Grant me the grace to take those hard mercies,
No matter how sharp or how heavy,
And use them to pave a road to You."
(from "*Moments With the Savior*" by Ken Gire)

WORK OUT
Take care of your covering today by drinking plenty of water, eating a healthy diet, and getting out into the fresh air to do your favorite form of exercise.

JOURNAL
In what way can you improve your care of your earthly tent? What is one change you'd like to make? Write it down and date it, asking God to help you make the improvement.

When God Says No

BODY BASIC
Psychologists have found that the results of disappointment vary: some people may rebound quickly; others may bog down in frustration, blame or depression. Positive emotions originate mostly in the left hemisphere of the brain, and the right side of the brain is responsible mostly for negative ones, such as anxiety and depression.

SPIRITUAL SPECIFIC
"...they were at their wits' end. Then they cried out to the Lord in their trouble, and He brought them out of their distress." (PSALM 107:27,28)

Has adversity delayed or derailed a plan you thought you were making with God's approval? Has He said "no" to something you thought He'd prompted you to do?

King David had his heart set on building a temple for God's worship, and he amassed materials for it and appointed thousands for leadership in it. Then God told David He'd chosen Solomon for the job instead. David, a warrior king, had shed too much blood to be the temple builder.

Yet David had been a fighting man through God's own instruction! It would have been natural for him to feel punished by God's "no." Instead, he announced that Solomon had the job, and then gratefully recounted all the things God had said "yes" to in his own life.

My college friend Jack, like David, believed he was following God's lead when he began making plans, and he was unprepared for God to change them. After graduating from seminary, he and his wife became missionaries in Costa Rica. Three months after they arrived, Jack's wife, who was pregnant, began experiencing terrible pain from what turned out to be rheumatoid arthritis. She had to return to the States for medical help. Jack joined her there the next month and realized that he needed to come home permanently to help her. The mission board agreed.

"So, I flew back in a depressed state to Costa Rica to arrange things," he relates. "I didn't want to admit my 'great plans for God' and my dream and adventure were over. My depression made it hard to function. I slept a lot. I took much longer than I should have to get permits and arrange for the shipping of our things back to the States.

"I searched for comfort in scripture, and Isaiah 46:9,11 really spoke to me. It said, "I am God, and there is no other; I am God and there is none like Me. What I have said, that will I bring about; what I have planned, that will I do." I saw that somehow God's hand was on our lives, directing us according to His purpose, and He would carry it out no matter what. So I was finally able to force myself to finish all the preparations, then headed back home in our Suburban."

Along the way, however, Jack found that a late season hurricane in Southern Mexico had washed out the highway leading home. "I was told it could be a month or more before the only road I knew about would be repaired. I became angry with God. I'd already postponed too long—why did He allow further delay? I felt sorry for my wife as well as for myself. She needed me and couldn't wait another month!

"About that time a man came up to me and asked if I was a missionary, probably guessing I was, since no other Americans were in the village. I wanted to answer 'no,' but said that I was. Then he told me that he and his family had fled for their lives from a revolution in El Salvador. And he shocked me by asking, 'Would you tell me and my family about Jesus?'

"I almost fell over. God opened my eyes to see that He really could 'accomplish His purpose' no matter where I was." The family believed. And because of the stranger's native Spanish, he was able to communicate with villagers and discover what Jack couldn't—a way out of Mexico, across some rough terrain. By the time Jack arrived home, his faith was at a new level. And his wife later gave birth to a healthy son.

Jack no longer gets depressed when his ministry plans run into a roadblock; he just prayerfully waits for God's "go" and then follows His lead.

SOUL THERAPY

Lord Jesus, You know better than anyone
The grief and agony that can arise
When the Father says "no."
But You willingly submitted,
Trusted His plan,
And sacrificed Yourself.
I'm going to need lots of Your help, Lord,
When sacrifice and suffering are required of me.
Please walk with me along the way, reminding me
That my earthly, obstacle-ridden path of faith
Leads eventually to the victorious "yes" of heaven.

WORK OUT

Life's ups and downs can strengthen us spiritually, and this up-and-down exercise builds strength in your calves. Stand with feet shoulder width apart and rise up onto your toes, balancing for five seconds, then return your heels to the floor. You can hold onto something for balance, or make it more difficult by leaving your hands free. Rise up and down fifteen to thirty times.

JOURNAL

Write about some of the highs and lows, "yesses" and "nos" that God has brought into your life and how you felt about them at the time. Looking back, has your perspective changed?

Silver Tongued?

BODY BASIC
The two-ounce tongue has a complex array of nerves and muscles that help us speak and swallow. Babies are born with a swallowing reflex, but speaking requires the tongue to flex into many shapes, which is why a baby may take years to be able to form sentences.

SPIRITUAL SPECIFIC
"The tongue has the power of life and death."
(PROVERBS 8:21)

The tongue is described in scripture in more negative than positive ways. It can be lying, malicious, back-biting, sly, deceitful and false. It is portrayed as an arrow or sharp sword which can wound. An untamed and unleashed tongue can spell disaster. As James 3:5 says, "Likewise, the tongue is a small part of the body, but it makes great boasts. Consider what a great forest is set on fire by a small spark. The tongue also is a fire, a world of evil among the parts of the body. It corrupts the whole person, sets the whole course of his life on fire, and is itself set on fire by hell."

On the other hand, "The tongue of the righteous is choice silver...".

(Proverbs 10:20)

Under God's control, the tongue can be filled with songs of joy, prayers of praise, and the word of God. "My tongue will speak of Your righteousness and of Your praises all day long." (Psalm 35:28)

Just as the tongue can be used for good or evil, so can common language. In the story of the Tower of Babel in Genesis 11, it says, "The whole world had one language and a common speech," but it was used for wrong purposes. Men united in a godless effort to build a tower for their own glory that would reach to the heavens "so that we may make a name for ourselves...". And because of that, God confused their language so they would not understand each other. They were scattered, and their plans were abandoned.

However, God *wanted* people to understand each other at another time—during Pentecost, when God-fearing Jews from every nation were gathered in Jerusalem to celebrate the annual feast. At that time, God sent His Holy Spirit, described as "tongues of fire," to rest on the twelve apostles (Matthias took Judas' place). And "as the Spirit enabled them," the apostles began telling the good news of Jesus in languages they had never learned. They amazed their audience, as "each one heard them [disciples] speaking in his own language." And about 3,000 believed and were baptized.

Even when we're speaking in our own native tongue, the Spirit's guidance is important. Without Him, well-meaning comfort and counsel to others can be misguided and hurtful. For example, Job's three friends, who came to console him in his misery, made good company only when they sat in silence and mourned with him. As soon as they began lecturing him in their own "wisdom," they not only hurt Job, but angered God.

Like Job's buddies, I learned the hard way how damaging the tongue can be, even when my motives were good. I had neglected to pray before trying to cheer up a hospitalized friend, and I made what I thought was a humorous comment during our conversation. Instead, I offended her without knowing it. When she recovered, she avoided me. Months later, I found out why. I was horrified at my own insensitivity and asked her forgiveness. She gave it. Now, before I visit anyone in need, I ask God to guard my tongue so that I say the right things or say nothing at all.

SOUL THERAPY

Merciful God, my tongue can be my worst enemy!
Please control it for me.
Help me to use it and my life language
The way You intended—
To build up Your people
And spread Your Good News.

WORK OUT

This tongue exercise should only be performed if you have a problem-free neck: Sitting straight and tall, hands relaxed in your lap, take a deep breath, then slowly exhale and stretch your chin gently toward the ceiling while pressing your tongue on the roof of your mouth. Then inhale and reverse the stretch by pulling your chin down into your chest while pushing the tongue down behind the bottom teeth.

JOURNAL

In what ways can you use your tongue to bring encouragement today? Write down some positive things you can say to a family member, fellow worker, or friend. Then tell them.

Visible And Invisible

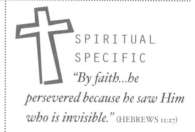

BODY BASIC
Wounds are visible; pain isn't. The brain is observable; thoughts aren't. The heart can be examined; love can't.

SPIRITUAL SPECIFIC
"By faith...he persevered because he saw Him who is invisible." (HEBREWS 11:27)

*T**he visible and invisible mingle in us as physical** and spiritual be-ings. Even the universe "was formed at God's command, so that what is seen was not made out of what was visible." (Hebrews 11:3) Jesus was "the image of the invisible God." And "by Him all things were created: things in heaven and on earth, visible and invisible..." (Colossians 1:15-16) Before He ascended into heaven, Jesus instructed His followers, filled with His unseen Holy Spirit, to be His well-defined representatives on earth.

In the book of Esther, God is never mentioned, yet His providence is apparent. Esther was a Jewish orphan exiled with her people and reared by her cousin Mordecai in Persia. She became that country's queen through an amazing, God-orchestrated series of events. With great risk to her own life, Queen Esther saved her race, the Jews, from extermination by the Persian king and his evil servant Haman, who plotted the Jews' destruction. Esther realized she had been raised up for "such a time as this."

We don't always feel like Esther, though. When God is not apparent in a situation, when it seems as if we're on our own, it's easy to feel afraid, angry, and forsaken. Job did. He said, "Somehow, though He moves right in front of me, I don't see Him; quietly but surely He's active, and I miss it." (Job 9 MSG) It is often only in hindsight that we are able to recognize God's partnership in a difficult time.

My church friend Brenda was in God's hands when she suffered a life-threatening and rare occurrence: blood vessels burst in her brain stem. No one could see with the naked eye what destruction occurred in her brain, but the after-effects were clear. She was paralyzed on her dominant right side. Unable to swallow, the fifty-year-old said, "I was mad at God and said, "Why me?' I got an immediate response: "Why *not* you?"

Brenda took that answer almost like a dare from God to keep going and not give up. "I said, 'Well, okay. If I have to go on, I will!' And He gave me an inner strength. Family, friends and God were always there, but I still got depressed a lot that first year. It was so hard! I had to learn to swallow again and re-learn to do all those little things we take for granted. Sometimes I'd just sit in the wheelchair and cry. But you can only do so much of that. I finally thought, 'I can't do this forever.' I felt God encouraging me to go on."

Irreversible setbacks, such as having her right eye sewn shut because of facial paralysis, still make her "mad, sad and disappointed. But I get over it and go on." And she's reached many goals, including snorkeling, scuba diving (if her husband is next to her), and taking long neighborhood walks with a friend.

Three years after the event, Brenda is still in therapy, regularly working out on exercise equipment. "I don't know my purpose yet," she says. "Maybe it is just to be an example to encourage others."

That part of Brenda's mission is very visible to all who know her. As I go into rehab for my exercise therapy, I've watched her soldier on, working strenuously and always improving. I'm inspired not just by her cheerful determination, but by her wonderful, lopsided smile with which she warmly greets everyone. God may be invisible, but His people and their example of faithful perseverance certainly get noticed.

SOUL THERAPY

Father, I need supernatural vision
To look beyond the grim realities of life
And recognize that You are at work in Your unseen way.
Though You don't lead me visibly
The way You did the Israelites with fire and cloud,
Or the Wise Men with a bright star,
You have given me Your visible word
To be a "light for my path."
Please light my way.
Help me to be a visible example of Your invisible strength.

WORK OUT
Smiling is good for facial muscles. To help a crooked smile, place your palms flat on each side of your face (cheeks) and as you smile, move your hands up to pull both sides into a full, exaggerated smile and hold for five seconds. Repeat ten times.

JOURNAL
After reading Hebrews 11: 1-16, make your thoughts about it visible by putting them down on paper.

Tooth Truth

BODY BASIC
*A baby's teeth, called milk
teeth, begin falling out at
about age six to make room for the
thirty-two permanent teeth he or she
will have as an adult. A tooth's hard
enamel covering helps it to last a long
time—archeologists have uncovered
human teeth that are thousands of
years old.*

SPIRITUAL
SPECIFIC
*Like a bad tooth...
is reliance on the unfaithful in
times of trouble."* (PROVERBS 25:19)

Teeth, which begin our all-important process of digestion, serve us well if they're healthy, but can cause plenty of pain if they're decayed or injured.

The earliest mention of a tooth in the Bible is in one of God's laws, "an eye for an eye, a tooth for a tooth," which was intended to limit an offender's punishment to fit the crime. (It was later changed by Jesus when He gave the people a new covenant.) If a master knocked out a slave's tooth, the slave was to be set free "for his tooth's sake." (Exodus 21:27) A common expression today may have had its roots in Job's lament: "I have escaped with only the skin of my teeth." In Psalm 58, David appeals to God to defeat men who corrupted justice and to "break the teeth in their mouths."

Gnashing of teeth in the Bible portrayed agony or fury and was part of the depiction of weeping in outer darkness, away from God. In his vision in Revelation, John describes locusts, sent out to torture those who refused God, as having teeth "like lion's teeth."

We put "teeth" into our faith when we live lives obedient to God. And that was my dentist friend Ralph's goal as he traveled on medical mission trips each summer, giving dental care and the Good News to patients around the world.

On one mission to Ecuador, however, problems plagued Ralph's team from the outset. Supplies were stolen, flights delayed, trunks of equipment didn't arrive. The missionaries felt dismayed and unsettled. They were all encouraged, however, when God answered prayers and solved each problem, one by one. But Ralph wondered why he still couldn't shake a strange feeling of restlessness. It dogged him. What was it?

After they arrived at their destination, while Ralph was working at a clinic with his team, a prison warden asked if they would come to his prison. "We felt pretty apprehensive," Ralph admitted, "and I wondered if that was what my odd feelings had been about. But, God had proven that His wall of protection was around us. So we went." The dental team provided medical services and shared the gospel with many who had never heard it.

That experience helped make it "the most successful mission trip I'd ever been on," Ralph said. "But it didn't remove the peculiar feeling. It still nagged at me—like I was supposed to do something else. It wouldn't let up. That last night we were there, when I still couldn't sleep at three a.m., I finally said, 'What is it, God?' and He let me know. He directed me to leave all my supplies and much of my equipment there! Most of it I used in my own practice, and giving it away would make my office temporarily run short. But God had already proved His provision through the many set-backs on this trip. So, the next day, I told the local dentist, who was also the prison dentist and a house church leader, what I was going to do.

"He began to cry," Ralph continued. "He told me he had been praying that God would help him provide services for the inmates, but he'd been feeling discouraged. Now, with our coming to help and sharing supplies, he felt his faith renewed and encouraged. I went home with my restlessness finally calmed, and my faith stronger than ever."

SOUL THERAPY

Thank You, Lord,
That You personally equip me
For whatever You call me to do.
When I feel disheartened, restless or unhappy,
Please give me insight and guidance as I pray.
Help me to "sink my teeth" into the instructions in Your word,
So that I can be an instrument
Of Your grace in others' lives.

WORK OUT

Flossing as well as brushing is important for hygiene and the health of your teeth and gums. As you brush and floss, think of ways you can put "teeth" into your faith.

JOURNAL

Jot down some ideas that you thought of, then choose one and do it.

Life Line

BODY BASIC
Blood is actually connective tissue and is unique, because it is the only connective tissue that is fluid. With its approximately 60,000 miles of blood vessels, the bloodstream not only transports the essentials of life to the body's cells, but also hauls away waste products. Since the seventeenth century, scientists have been trying to find a blood substitute, and have experimented with everything from vegetable oil to milk to beer. Now, modern researchers are close to perfecting an oxygen-carrying "artificial" blood for treating critical patients. But nothing works as well as the real thing.

SPIRITUAL SPECIFIC
"The life of the creature is in the blood." (LEVITICUS 17:11)

If Jesus fell down as a child, His scraped knees would bleed like any other child's. Fully God, He was also fully human, except that He was sinless. When His perfect life ended on the cross, His blood paid the death penalty for mankind's sin. Jesus' sacrifice had been foreshadowed all through scripture. Only the blood of a perfect, unblemished animal had ever done the job of temporarily making atonement for sin. Animal sacrifices could never *remove* sin, however, so for hundreds of years priests repeatedly made ritual offerings on behalf of the Jewish people.

Jesus' sacrifice, which *did* remove sin permanently, was also foreshadowed in the story of the Exodus. The blood of a sacrificed, unblemished lamb smeared on their doorframes protected Jewish homes from the angel of death, whom God sent in judgment to destroy the Egyptians' first-born males. God told His people, "When I see the blood, I will pass over you. No destructive plague will touch you when I strike Egypt." (Exodus 12:13) Unprotected by the blood, every Egyptian household lost its first-born.

Jews have commemorated the Lord's Passover ever since. And it was during a Passover celebration centuries later that the blood of God's Lamb, Jesus, was shed on the cross. His was the final sacrifice: full, perfect and sufficient. I eagerly accepted Christ's gift years ago and received new spiritual life. But I never thought I might require another person's blood to save my physical life, even if I needed surgery.

Just before I was wheeled into the operating room for elective female surgery, I was encouraged once more by a nurse to sign papers agreeing to a transfusion if necessary. (I had declined to do it.) At my family's insistence, I agreed at the last minute, even though I felt sure I'd have a problem-free surgery with no need for a transfusion. After all, I was being lifted up in prayer by many, and I was in good health. Why would I need blood? As it turned out, a tiny, unnoticed puncture of a blood vessel during the surgery caused me to almost bleed to death.

I received five units of life-saving blood. Although I was glad to be alive, I puzzled over why God had allowed the blunder, especially after all that prayer. I lay in the hospital bed in the middle of the night, feeling sorry for myself, unable to sleep or take pain medications because narcotics made me sick. I couldn't lie still for long, because everything hurt. So, all night I prayed and walked the halls, pulling my IV stand along with me, then collapsed back into bed and read my Bible, and after a while began the cycle again. Lonely and confused, I asked God to encourage me somehow.

As dawn finally broke, that prayer was answered when I turned to Psalm 86. It was as if the psalmist were describing me and speaking for me! His words comforted and reassured me. Then the final verse jolted me: "For great is Your love toward me; You have delivered me from the depths of the grave."

He had—not once, but twice! Once through Jesus' blood, and once through transfusions. My discomfort was nothing compared to those gifts. I was suddenly transfused with gratitude, and I wept with thankfulness. My spirits lifted.

Shortly after that, a new nurse came into my room bringing physical help, too—a non-narcotic drug which eased my pain. Ever since then, I carry a deeper appreciation for every gift of God.

SOUL THERAPY

Creator and Sustainer of life,
Thank You that Your blood
Swept away the waste of my sins,
And delivered the essentials of mercy and forgiveness
To my soul.
Thank You not only for the gift of earthly life,
But also for the greater blessing of life to come with You.

WORK OUT
Circulation of the blood is enhanced by movement. If you can, jog in place for three minutes.

JOURNAL
Meditate on what Christ's sacrifice means to you and write about it.

Name It!

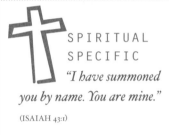

BODY BASIC
*There are more than 650
named skeletal muscles in
the body, and every other part of the
body has a name, too. Even diseases
are named, often for the doctors who
discover them.*

SPIRITUAL
SPECIFIC
*"I have summoned
you by name. You are mine."*
(ISAIAH 43:1)

*M*an's first act of dominion over the creatures* around him was
naming them. And, Adam, which means Man, gave his wife the
name Eve, "because she would become the mother of all the living." Every
descendant of theirs had a name, too, and according to Scripture, each
name had significance

In the Bible, God sometimes changed a person's given name to reflect a
life-change. When Abram was ninety-nine years old, God appeared to him
and confirmed a covenant with him. He told Abram, "You will be the father
of many nations. No longer will you be called Abram; your name will be
Abraham, for I have made you a father of many nations..." Abraham's barren
wife Sarai, which meant princess, also was given a new name at age ninety.

God said, "As for Sarai, your wife, you are no longer to call her Sarai; her name will be Sarah. I will bless her and will surely give you a son by her. I will bless her so that she will become the mother of nations." (Genesis 17:15-16)

New Testament name-changes included Jesus altering Simon's name, which meant something like "pebble," to Peter, or "rock." Levi, the dishonest tax collector who repented and accepted Christ's invitation to be one of the twelve disciples, was given a new label by Jesus, too: Matthew, "gift of God." A murderous persecutor of Christians, Saul, converted to Christianity and was renamed Paul. The new names demonstrated that God had no doubt what each of those people could and would become. And He still knows it about each of His children.

God also bestowed some names before birth. Before John the Baptist was conceived, the angel Gabriel told his father, the aging priest Zechariah, "You are to give him the name John." And Gabriel told Mary that her divinely conceived child's name "will be Jesus."

God gave the Israelites His label for Himself: "I AM." Yet God's Son, Jesus, called Him "Abba," Daddy, and gave us the right to call Him that, too. God's name is above all names. He knows the end from the beginning. He *is* the end and the beginning, the Omega and the Alpha, Who creates all life and makes no mistakes.

When he was born, my friend Stewart was named by his unwed birth mother. Three days later, his adoptive parents renamed him. Although he was content in his loving home growing up, Stewart felt troubled sometimes, wondering why his birth mother had given him up. When he was middle-aged, he learned his birth mother's identity and met her. She told him that she had always prayed for him by the name she'd given him at birth. She had no doubt that her son's Creator knew who he was. And Stewart replied that even when disquieted as a youngster, he'd felt comforted by a sense "that someone out there was praying for me."

Eventually in their poignant meeting, mother and son discovered that their common faith had sustained each of them. Neither worried that Stewart's earthly name-change might have confused God. They both knew that their all-wise Father, Who knows the number of hairs on each of our heads, was intimately familiar with each of them. And in answer to the fervent longtime prayers of Stewart's mother, He had brought them back together again.

SOUL THERAPY

Personal Lord, it excites me that You know my name,
And it's written in Your Book of Life.
Please show me not only who I am
In Your sight,
But who I can be with Your help.
And with all that you've given me,
Enable me to glorify Your name,
Which is above every other name.

WORK OUT
*"The Windmill" is this exercise's
name. Begin by standing with your
feet wide apart, arms straight out
like a "T." Reach with your right
hand to touch your left foot (or
knee), then come up and without
stopping, reach the left hand to
the right foot (or knee). Continue
alternating smoothly ten times.*

JOURNAL
*How does it make you feel to know
that God has summoned you by
name? Record your thoughts.*

Fighting
The Invasion

BODY BASIC

We possess five kinds of white blood cells, and each kind has a specific role in defending the body. These cells "know" where to go in the body, because they are attracted by certain chemicals that are released by infected or damaged tissue. In protecting the body against invading organisms, white blood cells are not confined to the blood stream. They can push through capillary walls to get to an infected or damaged spot, and then they begin their healing work.

SPIRITUAL SPECIFIC

"When Jesus saw her, He called her forward and said to her, 'Woman, you are set free from your infirmity.' Then He put His hands on her, and immediately she straightened up and praised God." (LUKE 13:12, 13)

*G*od created the human body with its own complicated processes for healing over time. But Jesus healed people easily and instantly. He did it through His forgiveness and divine power. Both forgiving sins and healing infirmities were equally effortless for Jesus. Sometimes He made someone well by saying, "Son, your sins are forgiven." (Mark 2:5) Sometimes He just commanded the healing to occur. Either way, He showed that He was God. And He left His followers with the commandment to pass on His healing gift of forgiveness.

Forgiving a wrongful act is often tough and may seem unfair. But God offers to help drive out the invaders of resentment (which actually means "to feel again") and bitterness so they won't infect our lives and hurt our relationship with God and others.

When God commands us to do a difficult task, He also provides a means of doing it. He shows us that in scripture. He ordered the hesitant, stuttering Moses to lead his people out of Egypt, and gave him Aaron's help as well as His own divine assistance. God commanded His people to build a traveling tabernacle for their wilderness worship, and He provided the materials by inspiring the Egyptians to give their own riches to the fleeing Israelites. God mandated that a blood sacrifice be made in order for His people to be forgiven. Then, in an unfathomable display of His amazing grace and love, He gave His own Son to be that sacrifice.

And because of His own sacrifice for *our* forgiveness, He expects us to pass it on.

And He assures us He will supply His power to do it, even when we feel consumed with anger and hurt. He also promises to take care of evildoers Himself. "It is mine to avenge; I will repay," He says in Deuteronomy 32:35.

Joseph, after his God-ordained rise to power, was in a position to help or punish the brothers who sold him into slavery when they came asking him for grain during a famine. After revealing to them who he was, Joseph said, "Don't be afraid. Am I in the place of God? You intended to harm me, but God intended it for good, to accomplish what is now being done, the saving of many lives." (Genesis 50: 19-20)

Unlike Joseph, we may not see any good come from the evil done to us or to someone we love. Driving out anger and hurt may be a process like Israel entering the Promised Land. Moses had told the Israelites, "The Lord will drive out those nations before you little by little; you will be unable to destroy them at once..." (Deuteronomy 7:22).

Little by little, we make progress, intentionally giving our resentments to God again and again—every time they resurface. Jesus reassures us, "In this world, you will have trouble. But take heart! I have overcome the world."

A powerful example of Christ's forgiveness was demonstrated through the life of one of my favorite heroines, Corrie ten Boom (whose story is introduced in "Hope" on page 85). After her release from Nazi prison camp, Corrie had spent many years speaking about Jesus and His grace, and after she gave one such speech at a church in post-war Munich, a Nazi officer whose cruelty she vividly remembered approached her. He said, "How grateful I am for your message, Fraulein. To think that, as you say, He has washed my sins away!" Then he extended his hand to shake hers.

Corrie felt frozen in shock and anger, unable to accept the offered hand that had dealt so much suffering to her, her sister, and many others. Agonizing, Corrie prayed for God's help in forgiving him, but, even after that, "I felt nothing, not the slightest spark of warmth or charity." Then, as she recounts in *The Hiding Place*, she prayed again, saying, "Jesus, I cannot forgive him. Give me Your forgiveness.

"As I took his hand the most incredible thing happened," she wrote. "From my shoulder along my arm and through my hand a current seemed to pass from me to him, while into my heart sprang a love for this stranger that almost overwhelmed me. And so I discovered that it is neither on our forgiveness nor our goodness that the world's healing hinges, but on His. When He tells us to love our enemies, He gives, along with the command, the love itself."

An older friend of mine has not made that discovery yet. He was abused as a child by an alcoholic parent, while the other parent stood by, doing nothing. As an adult, my friend maintained a strained but courteous relationship with his parents, yet his internalized outrage resulted in health problems. Even though his parents have now died, my friend still feels powerless to let go of his hurt and anger. I am praying that he can tap into God's forgiveness the way Corrie did. When he does, he will set a prisoner free: himself.

SOUL THERAPY

Forgiver of my sins,
Thank You for Your grace.
Please help me to draw upon Your Holy Spirit's strength
So that I can extend Your undeserved forgiveness to others.
Exert Your power and love within me
To fight off the harmful things that invade my spirit—
Especially resentment, anger and hurt.
Perform Your healing work within me.

WORK OUT

Do you need to forgive someone?
Prayerfully turn to the Savior
to help you. Ask Him to fill your
heart and mind with Himself and
His forgiveness. He can enable you
to "take captive every thought to
make it obedient to Christ."

(2 CORINTHIANS 10:5)

JOURNAL

Write what you hope to do with
God's help.

To Believe
And Know

BODY BASIC
Health and disease involve both psychological and biological factors. Because of that built-in mind/body connection, researchers in controlled medical trials give one group of patients a medication, while supplying a second group with an identical-looking placebo or "sugar pill." Researchers can then learn if the differences observed in the patients are due to the medication or to the power of suggestion.

SPIRITUAL SPECIFIC
"I know whom I have believed..." (2 TIMOTHY 1:12)

We believe things, and we know things. The power of suggestion, or what we expect and believe, can be strong. But belief is not scientific certainty. Researchers depend on science's observation, study and experimentation to give them provable facts, so they can *know* something is true.

Jesus didn't need man's science to prove He was God. He demonstrated His power over all things—life and death, nature and weather, illness and health, demons and more—in order to give His disciples their own knowledge of who He was. And that knowledge solidified their faith.

John declared, "We have seen His glory. The glory of the One and Only, Who came from the Father full of grace and truth."(John 1:14). The disciples were eyewitnesses not only to Christ's miracles, but also to His transfiguration, His crucifixion and resurrection. They passed on in testimony and in Scripture what they knew. When Thomas would not believe his friends' eyewitness accounts of the resurrected Christ, the Lord graciously appeared to Thomas. Then Thomas *knew*—"My Lord and my God," he exclaimed.

We no longer have visible proof, like those who walked with Christ. Our knowing is not scientific. It is an inner knowledge, given to us by the Holy Spirit. The Holy Spirit is described as "the Spirit of wisdom and of understanding, the Spirit of counsel and of power, the Spirit of knowledge and of the fear of the Lord." (Isaiah 11:2)

The Holy Spirit speaks to minds and hearts. He spoke to me years ago about something He wanted me to do, clearly saying in my mind, "I want you to write a body devotional book." I was startled by the "voice" in my head, but I knew who it was and was glad to obey. Being a children's author, I excitedly began writing a book of devotionals for young readers about the human body. Looking back, I realize I didn't pray for further direction. I just assumed I knew what God wanted and started "helping Him" do it. My effort fizzled. Confused, I filed away my ideas.

Ten years later, physical problems led me to a prayer of desperation: "God, I know that following You can mean suffering. But how is *this* for Your kingdom? I can't do anything!" And His answer—not in words this time, but as a flash of knowledge—was that I would have to go through suffering before I could write about it. I suddenly understood—He was preparing me to write that body devotional book.

Knowing my purpose gave me new eyes to see every frustration, pain and limitation. He gave me fresh insight into the fact that He doesn't need *my* energy or health to accomplish His purposes. He just wants my submission and obedience.

Since my own activity was limited, I had time to write, and it didn't take much energy to sit in my easy chair and do it. The joy of my life became discovering new things in God's Word, watching Him develop ideas without my interference. I began experiencing the "abundant life." Before, I *believed* in God; afterward, I *knew* Him. I encountered Him first-hand. And it all started with illness.

Throughout Scripture God says, "Know that I am God." Knowing may mean suffering, but in the end, God promises, it's worth it.

SOUL THERAPY

Father, I believe *and* know,
But I know only in part.
I need *lots* of knowledge as well as faith
To make it through hard times.
Please help me to know You better—
The way You want to be known.
And when despair batters the door of my heart,
And suffering tears at my faith,
Let my knowledge of You fortify my trust,
So I can join You in whatever work You have planned.

WORK OUT
Look up and read Isaiah 40:11-14 and Ephesians 1:17-23.

JOURNAL
What do those verses tell you about God? What does He want to do for you and give you? Copy some of Paul's prayer for the Ephesians, and pray it for yourself.

Wilderness Heat

BODY BASIC
The body has more than two million sweat glands to help cool it, and depending on temperature and humidity, the average person loses one-half to one-and-a-half quarts of water a day through sweating. However, during a heat stroke, the body loses the ability to regulate its temperature. When that happens, body temperature can rise to 106 degrees or higher, leading to possible brain damage and even death.

SPIRITUAL SPECIFIC
"At once, the Spirit led Him out into the desert for forty days..." (MARK 1:12)

The desert wilderness is a prime place to have a heat stroke. Many American soldiers in the Middle East, even if they drink plenty of water and are in good physical shape, suffer from heat exhaustion and heat stroke if they are not slowly and adequately acclimated to that environment. The desert is tough on the human body.

The Bible is full of desert experiences—times of testing or of wandering, confusion and fear. But in those experiences, people learned about God. When she fled to the desert, Hagar, Abraham's slave who bore him the son Ishmael, experienced God's kindness, watchfulness and provision. The desert-wandering Israelites were guided by God, who was ever-present in a moving pillar of cloud by day (perhaps to shade them) and pillar of fire at night. (Exodus 13:21) He provided for all their daily needs there, too, even bringing a stream of water from a rock. He gave them sweet manna, "thin flakes like frost" which appeared six days a week on the desert ground after the dew was gone. (They gathered two days' worth on the sixth day.) It was the bread the Lord fed them with for forty years. (Exodus 16)

In Scripture, desert testing served a purpose. God developed Moses' character there and spoke to him from a burning bush, telling him to lead Israel out of Egypt. Jesus, immediately after his baptism, was sent out into the desert by the Holy Spirit. Weakened at the end of forty days there, Jesus was tempted by Satan. He resisted the temptation, demonstrated His perfection, and emerged ready to begin His mission.

We all go through one or more desert experiences of some kind, whether they're physical or spiritual. Sometimes we put ourselves there. Sometimes we are sent.

My friend and author Ken Gire talks about his desert experience in *Windows of the Soul*. After seminary, Ken began serving God in the way he felt most qualified and effective: writing. However, after working hard for years, his savings gone, his house up for sale, and nothing to show for his efforts except publishers' rejection slips and his own depression, Ken wrote in his journal, "I have come to a point of emotional and spiritual exhaustion. Drained dry, a drop of life at a time."

Even though he felt abandoned, Ken continued to watch for God, and he learned many difficult lessons. He battled depression for months. In the end, he writes, "When I first listened to the call of God to write, little did I realize it was a call to the wilderness. But it was there, not in seminary, that God prepared me to be a writer. The wilderness was a place of pain, humiliation, uncertainty, loneliness and desperation. All of which were necessary for me to experience if I was to be the writer I needed to be. Seminary prepared me to use my gift. The wilderness prepared me to live my life."

Whatever the purpose of our wilderness trial, in it we can count on Jesus to sustain us. He will help us take the heat and come forth as refined gold.

SOUL THERAPY

Lord, I dread desert experiences
With their emptiness, thirst and loneliness.
But I thank You that You will always accomplish something within me,
As long as I turn to You in my wilderness wanderings.
Please shelter me and provide for me as I learn hard lessons.
Don't let the desert scorch me dry.
Instead, let your Living Water restore and renew me,
Until at last I can lie down in green pastures.

WORK OUT
Sweating is actually good for you, because it releases toxins as it cools the body. If you can't exercise hard enough to produce a sweat, sitting in a sauna (with a doctor's okay) can do the same thing for you.

JOURNAL
Reflect on a desert experience in your life and note how you were changed from it. If the heat of adversity seems to have melted your faith instead of refining you, express your feelings and ask God to restore your trust.

SHAKEN TO THE CORE

Fingers

BODY BASIC
Fingers have many uses, but no muscles. The fingers' strength comes when tendons transfer force to them from muscles in the forearm and palm. Fingertips are sensitive because of a high concentration of nerve endings.

SPIRITUAL SPECIFIC
When the Lord finished speaking to Moses on Mount Sinai, He gave him the two tablets of the Testimony... inscribed by the finger of God."
(EXODUS 31:18)

God's figurative finger etched the Ten Commandments in stone. His finger was acknowledged by Pharaoh's magicians as sending the plague of gnats. To a terrified King Belshazzar, fingers of a human hand appeared and wrote on that wicked king's banquet hall wall God's message of condemnation and death for him. (Daniel 5)

Jesus used His fingers to heal, putting them into a deaf man's ears. He told doubting Thomas to put his finger into the nail holes in His hands so he could believe. Jesus also said, "...if I drive out demons by the finger of God, then the kingdom of God has come to you." (Luke 11:20)

Our fingers have their own unique prints to remind us we're each one of a kind. And often our gifts are expressed through the intricate work of our fingers.

My childhood friend Katherine has gifted fingers that began making beautiful music on the piano when she was very young. She has become a renowned pianist who now travels the world giving concerts. As an only child, Katherine always enjoyed being what she called "a daddy's girl."

Grief overwhelmed her in her forties when her father died. She said, "My heart was so heavy. I knew Dad was in heaven, but I missed him so much that I couldn't overcome the pain in my heart. It lasted for years! I wondered why I was mourning so long when I was a Christian. I couldn't allow myself to think about Dad, and I didn't even dream about him at night."

Katherine began developing physical problems with pain in her joints so severe that she was forced to cancel concerts. "I tried everything to get well," she said. "And finally, I relinquished myself to God, saying, 'If this is what You want for me, and it's the road I have to take, I'll try my best to handle it with Your help. But if You want me to get well, please show me the way.' After that, I saw so many God-touches! Helpful books and encouraging messages from friends were heaven-sent."

She was directed to hypnotherapy to uncover any subconscious emotional issues that were triggering her physical problems. Under hypnosis she recalled a childhood feeling of abandonment when her father, an airline captain, would leave home for several days at a time. That subconscious insecurity had resurfaced when her father died. The therapist instructed Katherine to let go of that destructive childhood emotion and instead picture in her mind something wonderful about her dad in heaven.

"My father had beautiful hands and long fingers like mine," she said. "Maybe that's why, as my mind searched for a picture, I suddenly envisioned a hand reaching down from heaven with another hand reaching up. It was just like Michelangelo's Sistine Chapel painting where God's hand is releasing Adam's, and their outstretched fingers are almost touching. The whole scene is peaceful. In my vision, it was as if God's hand were my father's, reaching out to me and releasing me at the same time. That became my mental symbol, and it brought me peace when I thought of Dad."

Katherine left the therapists office "tremendously relieved." But God wasn't through reaching out to her. That week, one of her music students brought her a souvenir book from his trip to Italy. On the cover was that Sistine Chapel picture. "I sobbed, knowing both God and my father wanted me to let go and get well. Within two weeks, my physical problems were gone."

SOUL THERAPY

Lord, when I'm grief-stricken or overwhelmed,
Please touch me with your loving kindness.
Point me in the right direction
Through Your word and Your people.
Heal me, Father,
So I can put Your gifts to good use.

WORK OUT
Let your fingers turn the pages of Psalms today and find a verse or promise that comforts you (I especially like some verses in Psalm 145).

JOURNAL
Record whatever verses you chose and why they help you.

Heart Failure

BODY BASIC
The fist-sized average human heart pumps nearly a gallon and a half of blood every minute. Heart failure doesn't mean the heart has stopped or will stop. It's a condition in which the heart can't pump enough blood through the body, and it can be treated with drug therapies and supervised cardiac exercise.

SPIRITUAL SPECIFIC
"For troubles without number surround me...and my heart fails within me."

(PSALM 40:12)

The heart is central to our physical life. The heart is also recognized as "the wellspring of life" in the Bible—symbolically being the home of emotions. Proverbs 4:23 advises us to guard the heart "above all else."

When we are emotionally devastated, we might identify with what the psalmist wrote in Psalm 22: "My heart has turned to wax; it has melted away within me." That Psalm, written 950 years before Jesus' crucifixion, prophesied how Jesus would feel as He underwent the agony of the cross, a gruesome means of death not even invented at the time of the prophecy.

Jesus quoted the opening lines of that Psalm before He died. Betrayed, rejected, humiliated, physically tortured and bearing the wrath of God for *our* sins, Jesus endured the most extreme mental, emotional, physical and spiritual torment. Therefore, His heart sympathizes totally with us when we hurt.

My friend Jane was heartbroken when her forty-year marriage ended in divorce. Devastated, she tried to rebuild her life, but grief and loneliness accompanied her everywhere. She told me that she prayed, wrote prayers in a journal and studied scripture to bolster her spirits. And as she studied, she reread a verse that had always seemed odd to her. "In Scripture, God calls Himself a husband, but the idea seemed too unreal, too intimate," she said. "But then I decided to ask God, since I no longer had a husband, 'Are you really my husband, Lord?' And when I asked Him, He answered in the form of a question back to me: 'What do good husbands do?'

"I started listing things: a good husband declares his love to his wife in small and big ways. He protects and guides. He provides companionship and an intimacy in heart, soul and mind. He rules in the house without oppression—unselfishly. He comforts his wife when she is sad or confused. A good husband will never leave his wife or forsake her. And sometimes he will surprise her with little expressions of love, bringing a gift such as flowers.

"Then, I suddenly realized that God *was* that 'good husband!' She continued, "I wrote down His promise in Hosea 2:19 'I will betroth you to Me forever; I will betroth you in righteousness and justice, in love and compassion.' And I was thanking Him for that when I looked outside my window and suddenly saw a gift He'd sent—one of those little surprises—flowers that had burst into bloom, growing for me to see and enjoy."

That unique revelation of God's partnership with her brought Jane new strength. An artist, she went on to build a business with her art. She also created an art mission which has taken her all over the world raising funds for the disadvantaged. As new doors have opened, Jane continues to witness God's many "expressions of love." And her heart is full once again.

The Bible says, "The Lord is close to the brokenhearted; He rescues those who are crushed in spirit." (Psalm 34:18 NLT) When we ask Him to, He builds up our failing heart.

SOUL THERAPY

God of love, when troubles surround me,
And my heart fails within me,
Please infuse me with Your strength and compassion.
Help me to connect more intimately with You,
And to remember that You treasure me,
Claiming me as Your own forever.

WORK OUT

To get your heart pumping, sit on the edge of a dining chair. Punch up toward the ceiling, alternating arms, ten times. Then kick each foot out alternately, straightening the knee ten times. Repeat the arm/leg sequence of ten repetitions for five more times.

JOURNAL

Pen a love note to God.

Running The Race

BODY BASIC

To run a race, or even to walk, muscles, joints and ligaments must all work together. If one is adversely affected, the others are hindered.

SPIRITUAL SPECIFIC

"Therefore, since we are surrounded by such a great cloud of witnesses, let us throw off everything that hinders, and the sin that so easily entangles, and let us run with perseverance the race marked out for us."

(HEBREWS 12:1)

The writer of Hebrews wrote to cheer on Christ's Jewish converts, because the persecuted church needed courage to continue "running the race" ahead of them. He told them to persevere in the faith, keeping their eyes on Christ. And he told them to look back at the unflagging faith of the heroes of the past, who were now a "great cloud of witnesses." Whether on earth or in heaven, God's faithful followers are to work together, encouraging each other.

Gayle, my physical therapist, always cheered on her clients, helping them persevere through difficult therapy. But, even as she successfully worked with others, she worried about having future children of her own with physical problems. "The thought of working with physical challenges all day and then coming home to more of them seemed too difficult," she told me. However, she and her husband, who is also a physical therapist, eventually chose to begin their family despite her fears, and their son and daughter seemed fine. Then one day, their three-year-old son Reese began crying with joint pain. The first diagnosis was juvenile rheumatoid arthritis. Gayle was shattered.

"I felt hurt and even a little betrayed to think that when I was trying to help others, God would allow me to have this heartbreak and struggle at home. I didn't immediately turn to God, because I was afraid I would start trying to bargain, or that I might get really angry at Him. And those were two reactions I didn't want to have.

"So," she continued, "I went straight into 'Mommy mode' and began caring for Reese in all the ways I knew best from my background. We took one day at a time focusing on what we could do to help him. As we began to let people know what was going on, I was amazed to find out how many people cared about us and our little boy. The amount of love and support that was offered to us through actions and prayers was overwhelming. With time, we began feeling as though God's arms were truly around us. We felt peace and comfort that gave us confidence that we would get through this no matter what the outcome. Although we didn't know how Reese would progress, we knew God had blessed my husband and me with talents and resources and the encouragement of others. I know Christ strengthens us, but God uses His family to strengthen our faith, too."

Doctors eventually discovered that Reese didn't have arthritis, but a lack of ligament support in his joints which causes arthritic pain symptoms. He may one day outgrow it.

As Reese continues his therapy, Gayle says, "I would tell others who are dealing with hard issues to focus on what you can do, utilize your resources, and receive the gifts from your support systems with humility and open arms. God works in many ways!"

SOUL THERAPY

Giver of every good gift,
It's hard to accept some of the challenges You hand me.
But, thank You for Your faithful people
Who turn to You on my behalf
When I'm temporarily too fragile to come.
Thank You for Your cloud of witnesses here and in heaven
Who are a triumphant testimony of Your sustaining strength.
Please empower me to follow their example,
And in partnership with You, to run with perseverance
The race set out for me.

WORK OUT

Stand on one leg and hold a tabletop or countertop with one or both hands. Keep your hips level as you move the free leg forward, out to the side, then backwards five times in each direction. Then switch legs. With this exercise, the leg you are standing on is building joint stability.

JOURNAL

You are a muscle in the body of Christ. Who can you help? Who has provided support for you? Note some strengths you have that you can use, then put them to work this week.

An Outstretched Arm

BODY BASIC

In most people, the width of a person's arms stretched out equals his body length. The forearm, elbow to wrist, is about the same length as the foot.

SPIRITUAL SPECIFIC

I am the Lord...I will free you...I will redeem you with an outstretched arm..."

(EXODUS 6:6)

*I*n Scripture, God's powerful, saving acts on behalf of His people were done with an "outstretched arm." Yet, even after God performed mighty miracles to free Israel from Egypt, Moses doubted Him when He told Moses that He'd bring a month's worth of meat to the grumbling Israelites in the desert. Moses said, "Here I am among six hundred thousand men on foot and you say, 'I will give them meat to eat for a whole month!' The Lord answered Moses, 'Is the Lord's arm too short? You will now see...'" (Numbers 11:21-25) And quail were blown in from the sea by a wind and brought down around the camp "to about three feet above the ground as far as a day's walk..."(11:.31) God proved His arm is anything but short.

Jesus, with His human arms, gathered children close to Him as He blessed them. And at the end of His ministry, it was Jesus' outstretched arms that performed one final, saving act for God's people: He stretched out those arms, not in mighty power but in submissive weakness, to be nailed to a cross and pay the penalty for our sin.

Joey, husband of my prayer partner, Bobbie, is a strong, middle-aged, ex-college football star who, after an accident, gained a new appreciation for God's protective arms as well those of Bobbie. Joey was on a ladder fixing their second story roof when the ladder began falling toward the concrete porch below. "I was about to land on my back or head, but thanks to God, I was able to fling myself off in the opposite direction," he said. "I landed on my right elbow and hip. The pain was incredible, worse than any football hit. I thought it would subside. It didn't."

Bobbie rushed him to the hospital for X-rays and surgery for his smashed elbow.

His hip was severely bruised, not broken. Soon after surgery and the news that he would never be able to completely stretch his arm out straight again, Joey went into rehabilitation, determined to prove doctors wrong. "I hated being helpless and dependent," he said. "So I wanted to accelerate things."

But he learned a hard lesson: "More is not necessarily better. In an athletic workout, 'more pain, more gain.' So, I didn't follow the doctor's advice to go slow and easy. I ordered a mechanical splint to help straighten out my arm, and daily I cranked it and held it to full extension until I couldn't stand the pain any more. I lifted weights too soon that were too heavy. And the elbow wasn't healing. I later found out my elbow socket was locked up by bone growth in the wrong places. When I bent my arm, the break *itself* actually acted as the hinge!"

After sixteen months of pain and improper healing, Joey had only thirty percent usage of his right arm. A specialist performed more surgery to put things right, and Joey began again.

"Sometimes it's hard to do things right. But I learned that even when things in my life shatter with almost unendurable pain, God can mend them and bring relief. I can't accelerate His timing. My scars remind me that worthwhile healing has to be done in God's timing."

SOUL THERAPY

My strong-armed Father,
Thank You that in every affliction
You reach out to me.
Please hold me close as I'm mending.
Cradle me in Your mercy,
And supply my needs.
Remind me that no matter how restricted I am,
Your arm is never "too short."

WORK OUT
With a small dumbbell or canned goods in each hand, arms by your sides and palms facing inward, slowly lift the weight away from your body until your body forms a "T," and your outstretched arms are level with your shoulders. Then slowly lower your arms and repeat the lifts ten times.

JOURNAL
List ways in which God manifests His power through the amazing capabilities of the human body or through the wonders of nature.

Tasty!

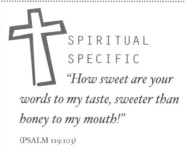

BODY BASIC
Every square centimeter of the tongue contains taste buds. But scientists have found that not only do we have different numbers of taste buds, but their density also varies. Therefore, taste sensitivity varies among people. The same food actually tastes different in different mouths. Because taste buds are resilient and are replaced every few days, the sense of taste is more resistant to damage than the other senses.

SPIRITUAL SPECIFIC
"How sweet are your words to my taste, sweeter than honey to my mouth!"
(PSALM 119:103)

*O*ur *Creator loves beauty and variety,* and He gives us different ways to enjoy and experience His gifts through our senses. We can see and touch food, but it is our sense of *taste,* enhanced by smell, which allows us to really enjoy it and savor food's unique flavors.

King David spoke of delighting in God the way we relish good food.

"Taste and see that the Lord is good," he said. David did more than just "see" God by focusing on His word, he "tasted" Him, and had a consuming desire for an ever-deepening relationship with Him.

We can still taste God the same way David did. And in the New Testament, Peter repeats David's advice in another way. He encourages Christ's followers to be *hungry* for spiritual food and to be nourished by it. Peter writes. "Like newborn babies, [you should] crave pure spiritual milk, so that by it you may grow up in your salvation, now that you have tasted that the Lord is good." (1Peter 2:2-3)

I never actually *craved* God's word, even though for many years, I'd enjoyed Bible study. The Bible has given me wisdom, guidance and comfort, and it has helped me know our God better. Even though it has been very beneficial, until recently it wasn't anything I truly longed for; it was more a discipline—like eating green beans, which I like, instead of eating chocolate, which I crave!

Then, when I suddenly was hit with my health issues, everything changed. My fear and confusion began to overpower my perspective. I needed God's goodness in a deeper, more comforting, way. So, like someone starving, I began devouring the Bible with a personal intensity I'd never had before. I asked the Holy Spirit to reveal new things to me in the Bible's old familiar words, to help me "taste and see that God is good."

And, like a miracle, God answered. Familiar stories came alive in a new way. Footnotes I'd never paid attention to in my study Bible became fascinating and enriching, and I studied the linking (parallel) passages I'd never taken time to look up. As I did, the whole Bible began blending together for me in an exciting way. Even a familiar word here and there jumped out at me, and I had a fresh appreciation for what it meant. Reading a verse first in my Bible and then in a paraphrase like "The Message" spiced things up, too. The only way I can explain how the same old thing suddenly tasted different is that the Holy Spirit did it for me. And even though I still had my physical problems, my soul was comforted, encouraged and soothed.

Then, on top of that, a friend showed me how to take a verse and make it into God's first-person words to me, by name—such as in 1 Peter 5:7, "Cast all your anxiety on Me, Marjorie, because I care for you" instead of the usual "Cast all your anxiety on Him because He cares for you." That technique made a well-known verse not just helpful instruction, but God's own sweet invitation.

I began to read expectantly instead of dutifully each morning, eager for what God might have for me. And I felt awed by Paul's statement: "Even if it was written in scripture long ago, [Marjorie] you can be sure it's written for [you]." (Romans 15:4 MSG)

My health finally improved, but I still pick up the "Good Book" each day with renewed enthusiasm, knowing that God's amazing truths have an eternally expanding, delicious flavor, especially when I turn my problems over to Him. There's something for every taste, and God invites each one of us to savor His bountiful feast.

SOUL THERAPY

Whether I'm experiencing life's bitterness or sweetness, Lord,
Please give me a constant craving for Your truth.
Satisfy my soul with Your tender message of love.
Thank You for the glorious variety of ways
That You nourish and sustain me
With your eternal—yet always fresh—words of life.

WORK OUT
*Treat yourself to a favorite coffee,
tea or other tasty drink as you read
David's praise to God in Psalm 103.*

JOURNAL
Record your reaction.

Joy

BODY BASIC
The brain has a "pleasure center," a certain area in the forebrain that produces sensations of elation when stimulated electrically.

SPIRITUAL SPECIFIC
"...for the joy of the Lord is your strength."
(NEHEMIAH 8:10)

*E*arthly amusements can temporarily stimulate our brain's pleasure center, but God offers a more lasting joy. His joy produces an inner feeling of well-being—a fruit of the Holy Spirit—which is not dependent on pleasure. Joy, even in unpleasant circumstances, is one of those deep, un-explainable gifts from God. Paul experienced those gifts. He wrote his most joyous letter, Philippians, while imprisoned for two years because of his stand for Christ. Paul's gladness comes from the inside, where he is full of Jesus, and his fullness of heart spills out in his words to fellow Christians. He celebrates, because he knows how his problems and persecution will turn out: if he lives, he can serve Christ, if he dies, he will join Jesus in heaven.

Jesus, too, knew joy even in suffering. Scripture says that Jesus, "for the joy that was set before Him, endured the cross." (Hebrews 12:2) What was the joy that was set before Him? *Us!* The whole reason He endured that torture and died in our place was to reunite us with God and make it possible for Him to enjoy us forever in heaven—and vice-versa.

Whatever you are enduring, Jesus endured even more *for you*. He wants to be the joy set before you, just as you were—and are—the joy set before Him. The world produces many things that try to steal our joy: pain, sickness, grief, stress, worry, fear. But Christ says, "I have overcome the world." And through Him, we can, too.

Debbie, who was introduced to me through a friend, told me over the phone about her pleasure in delivering the glad news of Christ to suffering people in Africa. She didn't mind the discomforts that came with the trip, because her heart was full of joy. Her ministry was central to her life. She tried to take good care of her health so she could continue to minister. One morning, after swallowing her prescribed medication for thinning bones, she took her dog for a walk. Along the way, she tripped and fell, fracturing her pelvis in three places.

After rehabilitation, Debbie got a walker, "But I was in a lot of pain," she told me. "I had a frozen shoulder, too, so using the walker was hard. I was totally vulnerable and dependent on others. I was no longer the helper I had always been." She reluctantly gave up a ministry she headed, and she felt that in other areas of her life "people had expectations of me that I couldn't meet. I was frustrated! And I was afraid my brittle bones might keep me from going to Africa again."

As Debbie fretted over her limitations, she began realizing, "I'm not indispensable to my causes. God could provide for them. I had to trust Him and His plan for me."

Through prayer, Debbie was able to better understand Jesus' suffering. "And I realized that my suffering was nothing in comparison with His. And compared to the people in Africa and what they endure, I was living in Disneyworld. No matter how limited I felt, I had provisions, friends, family. I began praying with more empathy for people suffering around the world. I felt so blessed that I wept! God gave me His joy as He changed my attitude and my life."

Later Debbie found another reason to be glad. Because of tests after the break, doctors discovered that she had been excreting calcium, and "that's why my bones were getting more brittle despite the medication." They fixed that with different medication.

SOUL THERAPY

Be the Joy set before me, Lord Jesus,
Through every adversity.
Only You can mold me into a disciple who can rejoice
Despite "grief in all kinds of trials,"
And I need Your help!
When it seems like You've given me more than I can bear,
Remind me of every blessing—
Especially the gift of my salvation,
Which fills me with "an inexpressible and glorious joy."

(1 PETER 1:8)

WORK OUT

The pleasure of participating in many activities can be limited by brittle bones brought on by osteoporosis. Vitamin D and calcium help maintain strong bones, as does weight-bearing exercise. With your doctor's permission, for fifteen minutes a day, walk outside to soak up the sun's Vitamin D while carrying a three-pound weight in each hand. Don't carry weights if you have trouble with your hands. (Wrist-wrap weights are okay.)

JOURNAL

After reading from Philippians, jot down some of Paul's expressions of joy as he encouraged his suffering fellow Christians.

What Holds You Up?

BODY BASIC
Bones not only help hold up the body, but bone marrow manufactures blood. In children, bones grow and support the body at the same time. Then, when bones quit growing in length, they can still become denser and stronger with weight lifting.

SPIRITUAL SPECIFIC
"Did you not...knit me together with bones and sinews? You gave me life and showed me kindness, and in Your providence watched over my spirit." (JOB 10:12)

God fashioned us so that with weight-lifting, bones strengthen. And through the heavy weight of life's problems, faith grows stronger, too, if we turn to God. In Scripture, God taught people about Himself as He interacted with them through various circumstances and trials. Whether walking with or wrestling with Him, running to Him or from Him (temporarily), arguing or agreeing with Him, each individual was strengthened by his own unique experience with God during those times.

One of those people was Moses, who met God via a burning bush and learned God's name, "I Am." He understood that he was speaking to the Almighty God of Abraham, Isaac and Jacob. But that wasn't enough to calm his fears when God commanded him to go to the Egyptian Pharaoh and demand freedom for His captive people. Even after God's reassurances to him, Moses said, "O Lord, please send someone else to do it." (Exodus 4:13) It wasn't enough for Moses just to hear about God's power; he needed to see that power for himself.

Through impossible situations, God showed His trembling servant what he needed to see, taking him to a new level of understanding. "I am the Lord..." God said, and proved His dominance over all nations and even creation. He dispatched plagues, divided the sea, delivered His people, disclosed His presence in a pillar of light and a cloud, dispensed forty years of food and water in the wilderness, and much more. Moses' faith grew as every obstacle was overcome.

My friend Lisa needed God to prove Himself to her in a time of grief, when her seemingly healthy fifty-three-year-old husband died suddenly from a heart attack. Her shock, grief and helplessness were so severe that she told me, "Without God making Himself real to me, I would not be here today. I *had* to have a Comforter and Stronghold. And He became that to me. I experienced His faithfulness and kindness. He gave me the strength to live." She leaned on Him moment to moment.

"I was able to comfort my children, go back to work, and move from our home,'" she continued, "Throughout the tragedy, and in each lonely, grief-filled day, I felt His blessing."

But the worst wasn't over. Just ten months later, Lisa's newlywed daughter's husband died of a seizure. Lisa said, "Nothing hurt as badly as seeing my daughter in pain. I fell to my knees, totally overwhelmed, and prayed for strength once again. I'll never be able to comprehend the incredible peace, strength and courage that lifted me to my feet. But I'll always be grateful for it."

Like one whose bones had been strengthened, Lisa felt God enabling her to carry her own heavy load as well as to help her daughter. The two grew in faith as God provided, and they pressed on. "I learned so much about who God is through that time," Lisa said. Then, two years later, she learned something else about God – He delights in being a Matchmaker. Lisa is now happily married to the man He brought to her.

SOUL THERAPY

Lord of all, You bear me up,
When every prop has been pulled out from under me.
Psalms says, "As a father has compassion on His children,
So the Lord has compassion on those who fear Him;
For He knows how we are formed,
He remembers that we are dust."
You know my weakness, Father,
And You offset it with Your strength.
Thank You.

WORK OUT

Strengthen your bones with this exercise. Standing or sitting with your abs tight, do twenty curls or lifts with three to five pound weights or canned goods. If you have ankle weights (don't use more than three pounds), use them as you do leg lifts.

JOURNAL

Have you ever been desperate for God's strength? How did He respond? Record those memories.

Communicating

BODY BASIC
In the nervous system, billions of specialized nerve cells relay messages to and from the brain by electrical impulses, some of which can move as rapidly as 250 miles per hour. Nerve damage from an injury or disease can halt "communication" with muscles, causing the muscles to waste away or atrophy.

SPIRITUAL SPECIFIC
"Why this waste?' they said." (MATTHEW 26:8)

When muscles begin to atrophy, it's usually because some problem has cut off the message system between the nerves and the muscles they control. Often, with therapy, the nerves and muscles can be "re-trained" to communicate, and a wasting muscle can be redeveloped. Without redeveloping communication, however, the damage to the muscle can be permanent.

Relationships can be impaired, too, unless people talk and listen to each other. Conversation connects us with others and with God. Habakkuk, a righteous prophet, was not hesitant to express his feelings to God. He boldly asked why God would punish Israel's wickedness by sending an even more evil nation, Babylon, to defeat them. He argued with God over His ways. But, through the conversation, Habakkuk's trust grew. He was still terrified of the future, but the prophet nevertheless began recounting God's merciful saving acts in the past, (Ch.3) and was finally able to say, "Though the fig tree does not bud and there are no grapes on the vines... yet I will rejoice in the Lord, I will be joyful in God my Savior."

I talked to a man named Rich in a friend's church who, unlike Habakkuk, found no reason to rejoice in God after multiple devastating tragedies in his family. Both of Rich's sons died before they were seven years old from a rare neurological disease. "For five years, my wife and I watched our children die," he said. "It was an aggressive disease. First they went blind, then their bodies atrophied, then they were fed through a tube. It was horrible. After our boys died, everything was about pain—even the memories. My wife's and my relationship fell apart, and we divorced. I contemplated suicide. Everything hurt so badly, and I couldn't see an end to it. I just wanted relief.

"Even though I'd been raised in the church and had always believed in God, I'd never really focused on Him," Rich continued. "I didn't feel very close to Him. After our tragedy, I was so mad, distraught and overwhelmed, that I still didn't communicate with Him much, except in anger. But I never stopped believing."

Nine years later, Rich met and married Jenny and adopted her daughter. Then heartbreak struck again. After four years of marriage, Jenny developed encephalitis, and died within a week. "I felt like I'd been crushed under a steam roller again," Rich said. "I still couldn't believe God would let those things happen to the people I loved. And even though I didn't *want* to turn to Him, even though our relationship was not the greatest, I knew He was there. And He was all I had. Without Him in my life, there would be no hope at all. I had nowhere else to turn.

"So, even though I'd never liked church, I went, just for the hour to sit and think about God and try to relate to Him. And gradually, I found strength and comfort doing that. It was a sanctuary for me—very beneficial. Getting closer to God and communicating with Him helped me deal with everything. If it wasn't for Him, I don't know where I'd be. It all comes back to God in the end.

"I'm finally realizing that life still has opportunities," he continued, "And my purpose is to have an effect on the people along my path. I'm glad I didn't give up and commit suicide. I'm happy I could be there for Jenny and her daughter, whom I love. And as I progress down the road, time and faith are softening the memory of those awful experiences. I still get hit off-guard with sadness sometimes. But I've found hope—especially in the promise that I'll be reunited with my loved ones. I've found God's light at the end of a very dark tunnel."

SOUL THERAPY

Lord and Messenger of Hope,
Thank You for remaining connected to me,
No matter how removed I may feel from You.
Only You can bring healing.
Only You know the whys that I can't understand.
And only You can give the peace
I am desperate for.
When I'm hurt and angry,
Please don't let my faith waste away.
Relay Your messages of love and hope to my soul
Until I'm strong again.

WORK OUT

As you do this exercise of Wall Sits, appreciate the nerve and muscle connections that make it possible for you to perform it. (This one uses muscles in the back, tummy, buttocks and legs.) Stand with your feet apart and about two feet out from a wall. Reach your hands back to the wall so that you can slowly lean yourself straight back into the wall until your shoulders and back are flat against it. Then, keeping your back against the wall, gently slide down about two inches or more, as if you were going to sit. Hold the position for twenty seconds, then slide back up and repeat five times. (If you want to sit lower, just make sure you never let your buttocks drop below knee level or let your knees bend over your ankles.)

JOURNAL

Communicate with God in your journal, composing a prayer about any broken relationship or heartbreak in your life. If you identify with Rich, ask God to help you restore your relationship with Him or the person with whom you've broken ties.

Through The Fire

BODY BASIC
Skin cells are killed by intense heat. A third-degree burn destroys the entire depth of the skin and can also damage fat, muscle, organs and bone beneath the skin.

SPIRITUAL SPECIFIC
"By day the Lord went ahead of them in a pillar of cloud to guide them on their way and by night in a pillar of fire to give them light..."

(EXODUS 13:21)

Scripture speaks of two types of fire: flames that represent God's presence and guidance, and the fire of destruction, which God sometimes uses in His wrath. When the fire represents God's presence, the burning object is not consumed—like the burning bush that attracted Moses' attention and through which he heard God call him into leadership; or the pillar of fire that led the Israelites through the wilderness. The mountain where God gave Moses the Ten Commandments "blazed with fire to the very heavens" (Deuteronomy 4:11-12), but the mountain was not destroyed.

It was an angel with the flaming sword of God's judgment that kept Adam and Eve from returning to God's perfect garden after they had sinned. The fall of man ushered in destruction instead of perfection—and fire became a potential enemy.

I talked with a firefighter's mother, Jeri, who told me the tragic story of her son, Destry. He had made it his life's work to save others from fire's destruction, and he also enjoyed leading others in praise and worship at his church. The thirty-two-year-old firefighter was heading out to play golf on his day off, when he was called and asked to join other volunteers in a fight against a rampant wildfire. It was threatening homes in his area of Oklahoma, so Destry quickly joined the other firefighters. But in a terrible turn of events, Destry's fire truck got stuck in a burning field, and wildfire engulfed it. As the driver, Destry was not wearing protective gear—it's not required of drivers—and he was critically burned.

For twenty-four days, his wife and two young children, his parents, and many friends and family gathered around his hospital bedside, praying. "He was such a special young man and had such a love of the Lord. But he didn't survive," Jeri told me. "As he lay dying, I prayed and said the twenty-third Psalm that I'd memorized as a child. I was so grateful I'd learned it, because I was so terribly heartbroken, and I was desperate for help. It was a horrific time, but the words comforted me."

After Destry died, Jeri's days were filled with grief, and her nights with panic attacks. "When the terrifying feelings would hit, I'd just keep repeating the twenty-third Psalm. It was such a help to be able to claim God's word when I couldn't even think. I never knew that scripture could have such power, but that's all that got me through those awful times. Also, I would pray for good dreams about Destry, and it was like a gift from God whenever I did. Once I asked Destry in a dream, where I saw him standing strong and healthy again, what heaven was like, and he just gave me a big smile. He was so happy!"

Even with an occasional good dream, Jeri's heartbreak was almost unbearable. "When I wasn't sure I wanted life to go on, God gave me life-saving strength. I still have some terrible times. But I have hope in what God promises each of us who believe, and I know that every day that passes, I'm one day closer to seeing Jesus and hugging Destry again."

Jeri's faith has been tried by fire, but it has not been consumed, because the Lord has been in it with her. She presses on, cherishing Destry's family and passionately working for a special cause: spearheading a campaign with Oklahoma fire fighters to raise funds for a remodeled ICU at the hospital where Destry was treated. It will be named for him.

SOUL THERAPY

Oh, God, tragedies sear their anguish so deeply!
Please walk with me through the fire.
Sustain me, my Comforter, through the valley of the shadow of death.
When I'm too despairing to speak,
Groan for me, Holy Spirit.
Fill me with Your peace that passes understanding,
And with the blessed assurance that my loved one and I
Will dwell in the house of the Lord forever.

WORK OUT
Memorize a few lines of the twenty-third Psalm each day until you can say it all. Then, then teach it to a child or grandchild.

JOURNAL
What way is God like a shepherd? In what ways are you like a sheep? Pen your thoughts.

Total
Remake

BODY BASIC
Each second, millions of the body's cells die and millions are born. Each day, the skin's dead epidermal cells—the outer layer—are washed away or rubbed off, and new cells that form below them push their way up to replace them. Gradually, we get a "new skin"—every four to six weeks.

SPIRITUAL SPECIFIC
"Therefore, if anyone is in Christ, he is a new creation; the old has gone, the new has come!" (2 CORINTHIANS 5:17)

*T**he Pharisee Nicodemus came to Jesus** under cover of night with his faith questions. Jesus let Nicodemus know that in order to see the kingdom of God, he had to be made a new creation through the work of the Holy Spirit. Jesus described it by saying, "You must be born again." After his talk with Jesus, Nicodemus apparently became a secret believer. After Jesus was crucified, Nicodemus, along with Joseph of Arimathea, took Jesus' body down from the cross (with Pilate's permission). They wrapped it in linen with spices that Nicodemus brought, then laid Jesus in a new tomb. Although both these men had not openly been disciples, by asking Pilate for Jesus' body and preparing it for burial, they showed their new beginning as courageous followers.

The new life that Jesus offers to create within us through His Holy Spirit is a result of our faith in Him. Even as our outer body deteriorates, nothing can harm our new inner spirit. At any time, at any age, we can be born again by repenting of our sins and accepting Jesus as our Savior.

A good friend of mine teaches Bible study to prison inmates, and she gave me the written testimony of a woman named Sue, who experienced new life as a result of my friend's ministry. Sue had been abandoned by her mother when she was eighteen months old, and she was left with her father, who was involved in the drug world and was in and out of prison. "I never knew security and stability in my life, but I longed for it," she wrote. "I've never known anything other than the life I was shown." And that life of drugs landed her in prison.

Through the prison ministry, however, Sue learned about Jesus and accepted His forgiveness, giving Him her life in return. "The transformation taking place in me blows my mind at times, because He's changing me from the *inside*," she wrote. "I've had to be tough and hard for so long in order just to survive, but I feel different now. My thoughts are not the same, things that used to be important aren't important anymore. I have hope today, and it's like nothing I've ever known. I'm excited—there's so much more I want to know and learn about Christ. It's my heart's desire to be the person He created me to be, and I want my children to be able to look up to me. I pray that God will have His way in my life and break the vicious cycle of my bondage to drugs, so that my children will never choose the destructive path I chose. Now I know my life is worth saving. I've laughed and cried from the joy I feel deep down inside."

Whatever you are going through or have been through, Jesus offers new life and a chance to start over. Paul told the Ephesians, "You were taught, with regard to your former way of life, to put off your old self, which is being corrupted by its deceitful desires; to be made new in the attitude of your minds; and to put on the new self, created to be like God in true righteousness and holiness." (Ephesians 4:22-23) Jesus provides the strength to "put on the new" each day.

SOUL THERAPY

Creator of every new beginning,
Please forgive me for those times
When I have failed to trust Your transforming power,
When I consider anyone's situation hopeless,
When I feel too set in my own ways to change.
You are the God of grace
And of every second chance.
Help me to deliver that message to a lost world.

WORK OUT
Flexibility stretches promote good circulation, which in turn nourishes new cells that are continually being created. Gently try these hamstring stretches: sit with both legs stretched out in front of you, inhale and lift your arms up toward the ceiling to make a straight "L" with your body. Then, as you exhale, reach toward your toes until you feel a slight stretch. Then inhale and return to the "L" position. Repeat fifteen times.

JOURNAL
Have you given up on someone else or on yourself? Write 2 Cor. 5:17 in your journal, and pray its fulfillment for that person or yourself.

Laughter

BODY BASIC

Human beings are the only species capable of intelligent laughter, and children laugh more often than adults. Laughing increases heart activity and exercises not only the diaphragm, but also abdominal, respiratory and facial muscles. It releases endorphins, our "feel good" hormones, and boosts our immune system, too.

SPIRITUAL SPECIFIC

"He will yet fill your mouth with laughter and your lips with shouts of joy." (JOB 8:21)

Laughing not only adds to our enjoyment of life, but also reduces stress hormones, which have a bad effect on our immunity. In the 1960s, Norman Cousins used comedy and laughter to help heal him from disease, and he wrote a book called *Laughter Therapy*. Whether or not laughter is actually healing, it is "good medicine" because it makes us feel better.

In Scripture, both the aged Abraham and Sarah laughed when God told them they'd have a baby. (Abraham was one hundred and Sarah in her nineties when Isaac was born.) At God's initial announcement, Abraham fell on his face and laughed in temporary disbelief. Sarah laughed to herself saying, "After I am worn out and my master is old, will I now have this pleasure?" They named their child Isaac, which means "he laughs." After Isaac's birth, Sarah exulted, "God has brought me laughter, and everyone who hears about this will laugh with me." (Genesis 21:6)

My friend Janice, who loves to laugh, cried for days after her cancer diagnosis. "I wasn't crying so much for myself as for my husband," she said. "He recently had lost a lot of people close to him, and even though I was ready if the Lord wanted to take me, I hoped I wouldn't have to leave my husband.

"Even though I was sad, confused and frightened by the cancer, my faith was strong. I was finally able to pray, 'If you've let this come on us, Lord, it must be very important. Help me every day to see the opportunities You are bringing me to share about You or help someone I might not otherwise think of.'" She expected it to be a time when she would do something for God. But instead, He did something for her.

"I knew God loved me, but He showed me how He can *pour* His love on us when we don't expect it—in small and big ways, He demonstrated to me how He cares about every single thing that He lets touch us. But His biggest surprise was what He did for me when I had to lie perfectly still on an MRI table for forty-five minutes. The nurse and doctor kept reminding me not to move so that they could precisely mark the tumor spots, and I was praying, 'Lord, help me stay still.' I really was afraid I couldn't hold the uncomfortable position for that long. I was saying scripture and singing in my head with my eyes closed, listening to the nurse's reminder warnings when suddenly—and I wasn't dreaming—I saw two angels in brilliantly colored outfits with unbelievable headdresses, and they were *dancing*! I was so astonished. God had never tried to entertain me before! I didn't want to open my eyes and lose the delightful, joyful scene. My heart was full of laughter, and the time flew by. The procedure was over before I knew it."

Janice had many other experiences of God's unexpected kindnesses as she recovered from cancer, but she remembers the funny one best. An artist, she said, "I've tried to paint that picture of the dancing angels, but I can't capture the brilliance or the joy. So I just keep it in my head. It still makes me laugh. It brings alive Jesus' promise, 'Blessed are you who weep now, for you will laugh.'" (Luke 6:21)

SOUL THERAPY

Lord of laughter and joy,
Let me laugh at myself and with You.
And if I'm overwhelmed with grief or fear,
If I'm battling disease or depression,
Remind me that one day I will laugh again.

WORK OUT
Rent a funny movie, read some jokes or get together with a friend who makes you laugh.

JOURNAL
Do you think God has a sense of humor? Describe in your journal where and how you see it.

The Right Stuff

BODY BASIC
Billions of bacteria live in the intestines and play a crucial role in digestion. These "friendly" bacteria dwell with yeast and other organisms in the digestive system, and if balanced, they help keep the body healthy. However, with an overgrowth of certain yeast, the resulting imbalance can cause problems not only in the digestive system, but in the mouth as "thrush," and in the throat, sinuses, skin and other areas.

SPIRITUAL SPECIFIC
"Be careful," Jesus said to them. "Be on your guard against the yeast of the Pharisees and the Sadducees." (MATTHEW 16: 6)

In the Bible, yeast or leaven is usually used in a negative sense, symbolizing sin, false teaching and hypocrisy. During the Jews' Passover festival commemorating God's protection from the death-plague in Egypt, Jews followed God's orders to get rid of all the yeast in their houses. They diligently swept, so that no trace of old yeast could be found. In the New

Testament, Paul spoke of the old yeast as "the yeast of malice and wickedness." He told the Corinthians, "Therefore let us keep the Festival, not with the old yeast...but with bread without yeast, the bread of sincerity and truth." (1 Corinthians 5:8)

The Bible points out that we are also to beware of man's "yeast" of sin, which can corrupt entire groups if not held in check. "A little yeast leavens the whole lump," Paul warns. (Galatians 5:9)

However, in one instance in the Bible, Jesus describes the right kind of leaven: God's kind. He used it as a symbol of growth in a person's life, growth in the right way, saying, "The kingdom of heaven is like yeast that a woman took and mixed into a large amount of flour until it worked all through the dough." (Matthew 13:33) Whether good or bad, yeast works its way through the entire lump.

Like leaven, one person's sin can permeate an entire family. In our family, one member's alcoholism brought pain, sorrow and loss to each of us. The alcoholic—a generous, loving, Christian—allowed his disease of alcoholism to rule his life, and it began ruling ours as well.

Unknowingly, we became "ill" too, with wrong thinking and habits that helped protect him from the consequences of his drinking, enabling him to continue his behavior. The disease finally flattened him in his later years, and he was forced to accept help at a rehabilitation unit. As family, we went for help, too. And that was a permanent turning point. When our alcoholic gave up the "sin yeast" and allowed "God's leaven" to take over, along with the support of family and Alcoholics Anonymous, he was lifted with the rest of us out of the pit. God infused us with forgiveness, and healing began permeating our family instead of hurt and resentment.

Although for the rest of his life our alcoholic was in recovery, and it was difficult to banish our fears of a relapse, we learned to "let go" and let God take control of every situation. And He faithfully filled us with His peace as He worked things out.

SOUL THERAPY

Bread of Heaven,
In the lumps of life,
I need Your leaven to hold me up.
Knead your love, truth and power all through me
Until they replace my discouragement, fears and bad habits.
Please forgive me of every sin
And remove every crumb of the wrong kind of yeast from my life.
Fill me instead with You.

WORK OUT
For a healthy digestive system, eat some yogurt with active yogurt cultures as you read about life by the Spirit in Galatians 5:16-6:2.

JOURNAL
List some things that permeate your life. Which ones should you "beware" of, and which should you intentionally cultivate?

Love

BODY BASIC
Brain research has shown that the brain region that is most active in early romantic love is the area associated with motivation and reward as well as basic human drives, such as hunger and thirst. Being newly in love involves a different brain system than the one that is specific to lust or long-term attachment.

SPIRITUAL SPECIFIC
"I have loved you with an everlasting love; I have drawn you with loving-kindness." (JEREMIAH 31:3)

God created human beings with a need to love and be loved that is as basic as hunger and thirst. And although human love can fail and disappoint us, God assures us that *His* love is everlasting. "God *is* love," John says twice. (1 John 4:8,16) And He first loved us. Nothing in all creation "will be able to separate us from the love of God that is in Christ Jesus our Lord." (Romans 8:38) God's love is in and behind all of His dealings with us, even when, from our perspective, bad things happen.

The Bible reaffirms that, saying God knows you by name. You are graven on the palms of His hands. You are never out of His mind. He sacrificed His only Son to save you. "This is love: not that we loved God, but that He loved us and sent His Son as an atoning sacrifice for our sins." (1 John 4:10)

God's love story in the Bible reveals His relationship with His chosen people, Israel, who alternately loved Him, receiving blessings, then rejected Him with tragic consequences. The final spurning of God came when people crucified His Son, their Messiah, Jesus. Nevertheless, that brutal ending could not extinguish God's powerful compassion. Christ rose from the dead and opens the door to eternal life for all who turn to Him and believe.

And every believer is told to share God's love. "As I have loved you, so you must love one another," Jesus told His disciples. (John 13:34) Nevertheless, a human being's imperfect love falls far short of God's.

Two of my husband's and my friends, Janet and her husband, were committed Christians who had been married thirty-two years. Janet had never expected their devotion to collapse. When her husband came home one day and told her he didn't want to be married anymore, she was unprepared and devastated. She spent days weeping and then feeling furious. "When your mate has an affair, it is rejection to the nth degree," she said. "It's a whole different category of hurt. I lay on the floor feeling sick and crying, 'God, I don't want this!' I had read in 1 Corinthians 13 that love never fails, and I said angrily to God, 'Love has failed me *big time!*' The next morning, though, I woke up and realized it is **God's** love that never fails. And it was God's love during those awful days that brought me much closer to Him."

Janet wrote out her feelings of fury and despair in a journal, expressed them to a Christian counselor, and then prayerfully watched for and listened to God.

"God used my circumstances to bring about things I never expected," she said. "While I was grieving, He restored a broken relationship with another family member. While my self-esteem suffered, He said, 'You can do this' and gave me the self-confidence to seek a new job. He eased my feeling of abandonment by deepening my relationship with my daughters and providing encouraging people to help me. And He continues to console me with His own comfort and strength, which I can *feel*."

Janet now is successfully at work in a new job, and she takes one day at a time, secure in God's unfailing love and growing in her own for Him.

SOUL THERAPY

Everlasting Lover of my soul,
Please help me through my heartache!
Remind me that I'm never alone.
And when I feel empty,
Pour Your forgiveness and love into me.
Please wipe away my sorrow,
And show me once again
That my future and my hope lie with You.

WORK OUT
Express your love or share God's love with someone today by word or deed.

JOURNAL
Write down ways in which God has demonstrated His love to you. Then write a love note back to God.

Strength
In Weakness

BODY BASIC
*Chronic pain, disability,
depression and feelings of
powerlessness often occur together.*

**SPIRITUAL
SPECIFIC**
*"My grace is sufficient
for you, for my power is made
perfect in weakness."* (2 COR. 12: 9)

The Apostle Paul had some sort of "thorn" in his flesh, an ailment that plagued him so severely that he called it "a messenger of Satan to torment me." Paul relates, "Three times I pleaded with the Lord to take it away from me, but He said to me, 'My grace is sufficient for you, for My power is made perfect in weakness.' Therefore I will boast all the more gladly about my weaknesses, so that Christ's power may rest on me. That is why, for Christ's sake, I delight in weaknesses...hardships...difficulties. For when I am weak, then I am strong." (2 Cor. 8-10)

Like Paul, many of us at some time have pleaded for God to remove our (or another's) thorn of pain or sickness. When His answer seems to be "no" or "wait," it's hard to imagine how God can use that trial for a good purpose. It is even tougher to delight in that difficulty. Most of us would rather live in a thorn- and burden-free Eden, instead of a wayward world where trouble and misery have taken root.

However, man's sinfulness and God's resulting curse did not thwart His objectives for His people. He uses the very curse of pain to help *restore* us into His image. Through trials, Paul explains, we are being "conformed to the likeness of His Son which is God's highest goal for His people." (Romans 8:29)

In *A Daily Word*, Ron Hutchcraft wrote that hurting develops in us a more Jesus-like sensitivity to others. Difficulties make us more patient. "You can't learn peace without some pressure. You can't learn faith without needs that are bigger than your ability to meet them. If you're going to get the pain, you might as well get the point! And that is to make you more like Jesus."

As I've struggled with the discomfort of disc deterioration in my neck and back, I've felt God developing in me some much-needed patience and perseverance. My empathy for others has deepened, too. Frustrating physical limitations have forced me to prayerfully rely on God to accomplish things I'm unable to do. And He has come to the rescue—sometimes sending helpers from out of the blue to get a job done. Even though I don't delight in my physical restrictions, I do appreciate how God has built my trust in Him through them. I can't help but see His strength when mine is gone.

And I've begun looking for other ways God might be using my pain. Could my purpose in the therapy pool be not only to strengthen my back, but also to share His Good News with some new friends there? Is my deepened empathy to be used to encourage others by listening to them? Can I help build another's faith by telling what God is doing in the midst of my inadequacies? I've decided to look for ways that I can cooperate with God so that His power is made perfect in my weakness.

SOUL THERAPY

Lord, pain often hobbles me
And interferes with things I want to do,
Including serving You.
But nothing gets in Your way.
So I pray Your power will be perfected in my weakness.
Let Your grace be sufficient for me,
And help me reflect that grace to others,
Even as I struggle to understand Your purposes.

WORK OUT

Turn on your favorite music to lift your spirits and gently move your body in rhythm. Or do this reaching exercise to the beat: stand arm's length away from a wall, then take half a step back. Feet shoulder width apart, abs tight, reach forward with the right hand straight ahead and touch the wall ten times, reach to the right about ten inches and touch the wall ten times, then to the left about ten inches. Repeat with the left hand.

JOURNAL

What is your "thorn in the flesh?" Write your thoughts about how God can use it to showcase His strength or to make you more like Christ.

Time Is Ticking

BODY BASIC
Using MRI techniques that track second-by-second shifts in brain activity, researchers have identified areas in the brain responsible for perceiving the passage of time. Our grasp of time is an important part of our sensory system, allowing us to respond smoothly to our world. We use it in everything from driving a car to catching a ball. A person's internal time-keeping system can be impaired by stroke, diseases or disorders, which can cause the person to greatly underestimate time's progression. If the brain's timing circuits are functioning well, however, we are capable of managing that precious resource to our advantage.

SPIRITUAL SPECIFIC
"For it is time to seek the Lord." (HOSEA 10:12)

*W*e *consciously and unconsciously operate by time.* However, God, who created time with the rising and setting of the sun, has no need of it. To the great I AM, there is no past or future; He lives in the eternal *now* and remains in control of all things, including time.

God displays His control over time in scripture. In 2 Kings (20:8-11) He moved the shadow backward ten steps on the stairway of Ahaz as a sign to King Hezekiah that He would heal him of a deadly disease. And, to help Joshua, God stopped the sun in the middle of the sky for a full day, until Israel could defeat her enemies.(Joshua 10:13) In other scripture, God set a time for certain things to take place—such as births or plagues or the ending of Israel's slavery—and everything happened just as He timed it.

King David was well aware that his days had been numbered by God. He prayed "Show me, O Lord, my life's end and the number of my days; let me know how fleeting is my life." (Psalm 39:5) David knew each man's time to exist is a "mere handbreadth" in God's eyes. Since today is the only day any of us possesses, a later psalm advises, "let us rejoice and be glad in it." Only God knows how many todays will be ours.

My friend Clay was in his forties, an involved husband and dad of four children, when his "today" was shattered by a diagnosis of kidney cancer. "When I got the news on the phone, I was alone," Clay told me, "And I felt instant fear—not the kind of fear when someone has a gun pointed at you, but a fear like you have already been shot! I said, 'Lord I'm not ready for this! Please help me!'"

God did. Clay saw help come through a friend who got him into immediate surgery to remove the diseased kidney. Afterward, Clay was given a clean bill of health, and in the following years, he grew in his walk with God. He underwent scans frequently to watch for any return of cancer. Nine years later, he still appeared healthy. "But doctors were mostly scanning and hunting in certain areas where experience had taught them the cancer might return. And the system wasn't foolproof—cancer can go anywhere," Clay said. "They failed to check my hip, and that's where they finally found it." It had been there long enough to metastasize into my lungs and pancreas. And the doctor said there was no cancer treatment for the pancreas."

Despite the medical failure, Clay didn't feel bitter or even quite as terrified as he had been the first time, "But I was really, really disappointed about the mistake. I told the Lord I appreciated all the years He'd given me and asked for His help in decision-making now. I did not want to make any decisions out of fear. And I didn't want to chase after life unless it was life with quality. I was afraid, but it wasn't a fear that took over. I'd been growing in my faith, and I knew that Jesus would enable me to walk down any road with Him."

Clay's wife, Martha, mobilized a prayer chain and began researching alternative treatments for Clay as he went through an experimental freezing of the main tumor in his hip. "Martha's prayer chain grew to involve almost every denomination—Mormon, Baptist, Catholic—people from California to Florida to Muleshoe, Texas! I didn't even know them, and they were praying for me! I was awestruck by their love and faith. That has been the biggest blessing in my life. Not only has God been a Friend through all this, but He's shown me that getting strength from others is a good thing, too. And Martha continues to help me build my faith along with hers."

Nevertheless, the "cancer monster" grabs them on occasion, and "sometimes Martha will just hold me and say, 'You can't leave me!' And when the monster grabs me, I open my Bible and read. I need God's word especially in those moments. I like the verse 'I can do all things through Christ who strengthens me.' That's a verse for all things in life, not just life-threatening ones.

"Most people never think 'this may be my last day,'" he continued. "But, time has become very precious to me. I have more peace and joy than I once did. I try to walk the way I should walk, to be more loving, to enjoy my wife, kids and grandkids, and to be thankful for every beautiful day. God is helping me look up more than I ever have before, to see things His way, and I've seen Jesus everywhere. I couldn't go through this battle without Him, but with Him I can."

At last report, Clay's screenings showed the tumors had been reduced with the alternative treatments. He lives fully with abiding hope, enjoying each precious moment.

SOUL THERAPY

My Creator, when You entered life as man,
You split time and history in two.
And by Your death and resurrection,
You opened the way for us into Your timeless Kingdom.
Thank You!
Please help me to live out my days on earth
With abiding peace and a servant-heart.
Walk with me every second,
Making each minute count,
Until You welcome me into your glorious, eternal now.

WORK OUT
Read a little about heaven in
Hebrews 12: 22-24 and John 14:1-4.

JOURNAL
What are you looking forward to
in God's kingdom of heaven?

Leg Work

BODY BASIC
The leg muscles are among the largest and strongest in the body, and the thigh bone is the strongest and biggest of our bones. The thigh muscles are especially powerful, because, unlike our four-legged friends, we depend on them to hold the body upright against gravity's force.

SPIRITUAL SPECIFIC
"His pleasure is not in the strength of the horse, nor his delight in the legs of a man; the Lord delights in those who fear him, who put their hope in his unfailing love." (PSALM 147:10-11)

In biblical times, people's legs carried them great distances in obedience and service to God. Abraham walked away from all that was familiar to go where God told him to go, and that obedience and faith made him God's friend. Moses led the Israelites across the parted Red Sea to freedom, and that miracle brought the nation of Israel closer to God. Jesus walked everywhere during his earthly mission, and He healed those who were lame. Steven used his strong legs to run alongside a eunuch's chariot, and when he explained the Good News to the eunuch, the man asked to be baptized then and there.

Legs carried people the wrong way, too—the prophet Jonah ran *from* God rather than obey Him, and he was swallowed by a great fish. Most of Jesus' disciples fled in terror when He was arrested.

Our legs can carry us closer to or away from God. He tells believers to walk humbly with Him and not to walk in our own ways or after other gods, not to walk in lies or lusts or the customs of men. But He leaves the choice to us.

Doris, whom I met at a Christmas bazaar where our booths were side by side, lost most of the use of her legs from polio. She told me she contracted the disease when she was six months old and has been in leg braces and on crutches all her life. But she has never let her disability stop her. With her husband, she raised a family and worked full time. In mid-life, however, she fell and tore a rotator cuff, and even though she had two shoulder surgeries, she could no longer use her crutches. She was confined to a wheelchair. "It's hard and frustrating," she admitted, "But the way I've always dealt with my limitations is to focus on what I *can* do."

From her booth she was selling the pictures she paints in her spare time as well as stationery and cards made from her artwork. She uses her cards to send notes of encouragement to others. "You have to look outside of yourself instead of looking in at your limitations," she says. "Thinking of others helps you. If you help other people, you'll always find something useful to do."

She likes to "keep an ear out," for others' needs so she can help meet them. "I don't try to save the world," she said. "I just try to brighten someone's day."

Doris has found her faith walk doesn't require legs. Her hands and heart are all she needs to reach out to others and to God. Reading her Bible daily she also says, "I write in a daily prayer journal. Then, when I go back and look through it, it's amazing to see how God has blessed me." When Doris prays, she ends with this: "God, I pray for a generous spirit, a grateful heart, and since I'll never be graceful, I pray to be gracious."

SOUL THERAPY

Lord, please carry me
Over all life's hurdles.
Empower me to do my appointed "legwork" for Your kingdom,
So that no matter what shape I'm in physically,
I can walk in Your ways and reach others with Your love.

WORK OUT
To strengthen thighs, do "squats," beginning by standing with your feet hip-width apart. With your arms at your sides and palms in, slowly squat until your thighs are almost parallel to the floor. Keep your head up and shoulders back. Then return to standing position and repeat.

JOURNAL
Look back over your prayers and entries in the first of your journal and see what God has done to strengthen your walk with Him.

Christril In You

BODY BASIC
*The inner workings
of the human cell can only be
seen with a high-powered microscope.
Magnification reveals each cell
contains a "powerhouse"—super-minute
mitochondria that fuel each of our
body's trillions of cells.*

**SPIRITUAL
SPECIFIC**
*"The mystery in a
nutshell is just this: Christ
is in you...You do not need a
telescope, a microscope or a
horoscope to realize the fullness
of Christ, and the emptiness
of the universe without Him.*

(COLOSSIANS. 2 MSG)

*A*s a believer in Christ, your fuel or "powerhouse" is the invisible Holy Spirit who dwells in you. He is *Christ in you.* When the Holy Spirit descended on Christ at His baptism, He came in the earthly form of a dove. When He entered the disciples after Jesus' resurrection, He appeared as "tongues of fire." Today, however, we don't see Him; we only experience the results of His indwelling, such as love, joy, peace, patience, kindness, godliness, etc.

In the Old Testament, the Holy Spirit was given only temporarily to people to empower them, and sometimes was taken away because of sin, as in King Saul's case. Since Christ, however, believers have permanently been given the Holy Spirit as our Counselor, Comforter and Spirit of Truth. Jesus said, "If you then, though you are evil, know how to give good gifts to your children, how much more will your Father in heaven give the Holy Spirit to those who ask Him!" (Luke 11:13).

The Bible describes what the Holy Spirit does: He groans in prayer with each of us. He empowers us, gives us wisdom and knowledge, loves and leads us, comforts us, and more. He dwells within us, making our body His temple. The Holy Spirit was the power that brought Jesus back to life.

God the Father, God the Son, and God the Holy Spirit are One and make up the Holy Trinity. That confusing concept is a "holy mystery." But to my mother, it was an unbelievable idea. Mom prayed to God, and she believed Jesus was a wonderful man. But, she didn't believe in Christ's deity, resurrection or miracles. "How could I, when I had never read the Bible or had anyone explain it to me?" she asked.

So, while Dad took my brothers and me to church, Mom stayed home. She finally decided she should join the church, too, since worshiping together as a family seemed like "the right thing to do." But, to join our denomination, she had to attend confirmation classes and be baptized. "I wanted to believe, but confirmation classes were mostly church history, and I never got the answers I needed," she said. "Baptism seemed unnecessary, because I thought I was already 'saved.' But I agreed to the ritual for my family's sakes, so I could join their church and be with them.

"I had always been honest, and I knew I would have to lie—in *church*—when I answered 'yes' to the question 'Dost thou believe in Jesus the Christ...' So I prayed for forgiveness as I stood with the priest and my family in a private baptism ceremony. As I stood there anguishing, asking forgiveness, listening to words that meant nothing to me, like 'Receive her, O Lord, as Thou has promised by Thy well-beloved Son...' suddenly it happened!

"I began to vibrate. I was filled with an electric surge of energy that pulsed through my bloodstream, and in that remarkable instant, I knew it was all *true*! The whole fantastic, unbelievable, miraculous truth. Christ's very presence was coursing through my body. He was part of me, and I was instantly part of Him. Nothing like that had ever happened to me; yet I knew what it was; I *knew*! Nothing showed outwardly—my hands were still steady on my prayer book. But my life totally and completely changed!"

Our entire family's life changed, too, because Mom's passionate new faith brought us all closer to Christ. And it has been He who has fueled us through every triumph and trial of life.

SOUL THERAPY

My Powerhouse, You are life.
And You make me a part of You when I ask You into my heart.
Thank You for opening the door to Yourself when I knock.
Thank You for fueling me
With Your "rich store of salvation and wisdom and knowledge."

WORK OUT
Treat your body, the Holy Spirit's temple, to whatever makes you feel better, whether it is rest, exercise, or a hot bath. Also, fuel yourself by reading1 John 14: 4.

JOURNAL
Record what it means to you that Christ lives inside you. How will that affect how you live today?

Motherhood

BODY BASIC
A pregnant woman's body provides nourishment as well as oxygen for the developing life within her, and also disposes of its waste products. Her antibodies help protect the embryo from bacteria. Once a baby is born, the mother's breasts produce a high-protein fluid with her antibodies in it called colostrum. Two to three days later, she begins manufacturing milk, which sustains the child's life.

SPIRITUAL SPECIFIC
"Near the cross of Jesus stood his mother..." (JOHN 19:34)

*T*he female is designed to carry and nourish* developing human life. In the beginning of time, Eve became "the mother of all the living." The Bible relates many stories of mothers, and in them we see motherhood producing more than children—it also results in joy, grief, jealousy, pride, rivalry, miracles and more.

In ancient times, barrenness was seen as a stigma, and many childless women agonized in prayer to overcome it. One of them was Hannah, wife of Elkanah. "In bitterness of soul Hannah wept much and prayed to the Lord. And she made a vow, saying that if God would give her a son, 'then I will give him to the Lord for all the days of his life....'" Hannah conceived and named her son Samuel. He became a great prophet who took God's word to Israel.

The Virgin Mary knew that her Son was God's, miraculously conceived. And when she and Joseph took Him to the Temple as a baby, she heard the troubling prophecy from Simeon that "a sword will pierce your own soul, too." But she never wavered from her nurturing, protective mothering. She stayed by Jesus' side until His last breath.

Whether or not a child is biologically our own, motherhood can bring great rewards and joy, but also a sword—agony over a rebellious child, distress over an injured child, or trauma with a victimized child. We grieve over a lost child and endure heartache because of a child's addiction or unhappiness. We're concerned for a handicapped child, and suffer when a child rejects our love. Childlessness, too, brings sorrow to those who wish for children. But whatever sadness we face, our God longs to nestle us close to Him, "as a hen gathers her chicks under her wings."

My friend Phyllis had a adult child she adored who became estranged from her after a misunderstanding. Phyllis tried everything she knew to do to patch things up. She contacted her child personally and through letters, prayed unceasingly for reconciliation, and spent a year and a half in a state of "complete emotional drain. Finally God convicted me that I mustn't live that way anymore. When all my emotional energy was taken by pain and regret, I had nothing left for my husband or anyone else. So I made the choice to give those overpowering thoughts and hurt to God and let go. He gave me the courage to do it, and then gave me the peace, strength and grace to get back to daily living."

It's been nine years since Phyllis's child has spoken to her. She prays for that loved one daily. "God has done so much in my life, and my walk with Him is much closer than it was nine years ago. Even though I still cry over my child sometimes, I have been able to regain joy in the midst of heartache. The secret is focusing on Him. He is in the center of my heart. He is my hope, and His hope contains joy."

No matter what happens in an earthly family, each of us believers is part of Christ's intimate family. Christ said, "Whoever does the will of my Father in heaven is my brother and sister and mother." (Matthew 12:49-50) And nothing can ever come between us.

Whatever sword or challenge motherhood may have brought to your heart—or whatever joys—our loving Father is glad to mother *you*, helping, strengthening and nourishing you with hope and wisdom as you carry on.

SOUL THERAPY

When my heart aches, Nurturing One,
And bonds are broken,
Please hear my cries and comfort me.
Restore my joy, even if You choose not to restore a relationship.
And just as You never give up on me,
Help me never to stop praying for those I love.

WORK OUT
If you have a Concordance, look up "mother" and follow trails that interest you about mothers in the Bible. (You can Google Mothers of the Bible, too.)

JOURNAL
Write a list of things you could do with God's help to follow His commandment to honor your mother (whether or not she deserves it) if she is living. If you are a mother, jot down how you could improve your relationship with each child or adult child.

The Perfect Father

BODY BASIC
As many as two hundred million male reproductive cells, or sperm, swim toward an egg to fertilize it, but only one sperm does the job of making a man a father. Once a sperm has fertilized the egg, no others are allowed to penetrate it.

SPIRITUAL SPECIFIC
A father to the fatherless...is God in His holy dwelling." (PSALM 68:5)

When *Abram, whom God re-named Abraham,* received God's promise of fatherhood, God said, "You will be the father of many nations. I will make you very fruitful...kings will come from you." (Gen. 17:4-6)

Jewish lineage was recorded in long biblical lists of forefathers, although an occasional mother was mentioned in some of those. And the request "bury me with my fathers" was common when a man was about to die. In Israel, ancestors were so important that every Jew's record of his lineage was kept safe in the Temple until that holy structure was destroyed in AD 70.

Fathers passed along an important, sometimes fought-over blessing, too. Jacob stole Esau's blessing from his father Isaac by deceiving him, and when Esau found out, he "burst out with a loud and bitter cry and said to his father, 'bless me—me, too, my father!'" Fathers were—and are—living examples of good and bad, blessing and cursing, wisdom and folly, faith and unbelief.

Those who are fatherless have always been of special concern to God, who is "a Father of the fatherless." Joseph was God's chosen adoptive father of Jesus, His Son. God took special care of the orphaned and exiled Esther, too, through her cousin Mordecai. She not only became queen of Persia, but saved her people from extinction.

God, the only perfect Father, is described all through Scripture. In fact, in a Bible Concordance, you'll find nearly five pages of references to "father" and related words. Some of the things God our Father does for us, to us, or in us, are described in various verses: He feeds, knows, sees, forgives, speaks to and prepares His children. He delivers, appoints, answers, seeks, loves and makes promises to us. He raises, judges, seals, sends, honors, sanctifies, glorifies and blesses. He is an involved Father, Who loves each of His wayward children.

Earthly fathers, on the other hand, often disappoint us. Even God's Biblical heroes like David and Solomon failed at being good fathers.

Some fathers abandon their offspring. Others abuse them. Some have expectations that cannot be met by their child, and still others never know or care to know the child they have fathered. But our Heavenly Father offers His healing and blessing to all.

My friend Rob tried hard to live up to his alcoholic father's great expectations. But Rob's efforts—even being Valedictorian of his high school class—were not enough to satisfy his father. Never feeling truly loved, Rob had a skewed relationship with his earthly dad, and that got in the way of his seeking a meaningful relationship with his heavenly Father. In mid-life, through his wife's and his church's influence, Rob finally discovered and accepted Jesus' love and sacrifice for him. And that connection brought him his long-needed sense of worth and blessing. Even though his heart still hurts because of his earthly father's failings, Rob's healing is in the hands of his perfect Father.

God invites us to come to Him and even to call him Abba, "Daddy."

No matter how dysfunctional our family background may be, God offers each of us a new life with Him.

SOUL THERAPY

Abba, I am so grateful for You
And Your unfailing compassion.
Please show me how to be a wise and loving parent,
And help me direct all children into Your welcoming embrace.

WORK OUT
Read from Proverbs, which contains many wise sayings of King Solomon to "my son" about the art of living and reverencing God.

JOURNAL
What are the qualities of a good father? Record ways you could be a godly influence in your own or another child's life.

Hair-Raising Lives

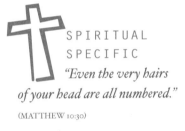

BODY BASIC
The millions of hairs on a person's body come in various sizes and shapes – stiff and short, long and silky, curly and so on—and are some of the fastest growing tissues in the body. Hair can be used to diagnose illness, to help with DNA identification or determine whether we have ingested toxic metals.

SPIRITUAL SPECIFIC
"Even the very hairs of your head are all numbered."
(MATTHEW 10:30)

*I*n Scripture, hair often represented strength, vigor and beauty. Kings and heroic figures were usually described with luxuriant locks. As a sign of grief or mourning, people often shaved their heads along with wearing sackcloth or tearing their clothes. Baldness was uncommon among the ancient Jews, and may have been considered disgraceful. Disrespectful youths taunted the prophet Elisha by jeering, "You baldhead! You baldhead!"

The hero Samson, a judge who was famous for his might, lost that strength when his hair was shaved off as he slept—betrayed by his lover,

Delilah. The importance of his hair was that it symbolized his special commitment to God, who gave him super-human power. Before Samson was born, the angel of God had told his mother, "No razor may be used on his head, because the boy is to be a Nazirite, set apart to God from birth...".

Thick locks of hair were a source of vanity for David's traitorous son Absalom and even caused his death. His hair entangled on a limb of an oak tree as he fled from his enemies on a mule, and his foes killed him as he dangled helpless there.

For women, long hair was considered a "glory." However, they were not to let their hair down in public—only prostitutes did that—and were to cover it when they prayed.

No matter how much hair we do or don't have, our detail-specific God knows its number. He created and cares about the smallest things in our life.

When my church friend Laura was only thirty-four-years-old, she found out she had cancer. As she began chemotherapy, she dreaded the side effect of losing her hair more than anything else. She wasn't sure if God cared about such details, but she asked her praying friends to request that He'd let her keep her hair. She cut it very short, and we prayed that God might encourage her with that little miracle we requested. We were surprised and delighted when He did! Keeping her hair kept Laura encouraged throughout her treatments.

Whether God says "yes" or "no" to a certain request, He still is involved in our situation, working out what He knows to be best in His overall plan. Believers are in His hands, where everything is filtered through His fingers and His love—even persecution.

Jesus warned His disciples that they would suffer persecution, betrayal and death "all on account of My name," but He promised them there would be no spiritual loss. He said, "...not a hair of your head will perish. By standing firm, you will gain [eternal] life."

SOUL THERAPY

Lord, please remind me,
When I'm tangled in life's trials
And feel like "tearing my hair out,"
That You are involved with me in every detail.
Thank You that when I'm knotted up with fear, doubt,
and burdens of every kind,
I can comb through Your word and find reassurance,
And simply ask for Your smoothing hand and know Your peace.

WORK OUT

Give yourself a scalp massage to stimulate hair follicles, while sitting as tall and straight as you can. Breathe deeply as you do it.

JOURNAL

God's omniscience—His knowing every detail about everything in His creation, right down to the number of hairs on our head—is just one of His mind-boggling attributes. List some of the other traits of God that are beyond human comprehension, and then praise Him for who He is.

Partnering In Support

BODY BASIC
An infant's bones are packed with red marrow, which produces both red and white blood cells. But by adulthood, most bones are primarily filled with yellow marrow, which is chiefly fat. Only a few bones still contain substantial amounts of red bone marrow, and among those bones are the twenty-four stacked vertebrae, which make up the supportive spinal column. It's only in partnership that the few red marrow bones can supply enough blood cells to meet the body's needs. If for some reason those bones cannot keep up with the demand, the kidneys send chemical signals to other bones to convert their yellow marrow into red to make up for the deficit.

SPIRITUAL SPECIFIC
"...So laboring, ye ought to support the weak..."

(ACTS. 20:35 KJV)

God designed the body with ways to support and take care of it-self. "The body is a unit, though it is made up of many parts," Paul says in 1 Corinthians 12. "If one part suffers, every part suffers with it; if one part is honored, every part rejoices with it. Now you are the body of Christ, and each one of you is a part of it."

While Jesus was present on earth, He brought together disciples that would act as His body when He left, upholding and helping each other as they carried His Good News to the world. And although He continually drew power from His Father, Jesus was also bolstered by His believing body, those He called His friends. After His death, those faithful friends, under the influence of the Holy Spirit, established the church, Christ's universal body.

As a church pastor, my friend Jordan felt it was his duty to comfort and support others, but he was reluctant to ask for help for himself. So when it came time to move his family into their new home, he attempted to do it without assistance. In the process, he injured his back, unknowingly breaking a vertebrae. Nevertheless, he continued on in pain until a second vertebrae snapped. The agony forced him to the doctor. Then, as Jordan tried to get off the physician's examining table, a third vertebrae crumbled. In pain-wracked misery, he returned home to a hospital bed and awaited the back surgery "to glue the pieces of my vertebrae together."

In the meantime, doctors diagnosed the reason for his trouble. He was in a late stage of a blood cancer called multiple myeloma, which was de-stroying the strength of his bones. "I got sicker and weaker, and it was a frightening time. My daughter was about to get married, and I didn't know if I'd live until the wedding," he said. "I was distraught!"

After surgery, Jordan and his wife Barbara drove from Texas to a spe-cialty cancer center in Arkansas for treatment. "As I went through the treatments, our church, friends and family, Barbara's class of first-graders and even my doctor and his children were praying for me. I had always been a 'do-it-yourself' man, but now my total dependence gave me a much greater appreciation for helping hands, prayers, and the people behind them. I had an army of spiritual support.

"I believe prayer is where the miracles take place," he said. "I became so aware of what a pleasure it is to be part of the body of Christ that sev-eral times I literally wept for joy when I was able to return to church. I had been the leader in the pulpit, and now my congregation was ministering to me. I discovered we're not meant to be self-sufficient. Difficulties teach us what love is and how much we need God and each other."

Jordan's body responded to the chemotherapy, and his cancer is in remission. He was able to walk his daughter down the aisle, and five years later was at his other daughter's bedside as she gave birth to his second grandchild.

SOUL THERAPY

Intricate Designer,
Thank You for the many astonishing ways
The body makes changes
So it can provide for its various parts in need.
And thank You that when I am crushed in body or spirit,
You and Your people dispense what I need.
Please let that love, wisdom and encouragement
Penetrate to the very marrow of my bones.

WORK OUT

To strengthen back muscles, get on your hands and knees on the floor. Tighten your abdominal muscles, then lift your right arm out straight and hold it five seconds. Put the right arm down and lift the left arm out straight for five seconds. With both hands down and abs still tight, stretch the right leg out straight behind you and lift it slightly, with your toes just brushing the floor. Hold for five seconds. Return to the hands-and-knees position and then do the same slight raise with the left leg

JOURNAL

Tell what being part of the body of Christ means to you.

Filled With What?

BODY BASIC

Alcoholism is a chronic disease in which the body becomes physically dependent on alcohol. The balance of brain chemicals is so affected by the excessive use of alcohol that withdrawal symptoms—tremors, seizures and even death—can occur when the alcohol is withheld. Genes may play a role in alcoholism, because studies show that the disease runs in families; the child of an alcoholic is four times more likely to become an alcoholic than the child of a non-alcoholic, even when raised in a non-drinker's home. Although there is no cure, alcoholics begin "recovering" when they stop drinking alcoholic substances.

SPIRITUAL SPECIFIC

"Do not get drunk on wine, which leads to debauchery. Instead, be filled with the Spirit." (EPHESIANS 5:18)

*N*oah, who walked righteously with God, spent a hundred years building the ark that would save him, his family and many animals from the flood that God sent to destroy the wicked people on earth. After riding out the storm and spending more than a year aboard the ark, Noah and his family finally stepped out onto dry land. First, Noah built an altar and sacrificed to God. Then this "man of the soil" proceeded to plant a vineyard. And when the vineyard produced, Noah got drunk on its wine. (Genesis 9:21) In this first biblical reference to wine, Noah's drunkenness not only disgraced him, but started problems in his family.

Wine, which purified water in ancient times and flowed freely during celebrations, had its proper place, in moderation. God never outlawed the drinking of wine—Jesus drank it and even created it from water—but He had particular commands about its use. God instructed Aaron and his sons, who were priests, not to drink wine or other fermented drink when they came into the Tent of Meeting, or they would die. God said to Aaron, "You must distinguish between the holy and the common, between the unclean and the clean, and you must teach the Israelites...."

Jesus said in a parable that the faithful servant should be waiting and watching for the Master, not abusing his privileges and getting drunk. The Corinthians in the early church were taken to task by Paul for abusing wine during the Lord's supper—"One remains hungry while another gets drunk"—and he reminded them to come in a worthy manner to the Lord's holy table.

Proverbs 24: 19-20 says: "Listen my son, and be wise, and keep your heart on the right path. Do not join those who drink too much wine..."

My friend Marcus, who attended my university, joined with lots of other college kids who drank too much. "We did it for relaxation, escape and fun," he said. Drinking hard and partying were common, so he didn't believe he had a problem. Later in life, however, destructive drinking habits finally landed him in a miserable place: "I didn't even want to keep on living, but I was too scared to die," he said.

His wife had "one foot out the door," when he finally admitted he needed help. He turned to the support group Alcoholics Anonymous. "Once I stopped drinking, I was scared I was going to break again," Marcus said. "But other AA members and God kept me going. I had to surrender. I had to admit powerlessness. I had to give control of my life to God, even when things were going well.

"I still carry some cards with sayings that helped me focus," he continued. "One says, 'Love the Lord and allow Him to love back—stay close.' Another says, 'This, too, shall pass.' A third one reminds me to laugh, another says to expect a miracle, and another says, 'Trust—let go and let God.' I've found that my faith isn't a luxury, it's a necessity. I'm dependent on God. And when I turned to Him every single day in devotion and prayer, I found strength 'one day at a time' for what is now twenty years of sobriety."

His time in the Bible and prayer brought Marcus into a life-changing relationship with Christ, and he said, "My battle with alcoholism has turned out to be one of my greatest blessings. It's brought me closer to God, and I try to never begin a day without praying to Him. It's my goal to serve, please, and honor Him—and I know I've still got a long way to go. But I have another saying that keeps me from losing heart: 'Progress, not perfection.'"

SOUL THERAPY

Sweet Jesus,
Pour Your Spirit upon me,
So that I'm filled with the delight of You,
Rather than the destructive pleasures of excess.
Please forgive me when I misuse anything You've created.
And, Lord, when I'm caught up in the turmoil of someone's alcoholism,
Give me wisdom to do the right thing.
Enable me to share Your love, grace and healing strength.

WORK OUT

The Bible advises us to be filled with the Spirit, which comes from Christ. Read Isaiah 42:1-12, which is prophesying Jesus and telling us in advance that He will free captives and "release from the dungeon those who sit in darkness."

JOURNAL

Write out a prayer for yourself or anyone you know who sits in darkness because of a drinking problem, and ask God to put that person's life on the right path.

Mind Over Matters

BODY BASIC
Because the body and mind constantly interact, emotions such as fear are whole-body experiences. Although everyone feels anxious or fearful in certain situations, extreme anxiety, panic disorders or phobias can disrupt a life. A phobia is a drastic, ongoing, irrational fear that compels a person to avoid the feared thing—such as fear of crowds, agoraphobia, or fear of closed spaces, claustrophobia. Although we can't prevent strong feelings, the brain's frontal lobes can help us gain control over how we express them, enabling us to plan and initiate our responses. And therapists have found that one way to effectively subdue panic attacks is with self-calming talk.

SPIRITUAL SPECIFIC
"So do not fear, for I am with you; do not be dismayed, for I am your God. I will strengthen you and help you; I will uphold you with My righteous right hand."

(ISAIAH 41:10)

*F*ear has plagued mankind since The Fall. Elijah the prophet, who is one of Israel's most famous heroes, was a faith-filled man who became fear-filled. (The story is in 1 Kings 18-19.) In the beginning, Elijah boldly followed God's instructions and defied evil King Ahab. The prophet confidently trusted God when he stood alone in a contest against 450 prophets of Baal. But, even after witnessing countless displays of God's power, Elijah ran for his life and hid in dread of one woman, Queen Jezebel, Ahab's wicked wife.

Nevertheless, God spoke to His cowering prophet and encouraged him by another show of His powerful presence, revealing His sovereign plan, and giving Elijah the promise of success. Emboldened, Elijah set out again and carried out God's orders.

Whether facing an outside threat or an inner fear, anxiety can limit life, and my massage therapist, Teresa, felt it limiting hers. She suffered from a lifelong terror, which she wanted to overcome. As a child, she had nearly drowned, and her dread of water had grown as she matured. When she watched the movie "Titanic" for the third time with her grandchildren, she felt herself hyperventilating. "I could tell my anxiety about water was getting worse," she said. "It was keeping me from doing something I'd always wanted to do: go on a cruise. I knew that the way I felt, I could never go." Determined to conquer her fear, she signed up for private swim lessons. Then she booked her cruise.

With her instructor in the shallow water, Teresa learned to float and swim well by the fourth lesson. But when it was time to cross the black line dividing the shallow from the deep water, she couldn't do it. Time and again, she stroked her way in that direction, but stopped at the line, unable to cross.

For an hour she stared at the sunlight reflecting off the deep water and said to herself, "Look, Jesus is there waiting!" And she heard the instructor's calming voice saying, "I'm right here. Nothing can happen to you." Still Teresa couldn't force herself to do it.

She said, "It was all in my mind. I was physically capable of swimming. I had help beside me. I knew God was with me. But until I could change my *own mind*, push out the dread and re-set my thinking, I was paralyzed when faced with deep water."

She went back to the pool alone for days, reassuring herself of God's help, envisioning herself crossing the line, reminding herself to "Be of good courage."

Finally, at her last lesson, praying with every stroke and claiming God's strength, she was able to at last propel herself across the black line into the sunlight. "It was the most incredible, freeing feeling!" she said. "Once I crossed the line, the fear disappeared." And a month later, she swam in the Caribbean with stingrays!

Whether anxiety is short-term or a serious problem that calls for psychotherapy, every believer has been given a built-in antidote: God Himself, whose name is I AM. When we ask in dismay, "Who is able to help me overcome this fear?" God answers, "I AM." When we wonder apprehensively, "Who is capable of turning around this impossible situation?" God says, "I AM." When we cry out, "Who is with me in this dark night?" God replies, "I AM." He promises to uphold us in His righteous right hand.

SOUL THERAPY

Father, I know that fear is the opposite of faith,
Yet I'm afraid of so many things!
Please help my unbelief.
Calm my racing heart.
Enable me to focus and rely on You
And Your boundless powerful Spirit, who lives inside of me.

WORK OUT
Memorize Isaiah 41:10.

JOURNAL
Record what you are afraid of and enlist God's help in overcoming it. Write down a step you will take to master that fear. Then write Isaiah 41:10 beside it.

Left And Right

BODY BASIC

Our brain's two hemispheres process things differently and divide up some of the brain's functions, yet they work in a constantly communicating partnership. For instance, when you run into an acquaintance, your left hemisphere, where speech is located, recalls her name, and the right hemisphere, which understands shapes and movements, remembers her face. In another division of duties, the left half of the brain controls the right side of the body, while the right half controls the left side of the body. That's because nerves to and from the left and right sides of the body cross in the brain stem. If a stroke occurs on the right side of the brain, the left side will be affected.

SPIRITUAL SPECIFIC

"As servants of God we commend ourselves...with weapons of righteousness in the right hand and in the left; through glory and dishonor, bad report and good report;...beaten, yet not killed; having nothing, yet possessing everything." (2 CORINTHIANS 6:4-10)

My friend Greg, a fifty-seven-year-old retired Marine and retired nuclear power plant worker, was on a construction job with his son, when his left hand started tingling. Then his left leg and foot "felt funny," and he began "walking like a drunk." Not knowing what was wrong, he took his son's advice and went to the emergency room. "By the time I got there, my leg and arm weren't working, and I was having trouble thinking," he told me. Greg had suffered the first of what would be three strokes in the course of a few weeks. He was awaiting open heart surgery when he had the third stroke. "It left me completely paralyzed – I couldn't talk, eat or move. And for a Marine, who was used to being tough, it was very scary not to be able to do anything. They didn't think I would recover well."

However, after months in a rehabilitation hospital where he worked hard and prayed harder, "I made some miraculous progress," he told me. "I was able to get around for short distances with a walker. So I was able to go for the open-heart surgery, even though I was still in rehabilitation. I was really nervous about it, and I was trying not to let my wife know, because she was already panic-stricken. She was sort of anti-God at that point, and when I tried to talk to her about her faith, I was the 'bad guy.' That added to my stress. I needed someone to pray with before I was rolled into surgery. Then, in an answer to prayer, a nurse came in and prayed for me. That helped a lot."

Greg had a successful operation. But kidney problems interfered with the pain medication and left him hurting badly. Besides that, the physical stress of the surgery set back his stroke recovery "so that I almost had to start over. I was battling on many fronts and feeling really jittery, too" he said. "My minister came to pray over me. And during that prayer, I felt God saying, 'Just relax. It'll be okay. I'll take care of you.' And, poof! I suddenly felt calm. Even the pain was better! I can't describe it, but I knew God did it. And it was a turning point for me.

"Before then," he admitted, "I had pretty much been a 'pew warmer'— I attended church, but the rest of the week I acted however I wanted. My faith wasn't as strong as it should have been. I didn't really doubt; I just wasn't 100-percent sure God would take care of things for me. All my life I had struggled. My dad committed suicide when I was four; I grew up with an alcoholic mother and was finally taken away from her and raised by an older brother. So I hadn't recognized all the ways God was in my life. I didn't give Him credit when, as a neglected child, I was helped by people I didn't even know. They brought food, took me places, did nice things for me. Instead of acknowledging God's hand in all that, I'd always believed that somehow *I* had to fix everything, *I* had to make things right.

"So when I couldn't fix anything—my health, my pain, my wife's unbelief or a devastating problem with a close associate that cost me my house, my tools and my truck while I was in the hospital—I was truly at the bottom. And when God spoke to me as my minister prayed that time, it was a miraculous eye-opener. I was able to give every one of my problems to God, and just focus on recovering. I spent a lot of time reading and studying the Bible. And I began seeing God working in ways I couldn't imagine—things just happened that I didn't have anything to do with! And one of them was that my wife became a believing Christian."

Greg says that as he persists in working toward full recovery, his faith continues to grow along with his interest in spiritual things. "The blessing is that my outlook changed," he said. "I still don't have possessions—God didn't restore them—but I'm not terribly concerned about that. I've seen how God takes care of me. He is caring and loving even when I'm being stupid. Even though my problems haven't disappeared, God has shown me He can make anything happen, and that's enough for me."

SOUL THERAPY

When I'm hit left and right with troubles, Lord,
Life is overwhelming,
And my first reaction is to try to "fix" it myself.
Please remind me to turn to You, instead,
My all-wise, ever-patient Partner.
Only You know what's best for me.
Only You are right in all Your ways.
Please take over!

WORK OUT

Stand and hold your arms out to your side. Begin a high knee march in place, and as your left knee comes up, reach across and touch it with the right hand. Then touch the right knee with the left hand and continue alternating for twenty repetitions as you march.

JOURNAL

What is a problem that you have tried and failed to fix in your life? Write it down and prayerfully give it over to God.

Successful Pulling

BODY BASIC
Muscles cannot push; they can only pull. Muscle shortening, or contraction, and relaxation produce almost all our body movements, but most muscles must act in pairs in order to create movement. They're arranged so that the shortening or contracting of one muscle or muscle group is balanced by the lengthening or relaxing of another. All muscular action involves give-and-take.

SPIRITUAL SPECIFIC
"Success, success to you, and success to those who help you, for your God will help you." (1 CHRONICLES 12:18)

God designed muscles to depend on other muscles to create the right movement, and people, too, work best when others are "pulling for them" and offering assistance when needed. All through scripture, God's people not only relied on God, but also on the reinforcement, counsel and encouragement of others. Moses' father-in-law, Jethro, urged Moses to delegate his responsibilities as judge, keeping only the most difficult cases. "The work is too heavy for you. You cannot handle it alone," Jethro said. Moses followed his advice.

Moses found a need for helpers again when he was holding up the staff of God in his hands, interceding from a hilltop for God's blessing on Joshua and his army against the Amalekites. Aaron and Hur were with Moses. "As long as Moses held up his hands, the Israelites were winning, but whenever he lowered his hands, the Amalekites were winning. When Moses' hands grew tired...Aaron and Hur held his hands up – one on one side, one on the other – so that his hands remained steady till sunset. So Joshua overcame the Amalekite army..." (Exodus 17:10-13)

Whether we need physical help or spiritual support or both, others play an important role. I was put in touch with D'Ann through a friend, and D'Ann told me how, through the very difficult experience of battling terminal cancer, she discovered the lift others can bring.

"The news that I only had a few months to a few years to live was devastating and terrifying," she said. "But cancer gave me new eyes to see what's really important." Faith, family and friends topped her list.

Prayers of family and friends encouraged her as she began chemotherapy. But the treatments made her so ill that she had to return to the hospital several times. During the ordeal, she was referred to CaringBridge, a website where a patient can journal, and friends and family can read and respond.

"That was one of God's greatest blessings," she said. "I was too sick to even talk to people on the phone. But through the website, people could reach out to me. And I received incredible messages from friends. I felt so loved and cared for. So cradled! I felt like I was being held in all these people's hands as well as God's. All my life I'd battled depression, and when I'm depressed, I feel like no one likes me. But that myth has been dispelled. People came out of the woodwork to show their love, and God used that to change my life and to help me live every day with joy and thankfulness. I now take every moment as the gift and blessing that it is.

"Even in the worst of times, God does bless us, but we have to recognize and appreciate those blessings, even if it's just the joy of being alive. I've gotten to experience the birth of my [now] year-old grandbaby. I'm so grateful I've gotten to hold and know her. I don't focus on the fact that I might not dance at her wedding. God didn't say we wouldn't have trouble in life. But sometimes the bad things teach us all that we have to celebrate."

SOUL THERAPY

Thank You, my Strength,
For pulling me through desperate times
And for sending me a support system
In family, friends and others.
Help me to celebrate every precious moment.
And as I near the end of this life,
Fix my eyes on You and remove my fear.
Let Your goodness and mercy follow me,
Until I come home to You.

WORK OUT

To work two supportive body systems—circulatory and muscular—try this stepping exercise: Find a step. Lead with your right leg first. Step up with the right foot, then bring the other foot up to that level, then step down with the right foot followed by the left. Do that for thirty to sixty seconds. Then lead with the left leg to step both up and down for thirty to sixty seconds. Repeat routine again. (You can do this holding small hand weights or canned goods, too.)

JOURNAL

Jot down some joys of being alive or some helpers who have pulled you up when you felt beat down. On the other hand, if you have felt abandoned by friends and/or by God, express those feelings in your journal. Then write beside that God's promise in Hebrews 13:5—"I will never leave you nor forsake you"—and record why His promise is more trustworthy than your feelings.

Shouldering Much

BODY BASIC
The shoulder is the most complex and mobile joint in the human body, but its great range of motion also makes it unstable and susceptible to dislocation and injury.

SPIRITUAL SPECIFIC
"For to us a Child is born, to us a Son is given, and the government will be on His shoulders, and He will be called Wonderful Counselor, Mighty God, Everlasting Father, Prince of Peace." (ISAIAH 9:6)

Burdens are literally and figuratively carried on the shoulders. The Israelites shouldered many of their possessions, including kneading troughs of dough, as they hurriedly fled Egypt. Aaron, Israel's high priest, wore a sacred robe with engraved stones mounted on its shoulderpieces; he was instructed to "bear the names [of the twelve sons of Israel] on his shoulders as a memorial before the Lord." When Moses delivered God's blessing to the tribes, he said of Benjamin, "Let the beloved of the Lord rest secure in Him, for He shields him all day long, and the one the Lord loves rests between His shoulders." (Deuteronomy 33:12) That blessing is for us, too.

With poles upon their shoulders, specially designated people shared the weight of carrying God's sacred chest or ark, His symbolic temple throne, from place to place. Similarly, oxen shouldered their work-load together; a yoke or wooden frame fitted around their shoulders helped maximize their strength. In a word picture, Jesus offered to "yoke" Himself to us and share life's burdens.

My friend Marty needed someone to share her burdens when she injured her shoulder, but she didn't ask anyone to help. "I knew I'd damaged something when I reached into the back seat of my car. But I just kept pushing on in spite of the pain. With time, my motion became more and more limited. For nearly a year I was handicapped, but I was still too stubborn to go to the doctor," she admitted. "Finally, when I couldn't even fix my hair, I gave up and went. The doctor sent me to a physical therapist for a frozen shoulder."

As she began stretching exercises with her therapist, they talked about their common faith. "One of the first things my therapist asked me was, 'What do you think God is trying to show you in this?' I was really startled, because we hardly knew each other, and that was a very penetrating question. I said sort of flippantly that maybe He was showing me that I needed to stretch. Why did I say that? Later I began thinking about it. I'd never stretched, even before exercising. And as I continued through physical therapy, it was a real eye-opener to see how important stretching is.

"*Was* God sending me a message? I thought back over the years and realized that God had been giving me clues for a long time that I needed figuratively to stretch—to move forward in my faith, to be bolder in my witness and in my prayer life, but I hadn't been paying attention. Now, because of my shoulder, He had my attention!"

Two years after her injury, Marty's shoulder recovered, but in the meantime, she began tuning into God's "clues." She started stretching out of her comfort zone in many ways, including writing two books, one of which is about spiritual growth. "I am being hugely stretched," she said. "And I'm sure I'm still in the process. God used my frozen shoulder to send me a message and a blessing."

SOUL THERAPY

Lord, I know You intend to stretch me
Until I become all that You've designed me to be.
And I realize pain is a part of that.
But when You require hard moves, heavy loads or long reaches,
Please yoke Yourself to me as You've promised.
Show me how to change.

WORK OUT

Don't stretch cold muscles. To warm up, gently do cross-over punches (rapidly punching at the air diagonally, one arm at a time) for about thirty seconds. Then, shrug your shoulders up and rotate them around backwards as if you're making a circle. Repeat five times. Then, stand in a doorway. Place your hands on each side of the door jamb, holding on to the jamb at whatever level is comfortable for you. (Putting your hands at shoulder height stretches shoulders more than if you put them at a lower level. Start out at a lower level, and don't overstretch!) Keeping your feet in place, gently lean forward, keeping your body completely straight as you lean, until you feel a stretch in the front of your shoulders. Hold a few seconds and repeat.

JOURNAL

Have you stretched spiritually lately by volunteering to do something out of your comfort zone? Compose a list of things that you are interested in, but are afraid of trying. Then ask God to help you step out in faith and give one a try.

Spinning Out
Of Control

BODY BASIC
*The inner ear, which
has many fluid-filled
channels, is responsible not only for
hearing, but also for balance. An inner
ear disorder, such as Meniere's disease,
can cause fluctuating fluid pressure,
resulting in vertigo, imbalance,
nausea and vomiting as well as ringing
in the ears, hearing loss and even
"drop attacks" in which a person
suddenly falls.*

**SPIRITUAL
SPECIFIC**
*"Now it is God who
makes both us and you stand firm
in Christ."* (2 CORINTHIANS 1:21)

Cindy's full life as wife and mother of six children along with be-ing a Bible study leader for my class was suddenly and drastically changed by a severe case of Meniere's Disease. "I began having lots of sound in my ear, and it soon became so loud I couldn't sleep," she told me. "I saw a doctor, but nothing stopped the high-pitched sounds that would shoot into my ears. Somehow, I finally adapted to that. But then, my occasional incidents of mild dizziness became more frequent and severe.

"I'd have two or three attacks a week," she continued, "And it got so bad that I had to hang on to something when I walked. I couldn't drive. I began having terrible headaches, then "dropping" episodes, where I suddenly fell to the floor. But even lying flat, I'd feel like I was still falling. I couldn't hold food down. I couldn't leave the house. Within three months, I had no hearing in my left ear.

"I became very, very afraid. That was the worst part—that incredible fear. I wondered if I'd lose all my hearing and never hear my children again. Would I be forever confined and miss the activities in their lives I wanted to share? The disease itself was debilitating, but the fear was worse," she admitted. "I could tell my husband and children were frightened, but I couldn't comfort them in my own terrified condition."

Through months of prayer, questions, tears, terrors and visits to many doctors, Cindy said, "I begged God to help. But I think fear kept me from any sort of depth to my prayers. I just wanted Him to *fix* it. I couldn't get past the physical realm. Medicines caused side effects, and doctors said there was nothing more they could do. I was so tired and so discouraged!"

Confined mostly to bed, Cindy kept a pan on the floor beside her for the times she got sick. One day hanging her head over the pan, vomiting and sobbing, she cried out, "God, my life is over!" And she sensed a startling reply from God: "Do you remember Who I am?"

"I was very surprised by the question, and in that moment the words of a song filled my head, a song I'd heard by Steven Curtis Chapman. The lyrics seemed aimed straight at me. The words were based on Isaiah 41:10: 'Do not fear, for I am with you; do not be dismayed, for I am your God. I will strengthen you and help you. I will uphold you with My righteous right hand.' And among the comforting messages in the song was the question, 'Do you remember Who I am?'

"It really made me think. Did I believe all I knew about God?" she continued. Lying there, she thought the question through. "I remembered what I'd learned my whole life about His promises and His power. And I finally said, 'Yes, Lord. I remember Who You are. I believe You. I know that You love me, that You know what I am going through, and You know what You're doing. But there is so much of You that I don't know. I don't have any strength left, but You do. Help me! I trust You.'

"After that I felt a flood of relief," Cindy continued. "I experienced an incredible joy and peace in His presence, so much so that nothing else mattered; He was enough! The spiritual healing was beyond words. It was like a physical change, too, because suddenly I was set free from that awful fear. The change in my heart helped me function better – I could even encourage my children. I *felt* God's love.'

"I thought I'd had a strong relationship with God before," she continued, "But everything after that went to a richer, deeper level. My prayer life changed, and I changed. I put notes all over my house with Isaiah 41:10 on them. When fears would re-surface about my hearing, I would say the verse and claim it. And God reminded me that I could still hear *Him*! And that meant everything."

Some time later, Cindy began getting some physical relief, too, when she reluctantly visited one last specialist who gave her an injection. It helped. After two and a half years, Cindy can now function, and her bad days are not as extreme. She had surgery to remove the inner ear on the left side, but she's facing hearing problems with the right. Nevertheless, she can press on, and she does so gratefully.

"There is so much depth to God we can't fathom," she said. "I am so thankful He has brought me to this place in my faith through this disease. I am forever changed! And as I continue to work on getting back my equilibrium, doing a lot of balancing exercises, I've found that even when I master an exercise in the light, I have to practice it in the dark, too. It is different in the dark. That's the way it has been on my faith journey."

SOUL THERAPY

Dear God, when everything is spinning out of control,
And the bottom drops out of my life,
Please steady me.
When my trust in You takes a nosedive,
When my focus is on my problem and not on Your power,
Remind me Who You are.

Increase my faith!
Bring me to that place of rich, deep closeness to You,
Where I find the solid ground of Your presence, peace and love.

WORK OUT

*Close your eyes while standing.
Focus on your balance, then inhale
and lift your arms above your
head. Place your hands together,
then as you exhale, lower your
clasped hands to chest level. Repeat
ten times as you extend and lift
your arms with inhalation and
lower them with exhalation. If
you are too unsteady for this while
standing up, sit on the edge of a
chair to do the exercise.*

JOURNAL

*Describe who God is to you. What
qualities does He have that give
Him the "right" to promise that
He can be your way through a
situation when there is no way out
of it?*

Man's Odds
Or God's?

BODY BASIC
The body is designed with remarkable self-repair mechanisms, but, unlike other body tissues, damaged brain tissue cannot repair itself.

SPIRITUAL SPECIFIC
"I have heard your prayer and seen your tears; I will heal you..." (2 KINGS 20:5, 6)

The human body has amazing capabilities, and many are yet to be discovered. But the body also has limitations. Only the supernatural power of God can overcome those limitations. The Bible tells of believers walking in a fiery furnace without being singed, prophets raising the dead, and Samson displaying supernatural strength.

Jesus allowed Peter to join Him walking on water until Peter's fears began sinking him. Jesus overcame His own physical death, rising from the grave. No matter how the odds are stacked, when God intervenes, anything is possible.

Joanie, the paratrooper in "Hidden Inside" (p. 104), who defied the odds in her recovery from injury, didn't imagine she would have a sequel to that story. But, she did. Just weeks after her strong left side became able to support her weak right side, Joanie suffered a severe stroke that paralyzed her left side. That setback made things look hopeless.

I prayed for my bedridden friend, my heart heavy, and all I could say was, "Please, God, help her!" I couldn't imagine what God was doing, but I was grateful for Joanie's new-found spiritual strength. I prayed it would endure.

Hardly able to speak or swallow, Joanie was angry, depressed, and had suicidal thoughts. But, with support of fellow Christians, she didn't turn away from her Lord. "And the Holy Spirit freed me of despair," she said. Nevertheless, she was terrified about her future. She went back into therapy with all that she had—a non-functioning left side, a very weak right side, a paratrooper's survival tactics, and faith that God would rescue her. Doctors warned her if she did not regain sensation in her left side within three months, it probably would never return fully. Three months went by, and no feeling returned.

Several months after that, I saw Joanie again at the rehab pool. She bounded over to me through the water, looking healthier than I had ever seen her. "Touch me. Feel this miracle!" she said smiling a beautiful, full smile. (When I had last seen her, her face was paralyzed on one side.) She told me she'd been sent home from the hospital with orders not to get out of her wheelchair. Even after the critical three months were up, she had kept up daily therapy, prayed, got a companion dog, and pressed on.

Finally, her once-weak right side grew strong enough to support the left, and she began to crawl, then stand with a walker, then set one foot ahead of the other, leaning hard on her walker. One morning, after months of prayer from many, she woke up feeling hardier and different. Better! And she got out of bed and stood by herself!

Her therapist was astonished. "What did you do?" he asked her.

"Nothing," she answered. "God did it."

Doctors were stumped as the miracle progressed: Joanie's right leg, which had been bent outward, straightened up. Her spine, which had been tilted forward, now holds her erect. Her left side has regained feeling and strength, and her body has balance, which it hasn't had in years. Doctors gave the miracle a complicated name, saying it was a rare occurrence. Joanie prefers the simpler name she has for her miracle: Jesus.

SOUL THERAPY

For my doubts that resurface when trials reemerge,
Please forgive me, my Savior.
Heal my weaknesses, both spiritual and physical.
And even if You choose not to make me well in body,
Please let it be well with my soul.
Help me to live my life proclaiming Your power and Your hope
To a world that needs to understand
That You can do anything, anytime,
No matter what the odds.

WORK OUT

To work out both sides of the body at once, lie on your back on a bed and do a lying march. Abs tight, bend both knees with your feet flat on the bed, and alternately pick each foot up off the bed as if you were marching. March for at least sixty seconds.

JOURNAL

The Bible is full of miracle stories. If you had witnessed those supernatural events like the Israelites did (plague protection, sea-parting, manna-provision, etc). would your faith be stronger than it is today? Why or why not? Why do you suppose that the Israelites who escaped Egypt because of those miracles fell away from faith? Jot down your thoughts.

That The Blind May See

BODY BASIC
Each eye's optic nerve has 1.2 million nerve fibers to transmit visual information from the eye's retina to the brain. Damage to the optic nerve causes vision loss. Every person has a "blind spot" in each eye where the optic nerve leaves the eye.

SPIRITUAL SPECIFIC
"I was blind, but now I see." (JOHN 9:25)

*J*esus *healed the blind more often than any other recorded miracle.* In one story, Jesus used a mud paste on the eyes of a man who was born blind, then sent him to wash in the pool of Siloam. The man didn't know if he was truly healed until he obeyed Jesus' command to wash. And when he immersed himself in those waters, he came up seeing for the first time in his life. It was an amazing miracle, but because it was done on the Sabbath, the Pharisees challenged Jesus for breaking Jewish law. They called in the healed man for questioning, accused Jesus of being a sinner and not being from God. Finally, after repeated questioning, the man said, "If this man [Jesus] were not from God, He could do nothing." Furious, the Pharisees threw him out of the synagogue.

When Jesus heard about it, He found the man and told him who He was. The man believed and worshiped Him. Although he had been cast out of the synagogue because of his faith in Christ, he was cast—seeing at last!—into the arms of God.

Life sometimes makes us feel as if we're groping through darkness. Or we may feel like we are existing at an in-between place—between the moment when Christ's hands are placed on our hurt and the time when we are finally healed. But the Light of the World is at work, even as we stumble through the gloom.

It was a dark time for my new friend Janina, when her eighty-two-year-old mother began going blind with temporal arteritis, an inflammation of the arteries that shuts off the blood supply to the optic nerve. Janina was panic-stricken. She rushed her mother to specialists, but even injections of steroids didn't help. Her mother was blind in a matter of days. "We had so many people praying, and we had hope that her sight would return. But, it didn't," Janina said.

Janina's mother felt fearful, despairing and depressed. "She felt trapped in the blackness. And I was battling sadness and guilt, thinking that maybe I somehow could have done something more. I also was overwhelmed with her care, and confused about how best to help her. I called my Bible study teacher, telling her all the bad things. She not only prayed for me, but reminded me of the truths we'd learned in our study. She said, 'God's love is in this, and His love to you through others is a gift. So open your eyes and heart to see His provision.' That wasn't what I expected to hear, but I decided to try it."

Janina and her mother began "living with new eyes. And we kept finding God!" she said. "He encouraged us and revealed Himself in so many ways. One day Mom and I ran into a homeless man that we had ministered to at a mission, and he came over and prayed for *us*! He was just one of our God-sightings.

"Over time, God provided Mom with increasing courage, perseverance and determination. And her faith and strength encouraged me. There have been many challenges in the last two and a half years, but there are also many blessings. God is developing good things in Mom and me as we depend on Him. Mom's example of joy, peace, patience and love shows

God's fruits of the spirit to her grandchildren and others. She exemplifies the Bible verse that says, 'He will make me fruitful in the land of my affliction.' He has done that for both of us."

SOUL THERAPY

Light of the World,
Despair and fear lurk in the darkness,
And I need You.
Please extinguish my gloom.
Brighten my outlook.
Make me aware of Your mercies,
Which are new every morning.
Show me how to be fruitful for You.

WORK OUT
To exercise eye muscles, sit tall on the edge of a chair, take a pencil and hold it about ten inches away from your face. Keep your head still and move only your eyes to follow the pencil as you move it slowly to the right until you can no longer see it. Then move it to the left, following it with only your eyes. Then move it up and down. Repeat five times in each direction.

JOURNAL
Record every way you have "seen" God this week.

The Needed Knee

BODY BASIC
The knee, a mechanical wonder, is our largest weight-bearing joint, supporting nearly the entire weight of the body. As the most-used of our joints, it is vulnerable to injury and osteoarthritis. The knee cap does not fully develop in girls until age three and in boys until age five.

SPIRITUAL SPECIFIC
"...at the name of Jesus every knee should bow in heaven and on earth and under the earth..." (PHILIPPIANS 2:10)

*M*any emperors in the Bible believed they were gods and com-manded their subjects to kneel before them or their image in honor and worship. King Darius the Mede issued an edict that all citizens pray only to him for thirty days or be thrown into the lion's den. Darius' favorite advisor, Daniel, continued to get on his knees three times a day to pray to God. He was found out, and reluctantly King Darius had him thrown into the lions' den. But Daniel was saved when God closed the lions' mouths. The awed king then commanded all his people to "fear and reverence the God of Daniel."

Similarly, Daniel's three friends had been thrown into a blazing furnace earlier for the same reason by Darius' predecessor, King Nebuchadnezzar. After the three men were bound and thrown in, the king looked into the furnace and cried, "Look! I see four men walking around in the fire un-bound and unharmed, and the fourth looks like a son of the gods." (Daniel 3:25) When the three came out unsinged, the king decreed that no one was to speak "against the God of Shadrach, Meshach and Abednego." Although God did not remove His servants from life-threatening situations, He walked with each man through them, miraculously protecting those who knelt before Him only.

But God's servants are not always shielded so completely. I read a heart-wrenching and inspiring story in "Voice of the Martyrs'" magazine (used with permission) about a Sudanese boy named Damare, who worshiped God. He was raised a Christian, and he held onto his faith when he was captured at age seven by Muslim soldiers. Sold into slavery, Damare still wanted to worship his real Master, Jesus. So he sneaked away from the camels he was tending for his slave master and attended a village church. When his master found out where Damare had been, he dragged the boy to the edge of the compound and nailed his knees and feet to a board. There he left him, screaming in agony, to die.

A man, who happened to walk by, heard Damare's cries and slipped into the compound to help. He carried Damare to a local hospital where they removed the nails and board. The kind man kept the boy at his own home for a year and a half until Damare, whose family could not be found, was adopted by one of his own tribesmen. Damare still can't run like other boys, but he told friends from Voice of the Martyrs, "I forgive the man who did this to me. Jesus was also nailed [to a cross], and He forgave me."

I knew little about the plight of the children of Sudan before reading Damare's story. And when I read his request that others join him in praying for the children of Sudan, I fell to my knees on their behalf.

SOUL THERAPY

My King,
Thank you for the privilege of kneeling before You in prayer,
And for Your promise that those prayers unleash Your great power,
Which knows no boundaries.
Please send Your miraculous deliverance
To people who suffer everywhere,
Especially Your martyred saints,
The Underground Church,
And the precious children of Sudan.

WORK OUT
If you have existing knee problems, ask your doctor for appropriate exercises. To strengthen a healthy knee's supportive muscles and ligaments, kneel "tall" on both knees as if you were in prayer. Then gently lower your buttocks toward your heels, and rise back up. Repeat ten times.

JOURNAL
Have you ever felt persecuted because of your faith? What helped you to stand strong?

Power Of Touch

BODY BASIC
Studies have shown that touch is essential for healthy development. When a baby is born, his best-developed sense is touch, through which he begins to relate to his surroundings. Children deprived of touch can develop "phychosocial dwarfism," a condition which stunts their physical growth. However, appropriate soothing and nurturing touch at any age can bring about psychological as well as physical benefits—a slower heart rate, lower blood pressure and a speedier recovery from illness.

SPIRITUAL SPECIFIC
"And the people all tried to touch Him, because power was coming from Him and healing them all." (LUKE 6:19)

Touch, the first of our five senses to develop in the womb, conveys meaning and allows us to experience our world. But under Old Testament law, Jews had to watch what they touched. Contact with an unclean thing, such as a carcass, a corpse or a crawling creature, made a person "unclean" until a sacrifice was made for him/her by the priest. Lepers could not be touched for the same reason. Holy things, too, were untouchable except by a priest, and even the priests had to meet certain criteria to be clean enough to lay a finger on them.

Yet the Bible tells of ways that God reached down to people with the comfort and encouragement of His touch. The prophet Elijah, who was exhausted and fleeing the murderous queen Jezebel, was touched two different times by an angel who said, "Arise and eat!" God touched the prophet Jeremiah's mouth, giving him His words to tell the Israelites. But it was only through His Son, Jesus, that God allowed people to touch *Him.*

The perfectly holy Jesus was not made unclean by touching anything. He even laid His hand on lepers. His touch had supernatural power, and "as many as touched Him were healed." (Mark 5:56) Jesus reached out not only with physical healing, but with love and forgiveness, too. He touched and blessed children who flocked to Him and encouraged everyone to come to Him as eagerly.

My parents eagerly came to the Lord each morning in prayer, holding hands, before they got up from bed. Then, when Dad died at eighty-three, and Mom lost her mate of fifty-three years, she was bereft. To her, waking up without Dad on his side of the bed was the hardest part of the day. One morning, she was lying in bed saying her prayers, missing Dad's hand in hers and feeling very alone. She asked God to send her comfort. She didn't open her eyes, but continued to pray for God to ease her grief. Then she felt a hand in hers. Startled, she opened her eyes and discovered she was holding her own hand!

She laughs about the absurdness of it, but says it soothed her nevertheless. "It was as if God, with His sense of humor, was saying, 'I'm here.' And that was all I needed for the moment."

No matter what loneliness, grief or trial we are suffering, Jesus touches our spirits with His own. "We don't have a Priest who is out of touch with our reality. He's been through weakness and testing, experienced it all—all but the sin. So let's walk right up to Him and get what He is so ready to give. Take the mercy, accept the help."(Hebrews 4:15,16 MSG)

SOUL THERAPY

Thank You, tender Savior,
That no need, grief, problem or person is out of Your reach.
Please touch me today with Your humor, Your love, or Your people.
And help me to pass on Your kind consolation to others.

WORK OUT
Touch someone's life with a note or call.

JOURNAL
Write down some of the meaningful people in your life, and how they have affected you. How can you pass on a kindness to someone who is feeling alone?

Plenty Of Purpose

BODY BASIC
With the increase of medical knowledge, organs once thought to be without purpose (and often routinely removed) have been discovered to be useful after all. For instance, instead of simply serving as a potential source of inflammation, the misunderstood appendix has been found to be helpful in immune functions. Immunologists and surgeons at Duke University Medical School now believe that the appendix produces and protects the useful bacteria in the digestive system. Doctors have discovered that normal tonsils, too, are good for general systemic immunity.

SPIRITUAL SPECIFIC
"...It is the Lord's purpose that prevails."

(PROVERBS 19:21)

The One who knows every organ's secrets has much to say in the Bible about His intentions for His beloved people. He raises up individuals for certain purposes (Exodus 9:16), and He is "firm in His purpose" (Job 36:5) which always prevails. He has set objectives, and He calls people according to His intent (Romans 8:28). He reminds believers that a meaningful future destiny lies in Him (Ephesians 1:11).

Carol, whom I met when she came to speak at our church, told a powerful personal story about God's prevailing plan. She related that at age fifty-one, she couldn't imagine that her drug-devastated life might contain purpose. Addicted to cocaine, she had lived homeless for seven years under a bridge on Skid Row in California. She felt a world away from the protected, loving Christian home in which she'd been brought up and the college campus where she'd received her degree.

"I never intended for my life to end up like it did," she said. But through a series of bad choices that began as a rebellious teenager, she'd become a drug addict.

After college, Carole had been able to function while on drugs, working as a pharmacy tech and stealing and selling drugs to buy cocaine. Then, she quit that job to nurse her bedridden husband, and, "When he died after a stroke, I crashed. I hit the streets and went under the bridge. My addiction was so great at that point that I just followed other crack heads wherever they went."

She blamed God. "I would stand in the middle of the street, shake my fist and curse Him," she said. "I'd scream, 'Look what You've done to me!' I was doing things for money that I never thought I'd do. I was so hungry that my stomach would eat on itself. There was no one to trust, no way to stay warm, nowhere to even find a drink of water. I felt hopeless and worthless. I hadn't bathed in two years. I'd chalked off my life—I was a dope addict. I'd die a dope addict. There was no hope for me."

Then one night, sitting in an alley "with a crack pipe in one hand and crack in the other, I was suddenly shocked and overwhelmed by the presence of God. And all at once, I couldn't take the dope! So I said, 'God if you are for real, show me. Help me.' It was the first time I had asked for help, and I really meant it. I gave away the crack and walked away from that life. God completely delivered me from my addiction. I was not the type for a rehab center, so I just walked around all day, trying to stay clean and avoid the Skid Row people, but still sleeping under the bridge. Not long after my prayer, a lady met me as I walked, took me in, fed me and let me bathe. She helped me for months.

"When I'd been clean for seven months, I went into a store to buy cigarettes and noticed a television set in the corner," she continued. "On the screen, a pastor was talking, inviting me to change my life and come into his Dream Center. I thought, 'Who would want me?' But he held out his arms and said, 'Come!' So I walked six miles to the Center. I went to church that Thursday and Sunday, and I asked Jesus to come back into my life. The Dream Center people invited me to start a year-long Christian discipling and rehabilitation program, but I fought the idea. All I wanted was to stay clean—that was the extent of my vision for myself. But I kept thinking, 'Could God really have something for *me* to do. For *this* life?'"

Finally, after a week's deliberation, Carole decided to try it. And after graduating from the program, she began working full time as the Dream Center kitchen supervisor. She met and married Manuel, pastor of the food chapel. "And I thought that was as good as God could possibly do for me," she said. "My dreams were so limited. My view was like looking at a big parade through a tiny knothole in the fence. But God's wonderful plan and purpose soon became clear to us: Manuel and I were invited to begin a homeless ministry for a church in Nevada."

After serving there for two years, they moved to Texas where Manuel is helping to found a bilingual church and where Carole serves as Women's Program Director at Faith Mission.

Carole is still amazed at her life. "God is so faithful; He never gives up on us. We turn our back on Him, but He's always there. What He starts, He will finish. Who else but God could take all the terrible things in my life and then use them to minister to others? There has not been one issue yet in a person's life that I can't empathize with. I know exactly what that person has been through. God's plan and purpose extend to every life, even and *especially* a throw-away life. Nothing is impossible with God. And I stand on that amazing truth."

SOUL THERAPY

My astonishing Creator,
I am awed by Your purposes.
Thank You that nothing gets in Your way.
No problem, no addiction,
No poor choice is too great for You to redeem.
Thank you that because of Your forgiveness,
My history is not my identity.
My worth is in You.
Thank You that You see Your finished work in me,
And You will always complete it.

WORK OUT

The purpose of this exercise is to strengthen ankles, shins, calves and upper legs to making walking easier. Hold onto a sturdy chair with one hand, place feet about six inches apart. Slowly lift both heels off the floor, rocking forward and up onto your toes. Balance on your tiptoes for five to ten seconds. Then lower your heels to the floor and balance on them as you lift your toes slightly off the floor. Hold five seconds. Repeat sequence five times.

JOURNAL

Do you have a sense of purpose? What do you feel inclined to do with your life for the kingdom of God? Ask God to reveal to you what He'd like to accomplish in and through you, and as you gain guidance, write down how you are being led.

Persisting Pain

BODY BASIC
*Pain, which informs
and protects us, is
transmitted by a complicated process
involving nerve endings, nerve fibers,
the spinal cord, the brain and chemicals,
called neurotransmitters, that send
nerve impulses from one cell to another.
Some neurotransmitters control mild
pain sensations, others govern severe or
intense pain. Pain can become chronic,
and in America, the Centers for Disease
Control and Prevention estimates that
more than seventy-five million people
suffer from chronic pain.*

SPIRITUAL
SPECIFIC
*"My back is filled
with searing pain; there is no
health in my body. I am feeble
and utterly crushed; I groan in
anguish of heart..."* (PSALM 38:7)

*I*saiah encouraged suffering people with this prophecy: "Strengthen
the feeble hands, steady the knees that give way. Be strong and do not
fear; your God will come...Then will the lame leap like deer, and the mute

tongue shout for joy." (35:3-6) Hundreds of years later, Jesus fulfilled that prophecy. And at any time, He will come again and make it permanently true for His children. In the meantime, however, humans everywhere will continue to suffer.

When limitations due to pain or any other cause keep us from doing the things we once enjoyed, frustration develops. Our self-esteem suffers. How do we handle the "grief" of saying goodbye to our dreams or even daily activities we once excelled in?

My friend Leonette had been handling pain and limitations fairly well after a major car wreck broke her arm and damaged her spine. She had pressed on, despite persistent problems, not knowing that most of her troubles stemmed from undiscovered internal injuries. Surgery many years after the wreck uncovered the internal damage.

But she hadn't seen the worst; after that surgery, Leonette became bed-ridden for three months with Epstein-Barr virus. "That was my lowest point," she told me. "When the brakes are completely put on in your life, it's mentally debilitating. I'd had lots of adversity, but I'd always managed to keep going. I didn't know *how* to rest; I wouldn't even sit down for lunch. I was obsessive! Everything had to be perfect, and my identity was tied up in that perfection. Suddenly, I was a high-stress woman, bedridden and feeling like I was cheating my family and everyone else."

As Leonette mentally struggled, she realized that she had to let go of *her* kind of thinking and let God control her frame of mind. "All I had the energy to do was read my Bible, and in my low state, I began understanding it differently. My identity had been tied up in what I perceived myself to be, but God began teaching me my true identity is in Christ. The Lord showed me it's not who I think I am, but Christ in me that makes me who I am. I had always been an achiever and a giver, so it was hard to be a receiver.

"I lay there wondering what possible purpose could be achieved just lying in bed," she continued. "But God achieved a lot! Through that time, He revealed how unbalanced my life had been, what resentments I still carried, and how I'd allowed stress to take over me. Things penetrated my soul that never had before. Bed turned out to be a blessing."

Leonette still lives in chronic pain and can't exercise strenuously or do many of the activities she once enjoyed. "But even though sometimes I look in the mirror and think, 'I don't like it,' God has taught me that I'm okay. Life's not about all those things I thought it was. I've got a new level of gratitude and joy for all the little things that I still have and can do. And I have a deeper relationship with Christ, which has made it all worth it."

SOUL THERAPY

Lord, pain can either hold me hostage
And make me bitter,
Or teach me how to depend on You,
Which makes me better.
I choose You.
When I'm aching,
Please remove my disappointment and discouragement.
Show me what I *can* do
That's in line with Your plans.
And, if You so choose, please heal me when the time is right.

WORK OUT
To help get your focus off of what hurts, get some lotion, close your eyes and massage the palm of your hand, especially the padded area between the thumb and index finger. Massage three to five minutes on each hand and practice slow, deep breathing.

JOURNAL
List some of the things you can take pleasure in no matter how you feel—then do one.

The Chemistry Of Depression

BODY BASIC
The average adult body contains sixty chemical elements and components. Those chemicals and their balance affect both health and mood. Researchers studying depression believe that not only can a person's behavior affect brain chemistry, but brain chemistry can also affect behavior.

SPIRITUAL SPECIFIC
"He requested for himself that he might die, and said, "It is enough; now, O Lord, take my life..." (1 KINGS 19:4)

Some of God's most successful servants, such as Moses, Jonah and Elijah, had desperate times of discouragement and despair. Even Paul, known for his rejoicing despite hard times, wrote that at one point during his ministry in Asia that he felt more pressure than he could endure, and he "despaired even of life." (2 Corinthians 1:8) Paul wrote the Corinthians, however, that a desperate time during which he felt "the sentence of death" happened "that we might not rely on ourselves, but on God...On Him we have set our hope that He will continue to deliver us as you help us by your prayers."

We are often assaulted by discouragement, stress and the blues, and those feelings come and go. However, sometimes a deeper depression, clinical depression, seriously hampers life.

Tommy, pastor of a 4,000-member church, was "hijacked" by depression, and I heard him tell his story on a radio program. When I called him, he shared more with me. "I was doing what I loved, and God was blessing it. I didn't know I could burn out," he said. "I worked about twelve hours a day, preached four times on Sundays, used my day off to teach a Bible study, traveled to teach at conferences, and so on. I exercised regularly, enjoyed my work and felt healthy. I didn't pay attention when my wife warned me to slow down.

"When my problem first struck," he continued, "It was physical, including body pain and insomnia. Then one day the bottom just dropped out emotionally. I can still remember the moment. Something in me snapped! I was in a black hole, and I didn't know why. It was very frightening. I had no idea what was wrong with me—I didn't feel anything, not toward God or people. At night, anxiety crawled on me like an animal. It was a dark, dreadful time. I couldn't even read. But I could think, so I thought on God and prayed continually. I had no energy, but forced myself to work out, and that brought me my only few moments of slight relief."

His wife took him to a psychiatrist, who explained that his high-intensity lifestyle had caused a chemical imbalance in his brain. "When a person is under constant stress, the brain chemical serotonin is inhibited, and with no serotonin, the brain will turn off emotionally. That's what happened to me. Within three weeks of taking a serotonin re-uptake inhibitor and resting, I turned a corner. But it was four months before I was able to return to the pulpit. And even after I recovered, I had to cut out seventy percent of my activities, so that I wouldn't get under that load of stress again."

Tommy now advises others who struggle with depression to first "remedy it as best they can, getting to a psychiatrist and dealing with whatever put them in that condition (such as overwork). They should take what the doctor prescribes, and understand that no matter how hopeless they may feel, there is hope. Secondly, I remind them that nothing happens outside God's providence—not even a disease of the mind. So instead of just enduring depression, we should try our best to learn through and from it. I learned that even though I may be faithless, God remains faithful to me."

SOUL THERAPY

When blackness engulfs me,
Hang onto me, my Savior,
And keep me from sinking.
Your word says over and over
Not to fear, for You are with me.
Not to be dismayed, for You are my God.
You promise to strengthen and help me.
So please do—lift me to the high ground of Your hope.
You alone know what I require, my Counselor.
Please bless me with the earthly and heavenly help I need.

WORK OUT
Physical (aerobic) exercise releases endorphins in the brain and helps create a sense of well-being. Take a brisk thirty-minute walk or bike ride in new surroundings.

JOURNAL
Note some ways you can know that God is with you, even in dark times when you can't "feel" Him there.

Ageing

BODY BASIC
From the instant an embryo forms, the body will grow for at least twenty years. Then, in a person's early thirties, the body begins changing in a different way—declining in function. The normal ageing process causes gradual losses to the sensory system as well as a decline in short-term memory and muscle mass. However, studies show that the ability to cope does not normally decline with age.

SPIRITUAL SPECIFIC
"Even to your old age and gray hairs I am He, I am He who will sustain you. I have made you and I will carry you. I will sustain you, and I will rescue you." (ISAIAH 46:4)

*A**geing is inevitable unless death intervenes,*** yet it doesn't hamper God. He can use His people at any age. Nevertheless, growing old usually delivers discouraging changes, health challenges and heart-wrenching losses that take the sparkle out of the "golden years." While the Apostle Paul was not to suffer the trials of old age, he had much to teach those who do. He endured terrific physical ordeals and losses for Christ's sake, but he comforts us with God's word: "…We do not lose heart. Though outwardly we are wasting away, yet inwardly we are being renewed day by day. For our light and momentary troubles are achieving for us an eternal glory that far outweighs them all. So we fix our eyes not on what is seen, but on what is unseen. For what is seen is temporary, but what is unseen is eternal." (2 Corinthians 4:16)

Spiritually, we can grow stronger and more God-sensitive at any age. And no matter what we may lose, we never lose Christ. Keeping our focus on eternal "unseen things" renews us. My husband's ninety-year-old grandfather, who became increasingly interested in the scriptures as he got older, jokingly called it "cramming for my finals."

As years advance, death draws closer to our own threshold, claiming friends and loved ones. Our older friend Mike is a gentle man who has demonstrated a faith-filled dependence on God through the health trials and deaths of three beloved spouses. His first wife, Marge, was a person I greatly admired for her joyful spirit in the midst of suffering. Mike told me their story. "When we were both just twenty-seven, Marge was at death's door for six months. We had a newborn baby and a toddler. I was doing a lot of praying, but I didn't know what to pray for. Marge was so sick! Was it an injustice to her for me to pray that she'd live, when I knew she would never completely recover? I had to learn to pray, 'Thy will be done.' I had to be totally dependent on God, because I realized only He knows best."

Marge did live, although a permanent tracheotomy and breathing difficulties caused problems for the rest of her life. Nevertheless, she lived fully and victoriously despite her limitations, reared their two children, and died at age seventy-one. "Even now, people bring up Marge's name as someone who inspired them with her strength of faith and cheerful spirit," Mike said.

After her death, Mike leaned hard on God through his grief and loneliness. And he prayed "Thy will be done" with many events that followed. Each time, that prayer brought him peace: when he developed prostate cancer at age sixty-nine and had open heart surgery at seventy, and then when he remarried and was widowed twice more before he was eighty, and when he believed he was having a second heart attack. (It wasn't one, but he required a pacemaker.) At age eighty-two, he married a fourth time, and once again he gave God the reigns as he helped his current wife battle her way toward becoming a cancer survivor.

"With age's difficulties, my faith has kept growing," Mike said. "I read scripture and devotions and continue to give to God the people and the things in my life. I believe that no matter how something turns out on earth, His will is always for the ultimate best."

SOUL THERAPY

Old age can be so full of hardship, Lord!
Help me not to lose heart as I lose my youthful vigor.
Please enable me to grow older with grace.
Renew my spirit all the days of my life.
Fix my eyes not on what is seen,
But on Your unseen and glorious realm
Where one day, I will join
All Your forever-young faithful ones and You.

WORK OUT
Begin reading Genesis 12-25, which tells of Abraham's life after age seventy-five.

JOURNAL
Who are some people you know who have aged gracefully? What are some of their traits? Record some ideas about how you can gracefully handle growing older.

Body-Central

BODY BASIC

The central nervous system—our highly developed brain, spinal cord and nerves—sets humans apart from all other animals. All our movements, sensations, emotions and thoughts are products of this amazing, responsive system that keeps our whole body in touch with itself, its needs and its surroundings. However, if the neck is broken and the spinal cord is injured, the nervous system can't operate correctly. That damage results in serious complications all over the body, ranging from partial to complete paralysis, asphyxia and even death.

SPIRITUAL SPECIFIC

"...We are like the various parts of the human body. The body we are talking about is Christ's body of chosen people. Each of us finds his meaning and function as part of His body. (ROMANS 12: 4,5 MSG)

*U*sing examples of the body's interdependence, the New Testament teaches us we're to develop—and take care not to break—our close connections with each other and with Christ, our Head. The Old Testament records how God's first body of people came into being. God chose Abraham to father a tribe, which became the nation of Israel. God instructed them to function on a higher moral level than the rest of the world, collaborating with each other uniquely under His holy headship. God set Israel apart to receive His law and personal promises, and through them, He produced Christ's human lineage. However, when God selected them to be His special people He said through His prophet, "I revealed Myself to those who did not ask for Me...To a nation that did not call on My name, I said, 'Here am I. Here am I.'" (Isaiah 65:1)

Jesus, who was fully God as well as an Israelite man, picked out twelve men to be in His inner circle of disciples. And, in doing so, He showed once again that He has His sights set on certain people, whether or not they fully comprehend who He is. Some of Christ's future apostles were fishing, and one was collecting taxes (a dishonest trade) when Jesus came into their lives. Several were brought to Jesus by a believing friend or family member. Many of Christ's growing body of disciples started out just as curious onlookers, including one short man, who climbed up in a tree hoping to catch a glimpse of the Miracle Worker passing by. Christ bestowed His mercy and love on each of them.

Once the apostles and other disciples knew Jesus and believed, they became distinctively united with each other and with Him. "Now you are the body of Christ, and each one of you is a part of it." (1 Corinthians 12:27) After Christ's death, believing friends and strangers encouraged and helped each other through many struggles and much suffering as they spread Christ's good news of salvation.

My cousin Zach didn't know Christ. And he had no idea he would soon be the recipient of help from a body of believers both known and unknown. When he strapped on his snow skis one day and took off down the mountain with a friend, he was only thinking about one thing: practicing the Nordic skiing he loved. Well-coordinated and strong, Zach was a natural athlete. A college senior, he hoped to qualify for some national ski competitions.

But everything changed when he took a disastrous wrong turn on a remote trail. He hit a tree full force. Knocked unconscious, he woke up with intense pain in his neck. And when he tried to sit up, he couldn't. "I realized I couldn't feel my body at all," he said. He was panicked.

His companion rushed to his rescue, splinted his neck with ski poles, and then hurried away to get help. Zach, alone and struggling to breathe—the spinal injury affected his breathing—tried to pray. He was afraid that if he fell asleep, he might not wake up. Because he didn't feel as close to God as he did to his grandfather, a believer who had died, Zach said, "I talked to Grandpop. He seemed right there with me." At one point, Zach fell asleep and was startled awake from what felt like a sharp poke in his side. But no one was there!

Although Zach wasn't addressing Him, God was nevertheless orchestrating the events that followed. First, Zach's friend, racing for help, ran into a hiker and her dog on a remote trail, and he directed the woman toward his fallen friend. Zach could only manage a faint whistle in answer to her calls, and she couldn't hear it. But, her dog heard! And he led the woman to Zach. She stayed with him, encouraging him until help arrived. As soon as the rescuers got there, she disappeared. No one ever saw her again. "I don't know whether she was an angel or not, but she was *my* angel," Zach said.

Once Zach was stabilized in the hospital, "it began sinking in that I might never move again. I was devastated," he said. "I was terrified of being helpless." During those dark times, the prayers of others, requested by his parents, boosted him. "I got letters even from strangers saying they and their churches were praying for me. It was so inspiring to be prayed for! I drew strength from those prayers and from knowing that so many people were rooting for me."

Miraculously, Zach's neck had broken in such a way that his spinal cord was not severed. In the next months, physical therapists were able to help him learn to walk and move again.

Zach now works as a marketing coordinator with an Olympic committee. Although he struggles with some lingering physical limitations, he has turned his own skiing dreams into helping others achieve their athletic hopes: He assists paralympic athletes as well as competitors in Special Olympics.

"Encourage one another," the Bible says. Zach is grateful for the support he received from Christ's body of believers, who know that our God invites us into His loving care even when we don't yet know Him, saying, "Here am I. Here am I."

SOUL THERAPY

Involved Creator,
Help me, as part of Your body,
Not only to move and breathe and have my being in You,
But to react toward others with Your loving care,
So that those who don't yet know You
Will want to.

WORK OUT
To work all the muscles together, try this hold-and-balance exercise: On the floor or bed, balance on all fours (hands and knees). Tighten abdominal muscles. Straighten and lift the right leg off the floor behind you. Don't strain trying to lift it high; just get a comfortable lift and hold it, while lifting the left arm straight out. Balance like that for ten seconds, then switch sides. Repeat five times on each side.

JOURNAL
Do you find meaning and function as part of the body of Christ? Write what that means to you, or how you could develop and deepen your understanding.

Voicing It

BODY BASIC
Humans are the only mammals whose voice box is positioned low in the neck. That position enables us to create a wide variety of sounds. The vocal cords stretch across the larynx and vibrate to produce various pitches. Each person's voice has its own distinct "voice print."

SPIRITUAL SPECIFIC
"I lift up my voice to the Lord for mercy." (PSALM 142:1)

*T**he better we know someone,*** the easier it is to recognize his/her voice. In a parable about sheep and their shepherd, Jesus spoke about His relationship with His own people by saying, "His sheep follow Him, because they know His voice."(John 10:4)

In the Old Testament, God's voice sounded different to various people, but those He spoke to heard Him and knew that it was God. Elijah heard God in a still, small voice. The boy Samuel heard God's voice so audibly that he thought it was the prophet Eli calling him from the next room.

Moses heard God's words, but the people near him heard only thunder. Peter, James and John were with Jesus on the Mount of Transfiguration when God said, "This is My Son, listen to Him." Later, Peter told others, "We ourselves heard that voice!" Saul heard the risen Jesus' voice on the road to Damascus, and the men with him heard the sound, but didn't understand it.

People through the ages have lifted up their own distinctive voices to God in repentance, grief, praise and petition. But even when a person's physical voice is affected or non-existent, it doesn't hinder God's hearing or understanding.

I've never met Evelin—I've only heard her voice in our phone interview—but she lives in a neighboring town and is friends with a friend of mine. A stroke victim, she told me she wanted desperately to speak after the stroke. "I had the words in my head, but they wouldn't come out. I couldn't whisper or get my lips to move," she said. "I was very, very frightened. I went three days with no speech at all, and the neurologist who admitted me to the hospital had not come back to see me." The doctor's seeming lack of concern troubled her. "I wanted to tell my family how terribly my head was hurting, so I could get medication, but I was fighting my own lips to try to get them to move. Finally, I thought, 'If they can't hear me, God can,' and I told Him how scared I was, that I didn't know what was going on, and please to send someone to help me. I didn't know how He was going to turn things around, but I knew He could.

"Suddenly, I was given the knowledge that I wasn't going to die," she continued. "That helped. Then, a nurse came in to try to help me learn to use my hands to shape my lips into making sounds. On the third day in the hospital, my internist was making her rounds and saw my name. She came into my room. I know God sent her. She told me I would have to fire the neurologist in order for her to get me a new one, and I used my hands to form the word 'fired!'"

Despite finally getting some relief from the terrible pain, Evelin went through several setbacks during her week in the hospital, "and I had no one to cling to but God." When she was able to begin therapy, the partial paralysis on her right side didn't bother her as badly as her lack of speech. She struggled not only to say words, but to re-learn the names of once-familiar objects. "My husband was told I might never recover. But through it all, I held onto God's promise 'I will never leave thee nor forsake thee' (Hebrews 13:5). I say that verse every day, no matter what my struggle. Everything took time, practice and determination, but my speech was finally restored, and my faith grew stronger in the process."

More than that, Evelin says, "my troubled marriage was mended. We realize now how important we are to each other. Something good came of it just as God promised."

SOUL THERAPY

Word of Life,
Thank You that I don't need a voice
To speak my heart and my needs to You.
I ask You to intervene on my behalf as I press through my problems.
Please whisper Your encouragement and promises to my spirit.

WORK OUT
If you have a problem-free neck, gently hold your hands behind your back, lift your chin up to the ceiling, and repeat the vowel sounds AEIOU three times. Turn the head to the right, chin still up, and repeat the vowels three times, then turn your head to left and repeat them again.

JOURNAL
Give "voice" to your thoughts by writing down some ways that God communicates with you.

Perseverance

BODY BASIC
Whether you are losing weight, building muscle, or retraining your brain, your body requires perseverance—a steady persistence in sticking with your course of action—in order to make the change.

SPIRITUAL SPECIFIC
"...For we know that suffering produces perseverance, perseverance, character; and character, hope. And hope does not disappoint us, because God has poured out His love into our hearts by the Holy Spirit, Whom He has given us."

(ROMANS 5: 3-5)

Breaking through barriers takes effort and perseverance. God broke into our world as a human being, Jesus. And He persevered, teaching, loving and forgiving, even as people rejected and persecuted Him. Christ still steadfastly loves us—He never gives up on His children, no matter how many times we disappoint Him.

Christ provided what His prophets and followers needed to persevere through tremendous trials as they carried God's word to others. And He helped them hold firm even in martyrdom; Acts 7:56 tells us that just before he was stoned to death, Stephen was given a vision of Christ standing at God's right hand in heaven, awaiting him.

Whether or not we suffer for our faith, persistence is necessary in life's trials, and faith provides a strong undergirding as we hang on. "Blessed is the man who perseveres under trial, because when he has stood the test, he will receive the crown of life that God has promised to those who love Him." (James 1:12)

To my friend Vickie, her trial—multiple sclerosis—felt like anything but a blessing. She tried to continue her work teaching her beloved preschoolers, but she finally had to give it up. "I didn't want to retire," she said. "And when I did, I missed the kids a lot—especially their laughter. I'd lost so much strength with the MS, and then I lost the joy of my job. I knew I needed to discover new strengths to compensate. I began reading self-help books and spiritual books to inspire me. And I prayed a lot—for pain-free days or just pain-free moments. I'd get still and calm, so my mind could quit spinning, and I would try to relax and just relate to God. In those quiet times I could find some relief. But I was still so frustrated!

"Physical therapy hurt physically, but even more, it hurt my self-esteem—it kept reminding me of what I'd lost, what I couldn't do anymore. I kept going, but I wanted to quit. It was so hard. Then suddenly, one day, unexpectedly, I did it—I reached a goal that had seemed unreachable just a few days before. It was an incredible victory. It made me decide to keep up the fight, because you never know—any day, any minute, you could break through and turn a corner. So I keep that hope and keep working. When it's hard to keep moving through life, I remember that breakthrough. And I know God can do that sort of thing in my life again at any time if I persevere."

Jesus, who gave up His glory as God and became a man of sorrows, understands everything we go through. He's listening to each of us and loving us, helping us to persist with hope.

SOUL THERAPY

Jesus, You are the master of adjusting and persevering,
And I want to be more like You.
But it's so hard!
Please infuse me with Your attitude and develop my character
As I make the changes required in my life.
Help me to fight the good fight, keep the faith,
And finish the course that You've set out for me.

WORK OUT

Persevere with this switch-up exercise until you develop a smooth rhythm: step sideways with your right foot, then back to the center with your left. Step sideways to your left, then back to the center with your right. Keep your stomach muscles tight. Repeat ten times. Then switch the leading leg and do it again. You can do the same thing stepping forward and then backward. (Start by stepping with the right foot, bring the left to meet it, then step with the right foot backward, left to meet it. Go forward and back ten times, then switch your lead foot.)

JOURNAL

Record your reaction to today's verse: Romans 5:3-5. Have you developed more perseverance as you've matured? How can perseverance help hope to grow?

Life And Death

BODY BASIC
From birth to death, the oldest documented age for a human is 122 years, although some have claimed to be older. Despite our best efforts, every human body perishes, and death can happen at any age.

SPIRITUAL SPECIFIC
"There is a nice symmetry in this: Death initially came by a man, and resurrection from the dead came by a man. Everybody dies in Adam; everybody comes alive in Christ. Christ...won't let up until the last enemy is down—and the very last enemy is death!"

(1 CORINTHIANS 15:19-26 MSG)

*D*eath of a loved one, especially premature death, produces incalculable grief. Death even grieves God, who sent Jesus to defeat death, "the last enemy." Because of Jesus, death is not the end of life, but the beginning of a new, better life in heaven. Death destroys the perishable body, but when we belong to Christ, it can't touch the imperishable spirit. And we are promised new bodies in heaven.

God's judgment for sin was: "From dust you are, and to dust you will return." The dust that God had used to create Adam's life became a symbol of death. But when the promised Messiah, Jesus, came thousands of years later, He freed us from sin's curse of death by giving His sinless life in exchange. And His resurrection and ascension into heaven opened the way for us to eternal life. In the Bible paraphrase, *The Message*, it says in Romans: "That's why Jesus lived and died and then lived again: so that He could be our Master across the entire range of life and death...".

Imagery in the Old Testament portrayed death and the grave as being a great "swallower." Proverbs 27:20 says, "Death and destruction are never satisfied." After Jesus, however, something miraculously different is proclaimed. Using the same imagery, Paul reassures believers in Christ that instead of being swallowed up by death, we are "swallowed up by life." (2 Corinthians 5:4)

That promise means everything to my friend Lesa, a physical therapist at the rehab center where I go. It's what keeps her going after the death of her seventeen-year-old son from a complication with medications. He was a beloved Christian leader in his school. "When he died, the horrible hollowness inside me was so painful I couldn't eat," Lesa told me. "At first, I was so consumed with despair and heaviness that I wasn't even capable of going to God. That's when believing friends and family covered me with love and prayer. They were a cloak of comfort, surrounding me so I didn't even have to think."

As time passed and Lesa began dealing with her grief, she still felt raw. "When you lose a child, there is a thin line between getting bitter and getting better. You can be mad at God and be rebellious and try dulling the pain with the wrong things. Or you can pray a lot, express your anger honestly to God, and fill your mind with the comforts He gives us in the Bible and through Christian books, counseling and His people. I get close to God by going out into nature, listening to Christian music, and reading everything biblically based about heaven that I can. A part of my heart will always be broken. But I can choose what I fill that broken place with. It's a daily thing. I try to get my mind off my earthly feelings and imagine my son with God in a glorious, light-filled heaven, experiencing great joy and freedom from pain. He's in a place we all want to be.

"My son was courageous; he was known for his faith and his hope," she continued. "In his honor, my husband and I want to take this tragedy and make a difference: my husband has begun a ministry for bereaved parents, and I am always watching for someone who has a need. Reaching out is a big part of healing for me. I'd never choose this as a way to grow, but there is no question that I have grown in faith through it. And I no longer fear death. I know where I'm going when I die, and my son and Savior are there."

SOUL THERAPY

Eternal King and Savior,
Thank you that because of Your sacrifice and resurrection,
Death does not have the last word.
Yet it leaves behind a horrible heart-vacuum
And life-sucking grief.
Please don't let sadness and hollowness
Have the final say.
In Your mercy, fill my emptiness and dull the pain.
Comfort and uphold me.
Reunite me soon in Your glorious kingdom
With all those that I love.

WORK OUT

If you don't have the assurance of knowing you are going to heaven when you die, make Christ's gift of salvation your own today. You can pray: Heavenly Father, I confess that I'm a sinner and can't get to heaven on my own merit. I accept Your sinless Son, Jesus Christ, as my Savior. I pray You will forgive me through His blood. Help me to start all over with You as the Lord of my life. Draw me into a close relationship with You, so that You are truly my Core Strength now and forever.

JOURNAL

If you make a commitment or if you re-commit your life to Christ today, record the event and the date in your journal. Then share the good news of what you've done with someone else.

The Ankle Solution

BODY BASIC
The ankle, a complex hinge of bone, muscle, ligaments and tendons, supports the body. Sprained ankles are one of the most common forms of all joint injuries.

SPIRITUAL SPECIFIC
"Taking him by the right hand, he [Peter] helped him up, and instantly the man's feet and ankles became strong."

(ACTS 3:7)

Our daughter Joanna was in tears. A basketball stand-out on her high school team, she'd sprained her ankle for the umpteenth time. She wasn't crying from the pain, although it was intense; she was weeping out of frustration. Despite taping her ankles, using ankle braces and high-topped shoes in almost every game, when she came down from a shot, one or the other of her ankles twisted. She "played hurt" most of every game and limped for days afterward.

In desperation, we finally took her to a physical therapist. He told us she didn't just have weak ankles. Her brain needed to be re-trained to know where she was in space! He explained that the central nervous system constantly monitors our body's position in space. Muscles and joints have specialized sensors that "talk" to the brain about our movement and position. The sensors detect changes in angle and direction and send it to the brain to make adjustments. Basically, Joanna landed wrong every time she came down from a shot, which she made from many angles, because her stretched tendons and other injuries had robbed her of the ability to sense and naturally correct her landing position. She had to "retrain" her feet to come down correctly.

Joanna faithfully worked through long weeks of physical therapy, exercising to strengthen her ankles and performing balance drills to straighten out her ability to land right. Then she played the rest of the year without injury.

She never played again with ankle braces—those, we were told to our surprise, only weakened her ankles further. All our parental best efforts to brace Joanna's ankles had fizzled. Now we had to focus on what would be a permanent solution.

That experience taught me a lesson about my own life. When I'm "playing hurt" and feel discouraged, I often try to brace myself with man-made supports—"comfort food," caffeine for energy, forgetting my troubles through entertainment, etc. But those things never permanently strengthened me. The only One who can brace me and fortify me at the same time is God, who delights in using my weakness to display His strength. It's something I know, but I have to remind myself daily so that I remember to turn first to Him for help.

Even though He doesn't heal my problem instantly like He healed the cripple who took Peter's hand, God always teaches me something. And with His guidance and strength, I can land correctly.

SOUL THERAPY

Lord, You are my trustworthy Support,
But I often get off-balance
When I am stretched in many directions
With pressures and commitments
And pains I can't control.
Please brace me for whatever challenges this day may bring.
Train me with Your wonderful wisdom
To bring my goals in line with Yours.

WORK OUT

To exercise your ankles, stand on one foot at the kitchen sink and balance while holding onto the countertop. Then, close your eyes, let go of the countertop, and try to balance for fifteen seconds with your eyes closed. Repeat three times with that foot, then do the same routine with the other foot. Be sure you have an easy way to catch yourself if you lose your balance. If you can't balance on one foot, just stand on both feet and then close your eyes.

JOURNAL

What man-made supports are you dependent on when you are hurt? Are any destructive in the long run? Write a prayer inviting God to be your permanent strength.

Holding Together

BODY BASIC
A protein molecule called laminin helps cells adhere to each other so that the body holds together. Under an electron microscope, laminin resembles a cross.

SPIRITUAL SPECIFIC
"For by Him all things were created...and in Him all things hold together."
(COLOSSIANS 16-17)

*O**ne day, as I worked out in the therapy pool,* I met Lucia, and we began talking. Solemnly, she told me that swimming pools remind her of a long-ago day when her life began to fall apart. She was watching her four-year-old son Brian take his swimming lesson when Brian went into cardiac arrest. By the time doctors determined the cause and discovered the correct medication for his heart, Brian had had several more arrests. He was comatose for six months. After set-backs and problems in the hospital, Brian regressed. His brain was damaged, and he awoke from the coma as a quadriplegic with no speech.

While Brian was in the hospital, Lucia's husband Kelly and both their families helped with Brian and with their six-month-old baby daughter at home. But even with family near, Lucia felt empty and alone, drowning in her anger, grief, fatigue and devastation.

"I grew up going to church," she told me, "But I didn't have a relationship with God. I knew about Him in my head; I knew how to pray, but I didn't feel close to God. With the tragedy, all I felt was blackness and hopelessness. And when we finally got Brian home, the family had to go back to their lives. I was exhausted with all the care—suctioning, monitoring, giving medication every two hours. Brian didn't sleep except from three to seven a.m. Our baby girl needed me, too. And being a military wife, I had to manage without my husband's help much of the time. On top of that, we had to make another move! I was desperate and depressed."

Lucia felt she would have completely disintegrated except for occasional, amazing support, such as a helpful friend and former neighbor from another base (whom Lucia had been missing and wishing for) who re-surfaced. And they discovered they were back-to-back neighbors. Another great help was a teenager who came into their lives and taught them how to be playful with Brian and laugh again. "Gifts like that were all that held me together," Lucia said. "But I wasn't giving credit to God. I wasn't seeing blessings as they really were—His gifts."

By the time Brian was twelve, the family was transferred back to Florida, the state they'd lived in when Brian's heart stopped. "We sort of joked that we hoped we weren't headed back for more trouble," she said.

It was back there that a weary Lucia began attending a church that Kelly found. "The people at that church had a light in their eyes, a warmth and joy that I yearned for. And it was there that I learned about having a *relationship* with God," Lucia related. "I went on a weekend spiritual retreat, a 'Walk to Emmaus,' and that's where I really 'got it.' It changed my life completely. I had hope, a sudden understanding that I was never alone. Jesus was with me. I felt His reassurance and His love. It's hard to describe, but it filled the hole inside me. And He became the glue that held me together. I began to believe in His miracles."

Shortly after the Emmaus Walk, Lucia desperately needed one of God's miracles. "My husband Kelly had a grand mal seizure, and they found a brain tumor. But when the doctor told us the terrible news, my first thought was that I was grateful to God that Kelly hadn't been in the air when he had the seizure. He'd been flying a one-man F-16. I was thankful, too, that this time it wasn't like with Brian—we knew what Kelly had, and doctors could do something about it.

"The diagnosis was very frightening, but it was also a very different experience to go through *this* trauma this time with the Lord. I felt His comfort and peace. I knew we were not in this hole alone. I had hope. I could see God moving, putting people in place to make things happen. Time after time He provided miracles—even the miracle of building my faith back when I began feeling low again, when I felt myself sinking, my confidence in Him wavering, because I was so full of fear. People's prayers and our church helped me then, too.

"While we waited long hours for surgery, I tried to keep my fears down by singing over and over, 'surely the presence of the Lord is in this place.' And suddenly a warm glow enveloped me, and I knew that Kelly would be okay." After an eleven-hour surgery, Kelly began slowly recovering.

"It's so amazing when you start seeing blessings for what they are—God's hand in things, helping. I was finally in a place where I could recognize it and think, 'this is God's love.' None of life's pressures were removed or lessened; my circumstances didn't change, but I changed. Having a relationship with Jesus made my spirit and my outlook different."

Despite a recurrence of the brain tumor ten years later (he recovered again, but lives under the threat of more recurrences), and despite overwhelming sadness when Brian died at age nineteen, Lucia has been held together by God—by the Lord's laminin—Whose strength never fails.

SOUL THERAPY

Loving Jesus, what a difference it makes
When my "head knowledge" about You makes its way into my heart.
Thank You not only for binding together my body,
But for uniting me forever with You.

WORK OUT

Make the form of a cross with your body by standing on your right foot and gently placing your left foot on top of it. Then hold your arms straight out to the side, making sure your abdominal muscles are tight and your back is straight. Hold the position for a count of thirty seconds, focusing on your balance (try not to weave back and forth) and the core strength it takes to maintain that position. Switch feet and repeat.

JOURNAL

What is your relationship with Jesus like? Tell about how you've developed in your faith journey and in what ways you'd like your relationship with Christ to grow.

Reset

BODY BASIC
In order to grow back correctly, a broken bone must be properly realigned, supported and held in the right position until healing is complete.

SPIRITUAL SPECIFIC
"...like a lion He broke all my bones...Surely it was for my benefit that I suffered such anguish." (ISAIAH 38:13, 17)

Writers of scripture often described physical or spiritual anguish as broken or aching bones. And correct healing from such breaks depended on the person's repentance, obedience, and reliance on God's mercy. David cried, "O Lord, heal me, for my bones are in agony. My soul is in anguish." (Psalm 6:2)

Some of King David's bone-wrenching pain resulted from false accusations against him by people he loved, such as King Saul and later David's own traitorous son, Absalom. Some anguish was caused by David's unconfessed sin with Bathsheba. But when David realigned himself with God through repentance and prayer, God healed him.

David was a favorite Bible hero of a friend of mine's son, Andy. My friend had taught her children well about Bible characters, and as a grown man, Andy was aware that walking with God includes experiences of anguish, trial and peril. But he told me that he felt he could face whatever life handed him, because his faith was firm. It was so strong, in fact, he said that when he was in his early twenties, "I half-bragged to my Bible study group that my faith couldn't be broken. Maybe it was my competitive, athletic mindset, but I was halfway inviting a challenge to strengthen my faith even more. It had never really been tested. Well, I got it!" Now looking back on the experience, Andy admitted, "I see that I wanted to gain unbreakable faith *my* way, not God's way. But God had a different plan—His ways are not our ways.

"I was in a great place in my life," he said. "I had an enjoyable job as a teacher and coach, and felt I could be a strong role model for kids. Along with that, I was finishing my second graduate degree, had a wonderful bride, and was going to Hawaii! I felt secure and successful, and dependence on God didn't seem necessary. I hadn't thought of my self-sufficiency as a problem, but I see now that it was—it led to pride, pride I didn't acknowledge until it took a huge hit, and my life became a living hell."

Andy was working as an administrator at a football game and took an unruly youngster aside, gripping his shoulder as he reprimanded him. "I was falsely accused of assaulting the boy. Vicious, nasty rumors flew, and I was fired from my job. Everything that could go wrong went wrong. It was the worst time in my life, and I was scared and angry at God. Everything I had been leaning on was taken away from me almost overnight, even my good name. And I was innocent! I appealed the school district's decision to fire me and went to court." The process took months.

Frustrated and leaning heavily on support from his wife, family, friends and church, Andy was greatly relieved when "finally, the hearing officer ruled in my favor and the DA dismissed the charge. I went back and completed the school year, but the damage had been done. The district did not rehire me the next fall, since I was not tenured."

His dreams shattered, his future in question, Andy said, "I had been thoroughly humbled. God had brought me down in a hurry. But immediately I knew why: I'd placed too much faith in myself, and my life had been all about the things that made me feel secure and successful. Those things were gone now, along with my pride. I didn't have anywhere else to turn except to God. So I placed my life and my hardships completely in His hands. I learned a drastic lesson about unbreakable faith: trusting God involves putting everything else aside, including bitterness toward my accusers. I'm still learning how to forgive, but God is patiently showing me how. And I'm growing as He heals me."

Humbled and more dependent on God, Andy agrees with King Hezekiah's line in today's scripture: "Surely it was for my benefit that I suffered such anguish." He is now a successful coach and teacher in another town.

SOUL THERAPY

Great Physician, only You can realign my thoughts
And "splint" my faith when I'm fractured by blows from others,
Or by my own pride.
Please forgive me for the sin of self-centeredness.
Help me to be You-centered.
Please reset my life according to Your plan,
So that I can forgive others
As You have forgiven me.

WORK OUT

The alignment of your posture can be altered by tight muscles and tendons. For this exercise, stand in front of a large mirror. First, spread your feet apart, then lift your arms above your head as you inhale. Next, bend at the hips and reach your hands toward the floor as you exhale. Hold this position to stretch your arms, legs and back for ten seconds; then, bending your knees slightly, roll yourself back up into a standing position. Look into the mirror and check your alignment: Are your shoulders back and level? Is your head tilted or straight? Is your body tall or slumped? Realign your posture by setting it straight, then repeat the stretch and posture check five times.

JOURNAL

If you've been falsely accused or hurt by gossip, record your brokenness in your journal. Then finish it with your own prayer, specifically giving God the areas of your life that you want Him to realign and hold straight.

A New Thing

BODY BASIC
When the brain is injured
and connections between the
nerve cells (neurons) are broken, speech,
thought and movement may be affected.
The brain must build new pathways
so the neurons can reconnect. Early
medical intervention and cognitive
rehabilitation can help the brain
recoup functions and can assist patients
in learning new ways to compensate
for losses. Researchers at the Defense
and Veterans Brain Injury Center in
Washington, D.C. studying 360 injured
veterans discovered that teaching
patients how to think through tasks
enhanced their brain's recovery more
than treatments which focused solely on
performing the tasks.

SPIRITUAL
SPECIFIC
"Forget the former
things; do not dwell on the past.
See, I am doing a new thing!
Now it springs up; do you not
perceive it?" (ISAIAH 43:18-19)

The Bible reveals God as Master of restoration and miracles. And He performed a permanent "new thing" through Jesus' death and resurrection—miraculously repairing the sin-broken relationship between His believing people and Himself.

God still authors miracles, and my friend Jennifer was a recipient of one. When Jennifer was five, her mother Chris and father Don responded to her cries in the night. Going into Jennifer's room, Chris heard her wailing, "My head! My head!" Then Jennifer lost consciousness.

Chris and Don called 911, got a friend to stay with their younger daughter, and rushed to the hospital. A CAT scan revealed that Jennifer had suffered a massive stroke. She was in a coma for two weeks—exhausting and frightening weeks for Chris and Don.

Chris told me, "I was so physically and emotionally spent from all the days in ICU with Jennifer, plus the almost sleepless nights (she and Don alternated night shifts) with beeping monitors, that on the way home one night, I just pulled over to the side of the road and cried out to God, 'I can't do this anymore! I don't know where to turn. You can do anything, but I can't.' And suddenly, as I prayed, I was enveloped in this feeling of love. A voice in my head said, 'It's going to be all right.' I just wept and wept. And that night at home, I had my first good night's sleep."

When the blood in Jennifer's brain finally receded, and she at last regained consciousness, Chris and Don needed God's reassurance and comfort again; Doctors had grim news. "A tumor had caused the brain to bleed," Chris said. "Jennifer was not only totally paralyzed on her right side, but the tumor was inoperable – it was in her thalamus with fingerlike projections throughout her brain. It was the worst possible diagnosis." And it added to an earlier shattering grief. "Before Jennifer, we had lost a baby boy at full-term, so now our hearts were broken again. By God's grace, though, we somehow were not angry or disillusioned with Him. We knew His cherished people had suffered all through scripture. We just wished it had been us rather than Jennifer." They felt totally helpless and threw themselves on God.

The only hope of a medical cure, a one-month round of radiation on the tumor, didn't work. Only the outside of the tumor was killed. Doctors gave Jennifer six months to live.

Chris and Don and their younger daughter, along with their church and friends, began asking God for a miracle. Jennifer went into physical therapy, but "it was a terrible time," Chris said. "She was in and out of the hospital every two to three months. As the tumor grew, it would cause another stroke. At age five, Jennifer was in such pain that she said, 'Mommy, I'm ready to go be with Jesus.' It was awful. And although I couldn't stand to think of losing her, I began to think that maybe the miracle we prayed for might be that God would take her home."

Hiding her despair from Jennifer, Chris leaned on God's strength to help her through. And Chris began noticing something new—Jennifer's comment seemed to trigger something inside Jennifer. "She grew fearless, stronger and more determined. Her faith and spirit encouraged *me*," Chris said.

However, steroids to keep brain swelling down added to Jennifer's misery. So with the doctor's permission, Chris and Don began slowly weaning her from them. Over the months "as we continued to lower the dose, she got better! She learned to walk again in therapy, regained bowel and bladder control, and even went back to school in a classroom for the handicapped."

Over time, Jennifer's strokes stopped. The headaches subsided. Later seizures were controlled by medication. Chris and Don began believing their daughter was experiencing the miracle they'd prayed for.

Jennifer, however, battled blood clots in her lungs and was in and out of the hospital. Even so, she was progressing. Years passed. After one bout with blood clots when she was thirteen, she was given a full body scan. Chris related, "Afterwards, her astonished pulmonologist came in, elated, and said, 'In the brain scan, we could see where the tumor had been. But the live one is *gone*!' It was an unbelievable moment. We were ecstatic—and so thankful! We announced it to our church, who'd been praying for us for eight long years, and they just erupted in celebration. God had given us our miracle."

Now thirty-six, Jennifer leads a productive life despite paralysis on her right side and dead areas in her brain. Contrary to doctors' dire predictions, she not only graduated from high school, but was in the National Honor Society. And with the help of a leg brace and surgically placed rods in her limp arm and foot, she played one-handed drums and tambourine in the school's marching band. She's been a teacher's assistant for seventeen years. She loves doing that, encouraging ill children, and reading to people at the Alzheimer's unit. "Sometimes I read devotionals to God," Jennifer said. "And I think He listens!"

SOUL THERAPY

Miracle Maker, Your power is so awesome!
Your love is so all-encompassing,
Your sustaining strength so generous.
Thank You.
Even if You choose not to send a miracle,
I praise You for Your comforting presence
To see me through,
And for every new thing that You accomplish
Along the way.

WORK OUT
Put your brain neurons to work by meditating on the promise of 2 Corinthians 5:17: "Therefore if anyone is in Christ, he is a new creation; old things have passed away; behold, all things have become new."

JOURNAL
Through God's "new thing," Jesus Christ's salvation, He has miraculously made all things new in each believer's life. Pen your reaction to that promise.

Conclusion

"*When everything was hopeless,* Abraham believed anyway, deciding not to live on the basis of what he saw he couldn't do, but on what God said He would do." (Romans 4: 14-23 MSG) And God says He will make us "more than conquerors" through Jesus Christ.

Jesus won the battle at Easter – He was dead, and God raised Him to eternal life. In the same way, He promises believers a victorious end to every grief and grim reality of "Good Friday." When God did "a new thing" through His Son, He opened the door into heaven for His fallen people. And, as Philip Yancey writes in Disappointment with God, "In any discussion of disappointment with God, heaven is the last word, the most important word of all."

Nevertheless, until that grand day when we leave earth behind, Paul says we must expect trouble, hardship, persecution, famine, nakedness, danger, and sword. Yet, he also reminds us as we battle on, we have not only a compassionate Comforter alongside, but also a mighty Savior fighting with us and for us, shaping and deepening our faith through the fray.

God describes heaven as a place so glorious we can't even begin to conceive of it, and several of the contributors to this book are now enjoying His promised rewards there. With faith and courage, each one ran a good race, finished the course, and is experiencing the joy of eternal victory. I pray the same for you and me.

Lord Jesus,
Please fill this dear reader
With Your peace and presence,
Your word and wisdom,
Your love, strength, and sustaining Holy Spirit,
So that no matter what shakes this beloved friend of Yours to the core,
He or she can walk victoriously with You
Until one day we all meet each other in glory.
– Amen.

Sources

Human Body: A Visual Guide, Beverly McMillan, Firefly Books, 2006.

Body Voyage (A Three-Dimensional Tour of a Real Human Body), Alexander Tsiaras, Warner Books, 2007

Body by Design: From the Digestive System to the Skeleton, Rob Nagel; Betz Des Chenes, Editor, U X L, an imprint of the Gale Group; 2000

The Way We Work, Getting to Know the Amazing Human Body, David Macaulay with Richard Walker, Houghton Mifflin Company Boston, Walter Lorraine Books, 2008

I Am Joe's Body, J.D. Ratcliff (based on the most popular series in Reader's Digest history and originally published as "*Your Body and How It Works*") Berkley/Reader's Digest, New York, 1980

The Complete Idiot's Guide to Psychology, Third Edition, Joni E. Johnston, Psy.D, Alpha Books, Penguin Group, 2006

Psychology Basics, Volume 2, Revised Edition, Editor Nancy A Piotrowski, Ph.D, University of California, Berkeley, Salem Press, 2005

Fearfully and Wonderfully Made, Dr. Paul Brand and Philip Yancey, Zondervan, 1980

The Attributes of God, Volume 2, Deeper Into the Father's Heart, A.W. Tozer, Wing Spread Publishers, 2001

Acknowledgments

Night Wrestling, Leslie Williams, Word Publishing, 1997. Used by permission.

Life Without Limbs, founder Nick Vujicic: web address www/lifewithoutlimbs.org

Voice of the Martyrs, PO Box 443, Bartlesville, OK. 74005, web site: www.persecution.com

A Daily Word With Ron Hutchcraft – Day 19, p. 41. Ronald P. Hutchcraft, Ron Hutchcraft Ministries, Inc., 2005. Used by permission.

Moments with the Savior, A Devotional Life of Christ, Ken Gire, Zondervan, 1998. Used by permission.

The Hiding Place, Corrie Ten Boom, with John and Elizabeth Sherrill, Bantam Books, 1971. Used by permission.

Disappointment with God, Philip Yancey, Zondervan, 2007

The Attributes of God, Volume 2, Deeper Into the Father's Heart, A.W. Tozer, Wing Spread Publishers, 2001

Godsight: Renewing the Eyes of Our Heart, Lael Arrington, Crossway Books, 2005

Hymns

[
Be still my soul;
The waves and winds still know
The voice that calmed them
In this world below.

Be Still My Soul,
by Katharina von Schlegel, 1752
]